Amiscellany

AMISCELLANY
My Life, My Music

JOHN AMIS

faber and faber
LONDON · BOSTON

First published in 1985
by Faber and Faber Limited
3 Queen Square London WC1N 3AU
This paperback edition first published in 1986

Filmset by Goodfellow & Egan Typesetting Ltd
Printed in Great Britain by
Butler & Tanner Ltd
Frome Somerset
All rights reserved

© John Amis, 1985, 1986

British Library Cataloguing in Publication Data

Amis, John
Amiscellany
1. Amis, John   2. Musicians—Great
Britain—Biography
1. Title
780'.92'4   ML423.A4
ISBN 0-571-13969-8

Library of Congress Cataloging in Publication Data

Amis, John
Amiscellany: my life, my music.

1. Amis, John.   2. Musicians—England—Biography.
I. Title.
ML423.A45A3 1985   780'.92'4[B]   85-1552
ISBN 0-571-13969-8

'To my friends pictured within'
and some who are not: in particular,
Michael Rose

Contents

Illustrations

between pages 160 and 161

1 Steve Race warming up the *My Music* team. (Photo: BBC Copyright)
2 On the waterfront, 1983, Chicago. (Photo: Betty Jowitt)
3 With William Glock at one of the early summer schools of music at Bryanston School.
4 Donald Swann and Michael Flanders at Dartington Hall. (Photo: Catharine Scudamore)
5 With my father at Dartington, *c.* 1955. (Photo: Catharine Scudamore)
6 With Peter Maxwell Davies and William Glock at Dartington, 1979. (Photo: Neil Libbert for the *Observer*)
7 Line-up of organizers and trogs at Dartington, 1979. (Photo: Charles Davis)
8 Benjamin Britten and George Malcolm at Dartington, 1959. (Photo: Catharine Scudamore)
9 With Sándor Végh at Prussia Cove, Cornwall, 1978. (Photo: Crispin Eurich)
10 Caught with bells in our hands: J.A. with Manoug Parikian and John Warrack. (Photo-montage: James Trimble)
11 An unpublished pedal composition by Peter Maxwell Davies. (Photo: Charles Davis)
12 Julian Bream and John Williams playing to a provincial audience of bullocks. (Photo: John Cooper for RCA Records)
13 Sir Thomas Beecham with the 17-year-old Noel Mewton-Wood, Queen's Hall, 1940. (Photo: Pictorial Press)
14 With Alan Bush. (Photo: Nigel Luckhurst)

Acknowledgements

Writing about Michael Tippett and Alan Bush I find that I have slipped in some phrases, even a whole sentence now and then, from previous articles about those composers so I am glad to acknowledge them: the first article was in *Michael Tippett: A Symposium on his 60th Birthday* edited by Ian Kemp, Faber and Faber, 1965; and the other was in *Alan Bush: An 80th Birthday Symposium* edited by Ronald Stevenson, Bravura Publications, 1981.

I should also like to thank Patrick Carnegy, my 'minder' at Fabers, for his comradely assistance – we had some very pleasing, even useful lunches together.

Preamble

By the 1950s Madame Binnie was old and round. I had thought she would examine my face and clothes to draw conclusions, but she was myopic and the light in her booth so meagre that all she could see was my right hand, which she had drawn into the pool of light: 'Hello, dear, what do you want to know?'

I didn't particularly want to know anything. I had to go to Hove to visit a sick friend, and Irene Worth had come down to Brighton with me for the day. As we got near the pier she had persuaded me that I must go and have my fortune told. Madame Binnie had told her several things that had come true. If I was sceptical about fortune-telling, which I was, Irene offered to pay the five-shilling fee. I pooh-poohed that but did as she suggested and said as little as possible on entering Madame Binnie's little booth.

'What do I do?' I asked her immediately.

'Well, it's the arts, dear, isn't it? she said. 'Words and music . . . . No, it isn't,' she went on, 'it's music first and *then* words.'

Correct.

When I consider the amount of talent that I have and the skill with which I have used it, I think I have been lucky to have had so enjoyable a life so far and to have met so many talented and interesting artists. I was forty before I had enough money to own more than one suit and was usually mildly in debt to the bank – which worried me more than them. It is the artists and creators whom I have met that have made me think of writing a book, not the parts of my life that relate to money, suits, banks and more domestic matters. That is why this book is not a continuous autobiography. I just don't think that much of my life – apart from the people I have met – has been all that interesting. Possibly because I am a Gemini, I have always had more than one job at a time. So what I have done in this miscellany is to write about certain parts of my life, packaging them – like Apollo or the London Philharmonic Orchestra, for example – though not excluding from those chapters other relevant or possibly interesting details. And in among those sections, in what seem the most obvious places, I have interleaved profiles of individuals who have been important to me and recounted my relationships with them.

By the 1960s Madame Binnie was older and rounder. (Alas, she has now gone to the great booth in the sky.) I was in Brighton again, and I thought I would go for a second five bob's worth.

'You're going on a journey, dear,' she started.

'That's what they all say,' I said.

'Take me seriously, please, or leave.' She was quite sharp. 'You're going on this journey in a few days' time. You will be surrounded by mountains and you haven't been there before. Have you seen a picture of the place where you're going to stay?'

I hadn't, nor had I any idea of the exact location where the singing teacher Lucie Manén lived in Igls.

'You haven't? Well, dear, it's odd. I see reeds around the house but no water, although there was water at one time.' (She was right about this, I discovered on arrival. Lucie Manén and her husband, Otto John, lived in a house surrounded by a dry moat. How did Madame Binnie know?)

I changed the subject. 'What about marriage, Madame Binnie?'

She smiled. 'You've had it, dear, haven't you?'

And indeed I had: I was married to Olive Zorian, the violinist, from 1948 to 1955. Divorced. My fault. 'Any more marriages?'

She looked very closely at my hand. 'Can't see any, dear. Certainly not for the next few years anyway.'

The strange thing is that I can't remember very much about the domestic side of my marriage. I have some mental snapshots of various events – concerts Olive played in, mostly with her Zorian String Quartet, some recitals, concertos, a Prom in which she played Arnold van Wyk's *Saudade*, the Mozart *Sinfonia Concer-*

tante (K. 364) with Sir Thomas Beecham conducting and Winifred Copperwheat as her viola partner, and later on her playing with Julian Bream's Consort – and I can remember places we visited together. But mostly I remember continuing situations and states of mind, happiness at first, strife later, each state moderated by our common and important gift for teasing each other out of a mood and tempered also by our almost perfect agreement about the quality of any given music and its performance.

Olive's own playing was not virtuosic, though she could most capably negotiate things like Mozart concertos, the first-fiddle parts of Britten, Bartók and Tippett, as well as Stravinsky's *Duo Concertant*. Her strongest point was her instinctive musicianship and, above all, her ability to float and spin a line. You can hear the best of her in the old 78 rpm recordings of the Britten and Tippett Second String Quartets and, on LP, the original recordings of Britten's *Saint Nicolas* and *The Turn of the Screw*. She died in 1969, at the age of forty-nine, of cancer.

In years to come I may be able to sort out in my mind some of the more domestic parts of my life; there are a host of friends and many events and places that I have not included in this volume. I think I will have to pass over my marriage with the words used by our dear old friends Jack Gant and his composer-pianist wife, Joan Trimble. They said: 'We love you both – separately. How you stuck it together for so long we don't know!' I think that living with one person is an art in itself – and I don't have it because I'm too selfish.

On the other hand, in my work I *like* playing second fiddle, whether the task is interviewing or, in the past, working for Tom Russell of the LPO or Beecham or Sir William Glock. But that is what the book is about.

Most of my working life these days is taken up with a kind of musical journalism – and that implies deadlines. Writing a book is a longer-term task, which is why it has taken me several years to compile this one. But as it gathered momentum I enjoyed it, most of it written away from London and the telephone at Eccleston Square, where I have lived for a quarter of a century. And I finish the book by typing this Preamble in the place where most of its pages have been written – in Neville and Molly Marriner's holiday house at Lyme.

J. A. Autumn 1984

(1)

Scenes from Childhood

My childhood was spent almost entirely in one house in South London. This was 9 Selsdon Road, a semi-detached red-brick affair with a laburnum and a lilac in the front garden, a little lawn at the back with vegetables and a loganberry bush at the bottom, backing on to more gardens, themselves backing on to the open grounds of a Jewish orphanage, the whole set on a hill leading up from West Norwood to Streatham, and down and across a valley. On the horizon was silhouetted the Horniman Museum. Just out of sight behind the orphanage was the Crystal Palace. Every Thursday night in the summer season from my bedroom window I could see the glow from the set pieces. I was tantalized by the bangs but I had a good view of the rockets. This was a feature of the summers until the last and biggest show of all when the Palace burned down, with the image remaining with me all these years of the goldfish in their pools boiled and then grilled by the conflagration.

I was born on 17 June 1922 down the hill and up again a bit, in Dulwich. My father had lived with his parents in Denmark Hill, Camberwell. Presumably the search for a house had brought them to nearby West Dulwich and then following my arrival, seven years after my sister Joan, my parents needed more space and found this not very pleasant house in SE27. Downstairs there was a hall, somewhere to put the barometer – 'Don't tap it,' my father would say, tapping it – and my father's bicycle, golf clubs and tennis racket. The front room was the living room, behind it the dining room and bookcases. The upright piano was sometimes in front, sometimes banished to the back so that I could bash away at it without disturbing the family quite so much. That is the awful thing about having so little space if you want to make music – knowing that you are overheard.

My father was more often out when I wanted to make a noise and both he and my mother were fairly tolerant of the shindy, but when my sister Joan was home from school the tension was considerable. She held the upper hand – often literally, otherwise with verbal weapons – until suddenly one day at the age of twelve or thirteen the Balance of Power changed and I began to boss her. I think my coming had seriously put her out. For seven years she had been number one; she was pretty and clever with her fingers, and then came the new squat little monster, my parents' favourite just by dint of juniority. At moments Joan and I had an extraordinary rapport, knew what the other was thinking or feeling, but all too often the difference in our ages, the proximity of our living areas and the fact that I could get away with murder while she was told off for minor offences inflamed her sensibilities, and made her morose and irritable.

There seemed to be so many crises in her life, caused maybe by things I knew nothing about, but I did see that her and my father's temperaments were in some ways too similar. There were endless skirmishes. I took after my mother at any rate in anticipating and avoiding confrontations whereas Joan never seemed to be able to resist bringing things to the boil. As soon as I was able to I escaped as much as possible, out for walks, playing games, but Joan was less outgoing than I was, could never make up her mind what to do with her spare time, didn't like taking exercise, wouldn't go out with boys if she could help it, couldn't even think what to wear a lot of the time, and therefore spent more time in the small homestead than was good for her. I recall tears and tantrums over piano examinations, term after term. She played quite well, could polish a piece for performance, but her nerves always got the better of her. Eventually she broke down and turned her back, not only on the piano but on the whole classical music repertoire. And the fact that I got more and more interested, more and more 'highbrow' in my tastes, did not improve our relationship.

I thought she was cruel to me but I am sure this was mainly because I was obnoxious and always knew how to curry favour with my parents. She had her pocket money docked whereas I could always wheedle more than my share. (Within reason, I must say.

I might get twopence over my weekly sixpence where her shilling might get knocked down to tenpence through giving offence.) Of course when I got near to the age of puberty I lusted after her. She was beautiful and she had wonderful breasts that I would have given anything to see, but in all those childhood and growing-up years I never saw a naked female at all.

Mornings I remember best when the dining-room table must have been in the front room because we could see only from the front of the house the ritual passing by of neighbours and my father's fellow commuters. If Mrs Kellaway, the undertaker's wife, started to clean the windows opposite that was all right, still time for another piece of toast. If 'Mr Lip', a German-looking man with a protruding mouth passed by, then it was time to be off. Remembering observing these people means that this must have been either during the school holidays or before prep or public school. There was time then to observe other things and people: the milk van whose horse got stung by a wasp, broke the shaft and lay down in misery; the leather-voiced man shouting 'Read your Bibles'; the local idiot lady; heart-throb schoolgirl Ruth Taylor from next door to the Kellaways ('I made me money in the 1926 flu epidemic, couldn't make the coffins fast enough'); the muffin man with the clanging bell and the tray on his head lined with green baize; the tricycle with the square navy-blue ice-cream refrigerator box, 'Walls, they're lovely!'

The view from the back of the house was a spacious vista. By night the valley was haunted by the noise of shunting trains, rolling stock that chuntered endlessly, even though the tunnels would occasionally blot out the sound for moments – then there was the din of the trucks giving out a sort of obbligato, different, higher pitches as the buffers hit each other, the chains clanking and then the quickening boom–boom–booms as the engine stopped and the trucks jammed rapidly backwards and forwards. By day the streets around were fairly boring, their geography mapped out by the people we knew or the people whose faces or habits I knew, and sometimes by the mysteriousness of neglected empty houses. Once further up our very own street there was straw on the road to muffle the noises for some sick person. But that must have been a very early memory indeed.

The first memory of all is not of home but of being in a hotel or restaurant in Ventnor, with my mother, and of my indignation because the waitress asked, 'And what will the *little* fellow have?' I would think that this was the memory of a story often retold except that I have a snapshot in my head of the table and the waitress standing beside my mother. Another early recollection is of being frightened because some idiot, probably our maid, threatening me one day, said, 'If you are not good, a man on a motor cycle will come and take you away to Africa.' As a result I was frightened out of my wits for some years whenever a motor cycle came along the street; I have never wanted to ride such a machine and, come to think of it, never much wanted to go to Africa (though I liked it well enough when I got there in 1983).

I wonder where that maid used to sleep, incidentally? I think she must have lived out because there was not a (fourth) bedroom for her. It just goes to show how cheap labour must have been in the twenties, although I believe that my father was earning as much as he ever did at that time. After the Wall Street crash and its repercussions his salary went down to £800 a year, not much to keep a family on. Holidays in Brittany became holidays in the Isle of Wight – Saint-Briac three years consecutively became a similar spell at Shanklin.

As my father was at the bank in Austin Friar's in the City every weekday and Saturday mornings too (there was usually steak for Saturday lunch), and since he was out most evenings, occupied by rehearsals for plays, committee meetings, tennis in the summer or gardening or a bonfire (always in his white trousers, to the despair of my long-suffering, washing mother), he was a rare commodity. Therefore I loved his company best. He was fun. I remember his goodnights to me when I was already in bed. He had a way of kissing on the neck and blowing a raspberry at the same time. He was inconsistent as a disciplinarian and I learned to gauge his moods. If refused in a request for pocket money or to be taken somewhere or bought something, I would bide my time and get my wish another day. (Poor Joan never learned this, to me, obvious fact of life.)

In the early days my mother was a ball of fire: did the shopping, cooking and cleaning (except for those few 'maid' years); mostly made her own clothes and my sister's; did all the darning, ironing and all the odd jobs too, and also took courses in upholstery and pewter work. No one else in the house could mend fuses or knock a nail in straight. She did all the fetching and carrying, and spoiled me rotten. As she grew older my sister came in for her share of housework and washing up, unwillingly. My mother was a good cook: roast beef, Yorkshire pudding, cakes of all kinds she excelled in, but most of the time, daytime especially, we had much simpler food. If she was out for the day shopping, I would be given sixpence to go down to West Norwood to buy myself a fourpenny piece of skate and two pennyworth of chips – a big meal.

My father never, I believe, told my mother how much he earned – on the advice of his mother and father. The result was that my poor mother, not exactly brilliant with finance, never quite understood what economy meant because she never had the overall picture. Especially since, when it came to holidays, my father would always spend freely. He also went for a solo holiday in the spring. Thinking about it subsequently I figured that he didn't care for her company much. Of course such a thing was not obvious to me as a child, especially since there was no bickering. I once asked my father, long after my mother died, whether, if it had all happened in the period after the Second World War, he wouldn't perhaps have left home and tried again. It was one of the few times that I asked such a probing question and it was dismissed quickly and angrily, but I thought I detected moist eyes.

My parents really were ill assorted. My mother, Florence, had apparently just got over another *affaire*, although I am sure that it wasn't a sexual one, and she said she married my father on the rebound. She was a model at Harrod's, as was her sister Ethel. Ethel married one of the bosses (Uncle Billy from Dundee) and struck it rich. Florence took my father, James, who worked all his life as a manager – whatever that meant – in a firm of merchant bankers called Seligmann Brothers. My father was not at the time of the marriage the jolly hail-fellow-well-met character that he was in later life. Photographs of him at that time remind me very much of Rachmaninov, jowly and gloomy. My parents' honeymoon began at Folkestone where they were supposed to stay the night and catch the packet boat the next day. But my father became suddenly terrified of the Channel-crossing to France and it was some days before he could bring himself to embark.

My first school was a local affair that I went to at the age of six, and my first piano teacher was a Miss Mabel Scott who taught Joan as well. She was German – her name was really Schott – and she boasted that she was a relative of Friedrich von Flotow who composed the opera *Martha*. What I remember about her is that I could twist her around my little finger, that she did nothing about my weak left hand nor my even weaker sense of rhythm and that she told me a story that haunted me for a long time. She had been to an open-air performance in Switzerland of a play based on *William Tell* and the protagonist had fired a real arrow which severed the head of the child playing his son. I continued with Miss Scott after I went, at the age of seven, to another and bigger school in Leigham Court Road.

What remains in my head from this one is waiting on staircases to march into assembly first thing in the morning, and that we had little paper silver and gold stars stuck on our work if it merited distinction. I also remember the journeys to and from school. Today kids get taken to school by their parents until the age of fourteen at least. After the first day or so at this second school, I always went alone. As always, typical perhaps of a Gemini, I explored every one of the possible routes there and back. One of the routes went through Broxholm Road where my Grandma Weight used to live.

I recall her benign, bland expression, her black clothes and lace – true granny clothes – and that she was not best pleased that every visit to her ended up by my persuading her landlady downstairs to play her gramophone, my favourite record being Rachmaninov playing his Prelude in C sharp minor, Op. 3 No. 2, on one side and 'The Bee's Wedding' on the other (with an idiosyncratic 'comma' in the latter before Rachy plays the tune – but that was a subtlety I did not appreciate until later).

Another route took me past the house where Stanley Lupino and his daughter Ida lived, and past a lofty elm tree which one day blew down in a gale with an almighty crack, missing me by a terrifying thirty yards or so. This elm was very close to the tennis club where I spent many happy hours, at first watching and then at fifteen or so as a playing member. Being shy, I was content to observe the habits and conventions of tennis society: how some people got out of playing with rabbits; how others were just too polite to extricate themselves from such situations (they were never to be good players themselves I found); how some players would crash their turn – in fact, how many things there were you could do without anybody questioning bad behaviour. I found parallels in animal behaviour, especially when several dogs met on waste land or common.

Cricket was a passion with me, played at school of course, but also in the garden, throwing the ball against the back wall of our house and then playing fancy shots – with a tennis ball, a hard ball less often because of fatal results to the windows. We played in parks, on commons and on waste land, parties of boys paralleled by the aforementioned parties of dogs. During one such session on the waste land I had a frightening experience. It had been raining; we had a ball made of stuff called composition, quite hard; the pitch was uneven. I bowled to another boy not well known to me and, although I was never faster than medium-to-slow, the ball hit him just over the eye and cut him quite badly. One of the boys said, 'Now you've gone and done it, he'll die,' and a neighbouring woman who applied first aid, frightened at the sight of blood no doubt, said something like, 'You boys ought to be ashamed of yourselves, hooligans . . . . ' I was disproportionately upset, went home 'in a state', and slept from early evening right through till next morning. I never saw the boy again, strangely enough, although I heard from others who had been in the same game that his cut soon healed.

At the age of eight it was time for me to go to my prep school, Dulwich College Preparatory – preparatory, in most cases, to going on to Dulwich College itself. I have been back to these two schools on only one occasion each and found them as diminished in size as theory has it. And I have never wanted to be a member of the Old Boys of either school. My father took me to Day One of the prep school but thereafter I made the journey by myself, either on foot or by bus. Needless to say, there were never any cars in our family. True to form I used many different ways of getting to school, and rather more coming home.

I would get up at the last possible moment. There is a special listening ear that you acquire if you are brought up in a house with only one bathroom and one lavatory. My father took cold baths and needed time to shave. The signal that he would not be out of the bathroom for some time was the noise he made in the bath, a kind of watery raspberry noise that I have only heard otherwise made by sea-lions. The two-minute signal was the ritual seven sneezes towards the end of his shaving – never more than seven, never less. By this time it would be 8.15 or so. By 8.25 I would have washed, within the letter of the act, had my breakfast in the kitchen and be on my way down the hill, along the orphanage fence, over the railway footbridge, past the Tannoy factory, hoping to catch the number 2 bus on the last leg of its journey to the Rosendale Hotel, or a number 3 on its way from a garage to join its proper route from Croxted Road towards London. If neither bus turned up or I was too late I would have to leg it smartly down the road beside the dreary cemetery, then into West Dulwich and up Alleyn Park Road to the prep school (or later, under the railway bridge and into the college grounds). Into the classroom for roll-call, then prayers in the hall.

I can remember the first day, all sitting about in the headmaster's study. Leggett, Bogarde – I can smell his sardine sandwiches as soon as I write the name, and his fishy bad breath – and Osler were three of the other 'new bugs'. The headmaster at that time was a frightening old lion of a parson called Leake, with a big face and a brindled moustache. Later his son Martin shared the job, and later still, confusing everybody, a man called Leakey bought (we all thought) his way in as a third. There were at one time 600 of us, I believe, in that not too large place, and yet our classes were never larger than twenty-four or so. Shy outside school, I was fairly sociable within it, although it was only in my last term, after four years, that I made a real friend.

When I started at the prep I had the rare gift of a photographic memory, but I soon lost that after a serious illness from which I very nearly died. What at first appeared to be scarlet fever turned out to be mastoiditis, the cure for which involved cutting the bone behind both ears to drain off poisonous fluid from the mastoid cells. It is an operation scarcely, if ever, performed nowadays, thanks to new drugs, but at that time (1931) it was new and tricky. With the fever my weight had dropped to 4 stone, and I was in a nursing home in Dulwich for at least two months, getting thoroughly spoiled – one aspect of the illness from which I scarcely recovered. My night nurse Phyllis was plain and blotchy but I fell deeply in love with her. Fifty years later I was crossing Westminster Bridge when a smell of buttered toast brought back the whole scene

– loving hands in the dark, my head swathed in bandages, that curious feeling behind my ears of deep and open wounds, with five yards of gauze bunging them both up, and the yucky smell of some medicament.

Behind all those bandages I was deaf and remained slightly so until eight years later when some knife-happy surgeon blighted my life by removing my left ear-drum, making my deafness complete on that side. The second operation was presaged by pains caused initially by a bully at Dulwich College. (I am tempted to name the yob – but not much.)

I went back to school, indulged by my parents because I had so nearly died, and never quite saw the point after that in trying as hard as I had before to be brilliant in class. I developed a resistance, for some reason, to being taught. If the teachers were good enough, or commanded my respect, or if I was plain scared of them, I would work and work well. In other words I would not apply myself except in certain cases and, alas, that attitude has made me what I am, and what I am not. I have always found conscious memorizing difficult. If only I had realized what a precious gift that photographic memory was.

I learned much more at the prep than at the college. At the college every teacher had a degree but few of them knew how to teach. At the prep few of them had degrees but a higher percentage knew how to teach. They had to. Best of all was a terrifying Swiss called Meyrat who taught us French, yellow-haired, with a high-domed forehead, ugly, often angry – first-class. Shepherd, Taylor, sarcastic Taggart, quick-tempered Leakey, they were all quite good. So was withering Witham, who despaired of ever getting me to understand algebra. I shared his despair, sometimes weeping with anguish underneath the dining-room table at home as I tried to unravel quadratic equations. But there were others who were frauds – obviously so. 'Fatty' Davis – did he imagine we couldn't see that he was reading it all out of a book propped up in his open attaché case?

Then there was dear old Chapman who tried so hard to keep his temper but we could not resist making him lose it because his voice went up a third in pitch and reverted to an Irish brogue. One thing I loved him for, though – and it was one of the big thrills in my young life. He would play the piano for the morning hymns at prayers and when it came to the last verse he would change the harmonies, make the whole thing richer, chromatic and magical. I cried sometimes for the beauty of it. No wonder I am still so harmony-conscious.

I managed eventually to get into the First Eleven at cricket and this was bliss. Sometimes the whole of the rest of the school would stay incarcerated while we, the Eleven, the élite, would go to the playing field. Oh, the smell of the new-cut grass, the air, and the game itself, even if I didn't do particularly well! Never have I been so happy and carefree.

There wasn't much bullying at the prep school except for one boy who frightened the life out of me and many others. Shaw's face was like an obscene mask. He was gross and had developed his diaphragm to such an extent that he would invite us to punch him there as hard as we could but it didn't ever hurt him. I never fought and I was never beaten. But I was disgraced once. One evening, leaving late after doing some prep for the next day, I saw a boy trying to force open the tuckshop door with a penknife. I knew him to be thoroughly incompetent so, being a prefect, I said, 'Cut it out; beat it,' but I didn't see any need to pursue the matter. About two months later, by which time I had entirely forgotten the incident – there was a holiday coming up or I was away from school with a cold or something – the boy apparently returned to the shop, broke in and when he was discovered by somebody else swore that it was my idea, that I had put him up to it and so on. I had completely forgotten the incident and my explanations were confused enough to sound guilty and I was de-prefected. The cloud was never removed and I left under it, or at least that's how it felt.

But it cannot have been quite as bad as all that because I enjoyed lots of things about that final year. I was part of two little circles. The boy I sat next to was called Silkin, John Silkin – just as good-looking then as he is now and a stalwart of the Labour Party. I never called him or anybody else at school by their Christian name – although perhaps I should say 'given' name in Silkin's case. My mother divided people she met into Jews and Others. 'He's a little Jewboy.' Like many other things my mother said, I thought it foolish, but it did permeate my thinking enough, in moments of stress, to call Silkin 'you bloody Jew'. He protested. I said, 'All right, you can call me a bloody Christian.'

'Yes, but it doesn't carry the same implications and it's unfair.'

I thought about it and I agreed and stopped calling anybody anything like that. We did bait one fellow because he was slightly crippled and had slurred speech. He fought back with a razor once. At morning and lunch break there was another sport, called Swann-baiting. But Donald deserves a chapter to himself. Here and now I'll say only that, although our friendship was curiously spasmodic, it was, for me, the most important one I had in my teens, especially since it was my first musical friendship.

One musical experience we had in common at the prep school was our delight in Mr Chapman's harmonically pepped-up last verses of hymns and also of the songs that he would occasionally play to us. (One of them was a Schumann song I have scarcely heard since called 'Sonnenschein'.) We also enjoyed records played to us by the new, third, headmaster, J. H. Leakey. Leakey took us once to a Robert Mayer Children's Concert, the first time I ever heard a symphony orchestra, and also, one memorable afternoon, to the ballet where we saw the work that all children seem to have experienced as their first one, *Les Sylphides*, followed by *Port Said* with music by one Konstantinov, and *Petrushka*, which was a knock-out experience with Leon Woizikowsky in the title role. I immediately went to the local record shop and ordered 'The Russian Dance' and 'The Coachmen's Dance' from Stravinsky's ballet, available on a ten-inch Decca record for the sum of one shilling and sixpence, much cheaper than HMV or Columbia records.

I had been passionate about the gramophone from a very early age indeed. I was often given as a birthday or Christmas present a toy gramophone that went 'phut' after about ten days of over-use. By that time I knew the little seven-inch records by heart and endeavoured to revive the dead gramophone by pushing the record round with one hand, sticking my fingernails in the grooves and singing the music. Eventually I was given a proper 'table-model' gramophone and I shall never forget the excitement of that first encounter, the smell of the polished wood and the packets of fibre and steel needles that went with it. We had few records at any time and all pocket money that did not go on sweets, laboriously saved up and augmented twice a year by birthday or Christmas gifts, went on records. The choice was agonizing but enthralling. Vocal gems from *Turandot*, the overture to *Die Zauberflöte*, Liszt's *Hungarian Rhapsody No. 2*, which developed a recurring groove near the beginning because the cellos and double-basses in Stokowski's famous orchestral transcription went so low and deep.

I could never afford to buy more than one record at a time so that I knew parts 3 and 4 of Franck's *Variations Symphoniques* better than parts 1 and 2. (That was Alfred Cortot with a splosh of wrong notes on the last chord.) Inherited from somewhere was a single-sided disc of Rachmaninov playing Chopin's Waltz in E flat (so I knew it when it came at the end of *Les Sylphides*) with a glamorous expanse of shiny black wax on the back. It was much thicker than a normal disc too. Certain pieces would inspire in me a sort of mental orgasm: the Franck did it in side 4 and so did a record that a grown-up friend once brought for me to hear by a composer I had never heard of called Delius. The effect that *On hearing the first cuckoo in spring* had on me was so obviously profound that the kind man, Harold Hersee, an amateur-acting friend of the family, generously gave it to me.

Life seemed to revolve round these revolving records for me. I would give my family for presents at Christmas, records that, by an amazing coincidence, I happened to want. I can remember asking my father once for the *Meistersinger* overture for my birthday. The poor man could not find it at the shop so brought me instead the intermezzos from *The Jewels of the Madonna* by Wolf-Ferrari. Mind you, I came to like those intermezzos a little later but even when I hear them today they still bring that initial feeling of tearful rage and disappointment. My father Jimmy was simply bewildered by my tears. I had been looking forward for weeks to the grand sound of the opening of Wagner's overture with its majestic tread and endless chains of harmonies refusing to come to a cadence. To be fobbed off with those wispy little Italian flute tunes and harp tinkles, quasi-archaic traceries — ugh! But soon he found the Wagner overture and I loved him for it. Loved the record too, not just the music but even the record itself, the dark green label, the gold lettering, the magic of the name of the conductor, Leo Blech (no relation to Harry), and the difference in texture between the grooves and the shiny bit in the middle with the double-looping lines where the needle would go on and on and on until stopped.

I shall describe later the ecstasy of hearing the records at the local record shop. Later on in my teens, weaned away from the classics temporarily by my sister, I would buy jazz records which were cheaper than the classics. Fats Waller fascinated me, so did Art Tatum, Fred Astaire, George Gershwin's *Rhapsody in Blue*, Alec Templeton's *Bach Goes to Town*. In my later teens came the first time I bought more than one record at a time. It was Rachmaninov's Piano Concerto No. 2, with Benno Moiseiwitsch as soloist and the orchestra conducted by Walter Goehr, 4 records, 16 shillings. If this was the sort of book that indulged in such fancies I would add, 'Little did I then think that one day I would meet some of the people whose names I dwelt on with such reverence – like Moiseiwitsch, for example, and Walter Goehr who I came to know quite well.'

The first wireless we had was of the 'whisker' variety and it was more remarkable as an object in itself than as a conveyor of music. Then came a Kolsterbrand (a name redolent of the times for anybody who had one, a small table-model machine with carved wood, inlaid with some kind of pre-lurex material, round the speaker) and this was what we sat round in the evenings sometimes – that is, when my parents were not out rehearsing. It was Gilbert and Sullivan in my pre-teens for the Norwood and Streatham Operatic Society; *Amazing Dr Clitterhouse*s and *Night Must Fall*s later on. My sister and I were left at home, and quite often she would go out to friends' houses and I would be left on my own, either to bash the piano or to listen to the gramophone or wireless. I was thankful when the era of Sullivan, tempered occasionally with Edward German (I made my stage début at the age of eight as a page in *Merrie England*) or Lionel Monckton, came to a close because while the rehearsal periods were on there was nothing but Sullivan round the piano in the evenings and my mother singing the tunes all day.

In the school holidays I rarely saw my school mates and, having got over the 'But Mother, what am I going to do today?' questions, I would spend most of my time, when not going out for long walks, with music. Sight-reading the piano scores of composers A–Z from the public library took up a lot of the time and then I also indulged in day-dreaming improvisations whose imaginary titles I logged in an exercise book. I still have the book and the opus numbers exceeded 500, but nothing was written down on music paper.

This proves, I suppose, that I was a listener type rather than a composer type. It never occurred to me to ask to learn how to write it all down or even to work it out for myself. (That came later.) It is interesting to compare, for example, the early efforts of Benjamin Britten and Richard Rodney Bennett, composers whose first efforts on manuscript paper were imitations of what music *looked* like – in other words, nice shapes on paper regardless of what it *sounded* like. Anyway, my titles, complete with details of movements and occasional haughty judgements, were all carefully set down. They often reflected the sort of music I had heard on the educating wireless. The *Radio Times* was my constant guide; and so were musical commentators like Walford Davies, that dear benign old fuddy-duddy. I can recall now him talking about the slow movement of Schubert's Symphony No. 9, the 'Great C major'. He opened doors for me all right, not just into new rooms, but into new landscapes.

My piano playing became fluent, my sight-reading quite fair, but alas! my sense of rhythm was bad. That was something that all my listening and my rather feeble teachers could do nothing to improve. It was always the stumbling-block when I played duets with Jimmy. However, we did get through a number of Haydn symphonies, Moritz Moszkowski – and I still really know the Brahms symphonies better as duets than as orchestral works, simply because that is how I heard them for the first hundred times.

The first person I met who made a living from music was Ronald Gourlay. He was also the first blind person I met. The Gourlays lived not far from us in West Norwood. There were Nance and Dad, Brummagems retired to London, and their children Ron, Phyl and Joan, who was very much the youngest. Ron was stout, probably in his forties when we met, drank a lot of beer and had made a career in the variety world. He was an 'Uncle' for BBC *Children's Hour*, to which I was an avid listener, and my first visit to Broadcasting House was with him. He composed one song that became a hit, a nice tune with silly words called 'The Dicky Bird Hop'. He whistled beautifully and was capable of trilling and phrasing in a way that took me about two years of hard practising and experimenting (while sitting in the lavatory) to emulate. Ron was usually in the company of three or four small girls, so I was lucky to get taken about by him sometimes. Of course I had the advantage over the girls in that I could begin to appreciate his extraordinary gifts as an improviser.

One of his turns on the wireless or on the music-halls was to ask the audience to suggest four or five tunes which he would then weave into a four- or five-minute medley, frequently combining two or even three of the tunes simultaneously. In public these 'impros', as he called them, had to be relatively simple but sometimes at home after dinner and a few pints of beer he would get quite inspired, especially if his other blind friend, a professional singer called Sinclair Logan, with a mellifluous baritone voice, were there too. One evening Ron improvised for three-quarters of an hour on the popular song 'The music goes around and around', ending up with a whopping great fugue. Sometimes the two musicians would recall how they had escaped from some institution for the blind, climbed out of a second-floor window, and wandered about all night before being picked up by the police in the morning.

The rest of the Gourlays were unmusical and I can remember one day being hoity-toity with Phyl who had kindly asked me to play her my latest thrilling birthday present record. It was the Polka and Fugue from Weinberger's *Schwanda the Bagpiper*. It lasted only eight minutes but dear Phyl talked all the way through the music, to my mounting horror and fury, and then at the end said, 'Oh, that's a nice record.' To which I replied, 'Yes, then you must hear it sometime.' I was glad to be sent out of the room for cheeking my elders.

The first performance of music I was taken to would have been some of the Gilbert and Sullivan operas but the orchestra must have been pretty bad and all I can recall of them is the look of the orchestra and how astonished I was that the sound I knew from the gramophone records was produced by that sprawling collection of men and women and instruments and music stands with a silly man (Percy Bright) standing in the middle having what looked like a public fit. But then I was taken to Streatham Hill Theatre for a professional performance of *Lilac Time*, probably with Richard Tauber as Schubert. Those wonderful melodies and the sound of the orchestra had the effect of making me weep throughout the entire performance. And the same thing happened a year or two later when I was taken to the same place for my first opera *Madam Butterfly*, with Maggie Teyte as the heroine. Tears still come easily when I am moved and, despite now knowing that this is nothing to be proud of – didn't Hitler cry easily? – I am somehow impressed when tears overcome me.

My first ballet was *Petrushka*; my first concert was a Robert Mayer Children's Concert conducted by Dr Malcolm Sargent at the Central Hall, Westminster, and my first evening concert was conducted by Sir Hamilton Harty. I remember complaining to my father that the whole thing was a swindle because Harty was not throwing himself about as Sargent had done – nor did he seem to be doing much elementary time-beating. Seeing that there were some empty seats behind the orchestra, and that this was my first visit to Queen's Hall, my father suggested that we should take a look at the orchestra from behind, where we would be facing the conductor and be able to see exactly what he was, or was not, doing. This was a most sensible idea because we could then observe that Hamilton Harty was doing it all with his *eyes* plus rather sparse gestures with his hands. The work was Brahms's Fourth Symphony which I knew well from our piano duetting. So I was able to appreciate how Harty got his results, and how just with a look he could produce a thrilling fortissimo or an even more thrilling pianissimo.

The only other pre-war concert that I can remember was one in which Solomon played the British première of Arthur Bliss's Piano Concerto, conducted by Sir Adrian Boult. That morning at home I had broken a string on our upright piano, the only time I have done such a thing. Blow me down if Solomon didn't break a string that very evening in Queen's Hall. And that's the only time I remember it happening at a concert. Apparently it was nothing for Beethoven to break about half a dozen per concert. In fact the only other occasion in my experience was when Noel Mewton-Wood broke a string while we were playing duets on two pianos. That stayed in my mind because Noel immediately yanked out the offending string and repaired it on the spot. I didn't know any other pianist who could have done that or who knew anything about the maintenance of his instrument – until, that is, I met Alfred Brendel a long time later. It is curious that pianists (and maybe organists) are the only instrumentalists usually incapable of doing minor repairs to the tools of their livelihood.

I shall never forget the day I first played on a concert grand piano. As I have said, we had an upright at home and a pleasant enough one it was. Curiously enough, considering the number of hours that I sat at it – six hours a day and more in school holidays – I cannot now recall the name of the obscure German manufacturer. (But then, have you tried that parlour game of asking the company to describe the face of their watch – does it have every hour marked, or only three, six, nine and twelve o'clock; are the numerals arabic or roman; what colour is it, etc.?)

At the age of sixteen I played in my first concert. This was at Dulwich College and I elected to play a duet with my teacher, Mr Burgess. He was a kind, self-effacing man, incredibly tall and angular, with teeth that seemed to be pouring out of his mouth. We were to play 'Italy', a quick tarantella by Moszkowski from a suite always known in the family as *From Poreign Farts*. (When my mother objected to the rude word my father or I would point out that we were using the German word 'Fahrt', meaning 'journey'.) There were always mock German jokes and accents in our family, arising from studies in Germany, not only from my father but from his brothers, Bill, the father of Kingsley, and Leslie, the bachelor one. When I met Gerard Hoffnung, and also when I was living in Swiss Cottage and Hampstead, the habit was renewed. Steve Race tries to get me to cut it down in *My Music* but I find it a useful shield for my embarrassment, particularly when I wish to correct something and don't want to appear to be pedantic.

Mr Burgess said that if I wanted to get accustomed to the piano to be used in the concert I could go and try it out during the lunch hour on the day. I entered the big empty hall and there was that great shining instrument dominating the stage. I think that the only time I had played on a grand piano before this was at the Gourlays, where there was a small brown grand. This incredibly glamorous object before me was jet-black, seemingly in mint condition, and seemed to stretch away for a couple of blocks. Alone in the hall I sat down at this sleek enormous Blüthner and played a few chords. It made sounds that were so beautiful they quite transported me. I played badly at the concert, partly out of fright, but as much because I was so much in awe of this 'wondrous machine'. However the concert included one performer who could and did control this shiny black Blüthner – to perfection, it seemed to me. Formerly this chap, in the sixth, was just a name to me: Lehmann, A. G. Now he became a hero. He played Mendelssohn's Piano Concerto

No. 1 in G minor and then, exquisitely, Chopin's *Berceuse*.

The college was a disappointment to me. Having tasted a little seniority at the prep, being in the cricket Eleven and being, before the Fall, a prefect, it was rather miserable to go to the bigger school and be a nobody once more. Even cricket lost its charm there because I was put in nasty little games on parts of the playing field where three or four games overlapped. Cover point in one game would be standing within a couple of feet of mid-wicket in another, and you had to be an Argus not to get hit unawares.

There were few teachers that I found any good. Some were so bad that we made mincemeat of them, young chaps fresh from their universities with no skill at controlling a class, no style and very bad accents in French and German. There was one master who did have style though, and that was Eric Parsley. 'Good morning, gents,' he is reputed to have negotiated that all-important first morning of teaching with. 'The name is Parsley, spelt the same way as the 'umble vegetable.' He not only had a good French accent, he wore white ties which was unheard of in the thirties – long ones, not bows – and he talked to us man to man, and man of the world at that.

There was also one absolute tyrant and that was Mr Tredgold, a thin, pinched spinster of a man with a lashing tongue. Punishments flew about in his class but he got results and yours truly flew to the top of his Latin class. I even developed a bit of style myself in translation. But there was no man-of-the-world stuff about Tredgold. It was dangerous in his class. He would start kicking the desk and it was the most menacing sound in the world. And if you were translating and made the mistake of making even the slightest unconscious gesture . . . . 'Amis, we are not a school of acting so kindly keep your hands still. I have a feeling that you are trying to disguise that your homework has been scamped, yes, sir, scamped. (*Kick*.) Do you hear me? (*Kick*.) SCAMPED.' We were not beaten for misdemeanours, only given lines or kept in for half-holidays, but it was the atmosphere that was so terrifying. I never see Britten's opera *Billy Budd* without thinking of Mr Tredgold – that's how tense it all was.

My companions at the college were a rather sweet-natured boy called Colin Bryant, who's now in flying and whom I still see occasionally; a rather raffish unhealthy lad called Dyches; a crazy chap called Jackson who was acrobatic by nature – if we went to the cinema I would pretend to push him as we came out of the circle and he would go crashing right down the stairs accidentally-on-purpose, to the consternation and sometimes indignation of old ladies – but my cronies, in the lunch hour especially, were Annatt, Brougham and Pope.

We were wisecrackers and developed rather cynical attitudes to life that I thought were rather depressing but seemed to be the only way. One ever so slightly artistic side to our coarseness was that we could all belch on definite pitches, our speciality being the quartet from *Rigoletto*. Was it Annatt or Brougham who could do the coloratura passages quite accurately? Difficult to remember except that his success endangered the performance with gales of laughter.

There was pressure exerted on every boy at the college to join the Officers' Training Corps or the Boy Scouts – and, if neither of these, then at any rate the choir. I hate the idea of the military – imagine trying to control anything as innately obdurate as puttees! – and the Scouts seemed to be ridiculous. It wasn't entirely laziness that made me escape all forms of extreme physical exertion; it was also the occasional violence involved in such activities. In the Easter terms, when the ground was too wet for rugby, there were awful 'run-rounds'. You were supposed to run for miles. I tried one and nearly collapsed, and got out of them somehow on all subsequent occasions. I also skipped most of the rugger – too much kicking and fear of injury. I likewise ducked the OTC and the Scouts. So began the awful business of grown-up emotions like conscience, fear of retribution and the injustice of the world. 'Lost innocence' turns to 'found guilty'.

I should really have been punished for not joining the OTC, for skipping the runs and the rugger, so I felt guilty. On the other hand I did not see why one should go with the herd. On the third hand I wanted people to like me. And if and when I left school, what on earth was I going to do, what was I good for? Music was my passion but at that time I had no thought that I could ever earn a living by it. Even in the school choir I had come a cropper one day when the music master finally discovered that I was the culprit singing an octave too low with my newly broken voice.

Life was not fair. My abiding impression of that time – it comes in dreams still – is of rushing about from classroom to classroom.

We did not have all our classes in our own classroom but had to go to the room where the master doing the next class was. Usually the next class was two buildings and five or six floors away. There was supposed to be a five-minute gap between one class and the next but so often the first master would keep you over time and the next one would punish you for being late. Oh yes, I admit I was lucky to go to a 'decent' school, lucky not to be bullied, flogged or forced into the Scouts or the OTC. . . .

Where I was *un*lucky was that my ears, having behaved themselves since I was eight, started playing up again when I was sixteen. It was decided that I should enter the Ear, Nose and Throat Hospital in Golden Square, near Piccadilly Circus, for a check-up operation. An ear-drum was removed (without parental consultation) and I stayed there a month recovering, pillow-fighting with other mastoid patients and learning about life from the other patients. They all talked about their jobs except one foul-mouthed but extremely entertaining man who turned out for his departure wearing a dog-collar. Another good friend to me there was a railway porter. It was all new experience for a lad who had led a sheltered suburban life. So was whistling at and talking to the prostitutes down below in Golden Square.

My parents decided to take advantage of my convalescence and absence from the school during the summer term – shame about missing the cricket – by taking me on a holiday, our first abroad for some years. We went to Ste-Maxime, not far from St-Tropez, and we stayed at a delightful hotel where my chief memories are of bathing, cafés in the street, and sitting in the lavatory at our hotel with mimosa blossom actually invading the large white-washed *lavabo*. In fact the hotel was called Les Mimosas and the management made me a birthday cake with mimosas in icing on it.

In view of my lack of scholastic brilliance my parents decided that I need not return to Dulwich College. My father would try and find me a job in the City and we would see what the future had in store for us in the autumn of 1939.

(2)

Donald Swann

He was Bumface and I was Barrel, undignified names but certainly at that time appropriate. I was plump and his face was curiously squashed together. He was quick to laugh, almost uncontrollably, contagiously, and also quick to lose his temper. In the playground during break a line would form, and opposed to it would be Bumface. Here he would only pretend to lose his temper and would try and penetrate the line. We were in different forms and it was not until I realized that he was musical that I got to know him, simultaneously moving into the same class for what was, for both of us, our last term at Dulwich College Preparatory School.

Every year there was an event called the Hobbies Exhibition. You entered your woodwork, artefacts, art works, Plasticine model of the Taj Mahal or whatever it was. The most ingenious was a really large pendulum with a pen on the end that made the most intricate patterns on paper. This exhibition was a horror for me because I didn't have any hobbies except music and I could not very well take our upright piano or the gramophone. In desperation I took my stamp album. But one year Bumface entered some manuscripts of some piano pieces he had COMPOSED, suites I think they were or sonatinas, spidery writing in black ink with the composer's name at the top: D. I. Swann.

At that time I didn't even know that his Christian name was Donald and it was a lot later that I discovered that his second name was Ibrahim. By golly, you had to keep your other names quiet at schools in those days, you would get so ragged about them. Even now I think twice before telling anybody that my second name is Preston in case the taunt should come back: 'prissy' or 'pansy'

39

Preston – the Battle of Preston Pans that we were always hearing about in History.

What kind of a Christian name was Ibrahim? No kind at all: his mother was a Mohammedan. She had been a nurse and had met Donald's Russian-born father, Herbert, when he was desperately trying to finish his medical training in the middle of a revolution. He did finish it; they married, and if their son had been born in Russia, he would have been a Russki because the Swanns had been settled in the country for so many generations. But by that time Herbert was a *locum tenens* in Llanelli – which is where Donald first saw the light of day.

His mother died just about the time I got to know Donald, although he did not talk about it, either then or later. Donald and I started visiting each other's homes, more often I his because it contained not only a piano but also a ping-pong table. We took the train from West Dulwich to the Elephant and Castle. Herbert was a GP living at 92 Walworth Road which backed on to the railway line about fifty yards from the station, near enough for us to whistle out of the carriage window so that the wall-eyed maid Ada could put out the macaroni cheese – it couldn't have been that dish every time but memory insists it was – together with tea, which Donald drank then, as now, Russian-style, very weak, no milk but lemon. His table manners were atrocious then. ('Poor little chap, he lacks a mother,' said mine.) He guzzled his drinks and always attacked sandwiches with both hands and, if it was fish for a change, let the chips fall where they may.

Herbert was a great charmer, bald-headed, and not only with a strong Russian accent but a habit of larding his speech and other people's with curious Russian sounds like 'unja', if you can imagine that vocalized very quickly. Marion, the elder sister, had hair parted in the middle and looked to me very foreign, obviously having taken on aspects of her mother's looks – and the mother hailed from down by the Caspian Sea somewhere. But usually Marion had not arrived back from her school and Herbert would be out visiting his patients or receiving them in the surgery down below.

The problems facing Donald and me on such occasions were: shortage of time and which to play first – table tennis or piano duets. As soon as the quick meal was over we would speed to one floor or the other. When the first bout of ping-pong was over there was a Gadarene rush downstairs to the piano. We played proper music from the vast library of four-hand music that every musical Russian family possesses – original works for the medium plus innumerable arrangements of quartets, symphonies, operas, everything imaginable. Part of the fun for me was recognizing well-known pieces from the Russian Cyrillic spelling or trying to decipher the names. Vast quantities of what looked like BAX would reveal themselves as BACH. We would beef through a Brahms symphonic movement perhaps, but mostly we improvised. Donald knew about harmony from the technical and practical point of view, so he kept the bass going while I threw in tunes and decoration at the top end.

After some time we developed sufficient empathy to know not only that we were going to modulate from one key to another but even to which particular key we were going. That takes a bit of doing. There was one silly tune that we improvised on for hours until Herbert would leave his surgery, come half-way up the stairs and shout for us to change the theme. He was going crackers down there with the monotony of it.

More ping-pong, music, ping-pong, music, then it was time to go. We would make the platform with seconds to spare. Once Donald actually managed to lure me into a Ladies Only carriage. He was left spluttering with laughter back on the platform while I blushed deep red at some spinster facing me in the forbidden carriage.

That last summer at the prep school with my new-found friend was truly halcyon, certainly the high point of my schooldays. I went on to Dulwich College from the prep school, whereas clever Donald had won a scholarship to Westminster as one of the King's Scholars. Our friendship continued, but was restricted firstly by the fact that Donald lived in at Westminster and secondly by Donald's own nature. Over the years I have come to realize that although he stands loyally by his friends on one level he blows hot and cold about the notion of actually being with them.

At times I have been possessive about friends of the opposite sex but not, I fancy, about those of my own sex. It worried me, upset me, that sometimes Donald did not seem to want to meet at all during the holidays. At other times he was keen. Yet always when we *did* meet the time was spent blissfully happily – by both of us as far as I could judge. My best friends are those with whom I can exchange musical pleasures, and verbal ones combined with humour. With all my male friends in particular there builds up a repertoire of private jokes, sayings, expressions, allusions. It almost amounts to a vernacular.

My only acquaintance in professional music was the entertainer Ronald Gourlay but the Swanns knew quite a number, many of whom were, like Herbert, Anglo-Russian. There was, for example, Donald's uncle Alfred J. Swan (only one 'n', curiously enough), who was a composer, an expert on Russian church music and the first biographer in the English language of Skryabin (whom he actually knew!) and a friend of Nicolay Medtner and Sergey Rachmaninov (golly!). Then there were the Collingwoods: Lawrance, composer, conductor, adviser to HMV, the Musical Director of Sadler's Wells Opera, and his Russian wife, whom he had met while he was studying in St Petersburg. I was introduced to these friends.

Up to the war Donald composed a bit. We were both fascinated by music that followed in the wake of Rachmaninov and the early Stravinsky ballets and by songs, especially those with chromatic harmonies. We particularly liked flashy, splashy introductions to songs such as are to be found in Medtner, Ireland, Warlock and Bax. Donald was a dab hand at inventing these incipits himself and would sometimes write the rest of the song too. One of the first was a setting (dedicated to J. A., what's more) of Byron's 'So, we'll go no more a-roving', which, after the squashy piano opening, gets down to the poem. The novelty of the setting is that the voice part is in four beats to the bar, but the piano plays in seven beats to the same bar. The extraordinary thing is it works and an audience doesn't spot it.

During the early part of the war Donald sometimes came to stay with me in the mock-Tudor mock village called Loudwater near Rickmansworth, where I was living with my parents, and working at E.M.G. Handmade Gramophones in London. I remember one Easter especially because we made it a Stravinsky Festival. I brought home everything of the great Igor after *The Rite of Spring* that I could lay hands on: *The Wedding, L'histoire du soldat*, the Octet, the Symphony of Psalms, all directed on records by the composer. Donald and I were fairly baffled by it all and we took refuge in the two pianos that we had in this house, playing our favourites:

Rachmaninov's Suite No. 2, very tricky – I found it difficult to keep up with Donald who always had a much better technique and sense of rhythm – and things like Arthur Benjamin's *Jamaican Rumba* and Lennox Berkeley's seventy-five second *Polka*, which we adored so much we orchestrated it. We even sent it to the composer who was quite nice about it although he thought that our using trombones was somewhat like cracking a nut with a steam-hammer. He was baffled, too, by our special effect on the off-beat last chord in which we not only scored orchestrally but asked the fifth desk of violas to shout, 'Oi' – ah, youth!

Playing two pianos was also the main enjoyment of the times when I went to stay with Donald in Isleworth, the home of Herbert Swann's second wife, Irene Bonnett. Irene was a violinist, a very professional kind of amateur player, a teacher who had studied at St Paul's Girls' School with Gustav Holst. Irene was not at home much, leaving us with her mother, a very old and somewhat eccentric lady, made all the more eccentric by the fact that her current memory was almost nil. Often the only way Irene's anxious question, as to whether Mother had had any lunch, could be answered was by looking in the kitchen and making deductions from the evidence of the larder and the washing-up situation. The old lady's memory was prodigious when it came to the past – as it were, her memory bank's deposit account. She could recite at least half a dozen Shakespeare plays from beginning to end, so we were mightily relieved if some quotation that came up was from Act V. Otherwise we might be regaled with a completely recalled, un-stoppable *Hamlet*.

Then Donald went off to Greece in 1943 to do his war work with the Friends' Ambulance. When he came back three years later he said he had a few new songs to show me and he came and played them. His muse had lost weight. These new ones were revue numbers and/or imbued with Greek rhythms. Curiously enough, 'So, we'll go no more a-roving' was prophetic because the 7/8 accompaniment sounds as if Donald had consciously given Byron's poem a Hellenic flavour. These new songs were written not before Swann met Flanders but before their collaboration.

In 1947 Donald and I went off on a jaunt together to Salzburg for the month of May. Students from Princeton had got the idea that they needed to meet their counterparts in Europe and, more important, that students on that continent, having been bottled up in their own countries during wartime, needed to get out of their bottles and meet their fellow Europeans. The venue was Leopoldskron, a one-time archbishop's palace by a lake just outside Salzburg. The deal was that you got yourself there and then everything was provided. The seminars were on various aspects of the American way of life: economy, history, literature, politics *und so weiter*.

After two or three years they decided to have a go at music, so some thirty students from all over Europe were invited. The selection was certainly odd because neither Donald nor myself were students, nor was Douglas Gamley, an Australian living in London, now well known as a conductor and arranger on the lighter side of heavy music. A fourth person from the United Kingdom who arrived later in the month was the music critic Arthur Jacobs, known as a writer and lexicographer and as the Director of Music at Huddersfield Polytechnic.

So we three arrived, expecting that the American way of life would reveal itself as highly efficient and smooth running. Wrong! The Princeton lot were charming but vague. The organization was as haphazard as the selection had been. Yet the final result was good, rewarding and meaningful. (One day in the office I saw a telegram sent to a German applicant which read, 'Regret unable to find place for you. Seminar overbooked.' But attached to it was a note reading, 'Too late. He had already arrived.')

There were French, Germans, Italians, Scandinavians and us Brits. The nations sat separately at the first supper. The food hovered uneasily between United States' and Austrian characteristics: American army rations, thinned out, watered down, and cooked with Austrian overtones – not very good but then Europe was still fairly hungry in 1947. After supper the national grouping prevailed, despite Princetonians doing their best to jolly us up. Donald muttered to me, 'My dear chap, I think the occasion calls for a spot of *Oklahoma*' – still fairly new but famous all over the world by name and sound.

He fetched his score, sat down at the piano and within three minutes everybody had bee-lined for the piano. Within ten minutes we were all singing. Within a couple of hours everybody knew everybody except the Americans, who retired in a big cultural sulk.

Oklahoma was not what it was all about – they were trying to promote higher things, not the America of Hershey bars, Coke, chewing-gum, Hollywood and *Oklahoma,* for Christ's sake!

An Austrian janitor who had been at Leopoldskron a long time told me later that after three days the music seminar had thawed to a warmth all the other seminars had reached only after three weeks. In fact some of the Princetonians got extremely worried. We were fratting too much and some members of the seminar were even exhibiting anti-American feelings.

Charles Jones was in charge of the musical programme and studies and he gave most of the lectures and led discussions. Charles is a composer (born 1910), originally from Canada but for many years now a New Yorker. He is liberal, genial, urbane. His compositions are gentle and civilized – rather like himself, cultivated but somewhat lacking in either lyrical passion or intellectual fire. Charles knew all the living American composers and he proved himself an excellent guide to the contemporary American musical scene which we Europeans were generally so ignorant of at that time. Through records I already knew Roy Harris, George Gershwin, Charles Ives and Aaron Copland in moderation, but at Salzburg we had a chance to get to grips with Carl Ruggles, Ives's vast *Concord* Sonata, Roger Sessions's exhilarating Symphony No. 2 and the music of younger men such as Alexei Haieff, Harold Shapero, Lukas Foss and others, either on records or in live performances, given principally by the pianist-composer Noel Lee and a French string quartet.

Most of us Europeans had, frankly, come for a free jaunt and we only gradually came to realize that the Americans, for all their vagueness in organization and their newness in composition, had something worthwhile to offer. The Germans were especially toffee-nosed at the beginning, apart from one exceptionally studious youth who bored us with his long speeches but gradually revealed a depth of culture that was formidable, his knowledge of French, German and American literature flooring everybody, especially the Princetonians. His name was Joachim Kaiser. He is now a well-known Munich music critic and has written a good book on pianists.

Several other musicians that I met at Salzburg became friends and/or famous: Boris Blacher (of the teachers), the composer;

Marius Constant, the conductor-composer; Noel Lee, and of course Donald Swann himself. Throughout the month Donald kept up the *Oklahoma* connection, despite black looks from the Americans. Another recurring phrase was Donald's line about the local mountain that stared him in the face every morning when he looked out of the window. 'Got to climb the damned thing,' he kept on saying. So about two days before the end of the month we set out to do just that, Donald, Doug Gamley and myself.

The Untersberg proved to be higher and more daunting than it appeared. Donald was in a hurry. Douglas kept somewhere between Donald, hundreds of yards ahead, and myself. The last hundred yards before the flat summit were solid steep ice, very difficult going. On top, we had ascertained beforehand, there was a hostel with a bar. As I downed my much needed litre of beer I announced, 'Dies ist meine erste und letzte Berg.' But I was none the worse for my unwonted exertion. Doug was in good shape and Donald seemed to be, although the effort had a bad effect on him. He suffered the following day from asthma, the first attack I think, and was quite ill during the whole of the following month, though not seriously so until we got home. We saw the sun set from the top of the mountain, slept like tops in the hostel, saw the sun rise and cantered down back to Leopoldskron.

When the summer school started in 1948 at Bryanston, somehow Friday night cabarets sprang up. The Amadeus String Quartet would do a cod version of a Bartók quartet to everybody's delight, except William Glock's. I can remember singing a parody of 'My heart belongs to Daddy' directed at Stanley Spencer in the audience – to his huge delight – with words that began, 'Oh, my heart belongs to Cookham'.

One year I got Donald to come and work in the office. He did, and we all had great pleasure by his presence, even if he was absent-minded at times. That was predictable. He also fell in love – as usual with an English Rose – and he took part in the cabarets, producing some fine pre-Flanders efforts. One of them was called 'Mediterranean blue', a concerted number that a small chorus could sing, and another called 'My sister Ruth' with words by Paul Townsend.

There were about eight verses of this epic, with solo lines

scattered throughout. One of these solo voices belonged to the famous wartime Brains-Truster C. E. M. Joad whose solo line, for which he lisped and bwoke his 'r's as usual, went, 'And the water-cweth contwactor fwom the thewage farm'. At one performance of this, led by Ted Jackson, our head 'Trog', with Donald at the piano, there was a collective black-out at the beginning of one of the later verses, the curious thing being that the same thought passed through all our minds – as we discovered when laughing about it later. We all said to ourselves in the blank moment, 'Oh well, the others will remember it.' Then followed that awful *total* silence.

Then, in the fifties, Michael Flanders came down several times to the summer school, which had, by this time, moved to Dartington, and he and Donald gave to our Friday night cabarets some of the revue numbers that they were already supplying for London shows. They also sang at other similar routs but it was mainly the summer school audience of two or three hundred that eventually gave them the idea that, instead of just singing the songs in private dos, they might take a theatre and do their own show.

They took a theatre in Notting Hill Gate. Summer-school members were circularized and helped to swell the audience and provide a sympathetic and enthusiastic sounding board. It was exciting for us all to be in on the birth of something that really took off and became a worldwide success. Donald's lyrical gift gave the numbers that extra touch. The harmonic interest, a dash of passion that lifted the songs out of the ordinary revue style, mirrored Michael's imagination, felicity with words and internal rhymes. Donald's playing in these shows never succumbed to routine.

It was curious, that show, because of the interplay of talents and personalities. Michael, with his background of theatrical family, was always the complete professional, and determined a little more than was necessary not to let the fact that he was crippled hinder that professionalism. He seemed to have a slight superiority because Donald's somewhat gauche stage persona became exteriorized in patter that slightly derided his own efforts, ignoring the very great gifts of his music and piano playing. Performing with a partner in a wheelchair calls for special patience, sympathy and tact, all of which gifts Donald exhibited with wonderful loyalty.

At the same time I could see that there were tensions and had the feeling that Donald felt as much trapped by success as enchanted by it. There was too much at stake in terms of reputation and financial security for Donald to get out of it . . . until many years had passed by – years during which Donald produced more serious music: operas on C. S. Lewis texts, and liturgical and other works. Some of these pieces had great merit, in part usually rather than in whole, but the big world was not interested in the whole, only the lesser world of small concerts, provincial tours and so forth. Donald formed vocal groups, one for sacred and one for secular music. They toured widely and gave pleasure, but they did not have the same sort of success that Donald had tasted in the Flanders collaboration. I think Michael had similar feelings and frustrations but I am writing about Donald.

The revue numbers dwindled. This was partly because years spent on tour blunted Michael's and Donald's edge and partly because they spent so much time on the road, long seasons in other continents, that there was little opportunity to concentrate on writing.

After Flanders died in 1975 Donald gradually made other performing liaisons: with Sidney Carter, the folk-singer; with Ian Wallace; with me, and one with the Reverend Topping, a kind of ecumenical chipmunk off the old block. They all died, these duos, because Donald killed them. I was particularly sorry that ours folded because the dates were enjoyable for both of us – or so it seemed to me. Donald once or twice said that the idea of doing a show with anyone else gave him the jim-jams and he once made some objection because his agent preferred him to do solo dates. I realized that he was at this time under some mental stress. He was spending longer and longer periods 'in retreat' and we had to cancel some engagements. But I never pushed him, insisting on the dates. OK, they brought in money – but they were primarily intended for our pleasure.

We had a ground plan of numbers – solos for each of us and duets. Various combinations were possible: an unaccompanied folk-song carol like 'I wonder as I wander' from me; 'Miranda', a Greek folk-song, or a Flanders number from him; songs by me with him at the piano like 'To the children' by Rachmaninov or (always a good starter, this) 'So, we'll go no more a-roving', or songs from his operas or operettas like a couple from the C. S. Lewis *Perelandra* and, my favourite, 'My heart is gone' from the abortive but delightful 1951/1851 show *The Bright Arcade*; then, together, point numbers like the Nadia Catouse 'England expects' (in 5/4 time, tricky) or, to end with, the Tolkien 'Bilbo's last song'. I suppose we did about a couple of dozen dates together and, bar the odd one or two, they ended in cheers and encores, usually two or three, finishing up with 'Mud' in various languages.

In between the music numbers, decided in advance, there was aleatory talk. We improvised our way, sometimes surprising ourselves with the material that came up. We knew we had to get from, say, Rachmaninov to a Hungarian Dance by Brahms, but it was left to me to lead Donald by the chat. With all his previous partners Donald had worked out his lines beforehand, especially with Michael's direction – they scarcely deviated by a word in the 'Hat' shows and that put Donald at a disadvantage because he is not an actor. But talking he was good at, provided that I could slow him down, which I did, from the manic gabble he thought was good showbiz.

We did festival dates, nothing stellar, but places like Boston, Canterbury, Belfast and Aldeburgh, all enthusiastic. There were some odd things. At Barnstaple, for example, the arrangers were attentive before and during the show, gave us drinks in the interval and then when the show was over and the encores done we retired to our dressing room thinking perhaps they might come to thank us . . . . After we had changed we ventured out . . . to the corridors . . . to the bar . . . to the foyer . . . not a soul in sight, a complete *Marie Celeste* situation. Mind you, the horn player Ifor James told me of a date when he didn't see anybody from the management from start to finish – except that after the concert, when he was changing, the door opened and a hand appeared which threw an envelope containing a cheque on to the floor.

After a couple of seasons Donald cancelled a few dates and said, with some embarrassment, that he thought, for the present, my dear chap, blah blah . . . and that was that.

A year or so later he wrote me a letter that I found too bland by far and I wrote him a sharp note back which I immediately regretted but that is the only small blot that has besmirched our friendship and we are now back on the best of terms. He even invited me to be his guest on a BBC Radio 2 half-hour show *Donald Swann and Friends* and we did some numbers together, including

'Bilbo's last song' and the Flanders words to the Mozart horn rondo 'Ill wind', and we *improvised* some chat. Quite like old times.

Once, in the late seventies, Donald rang me up with the news that Leakey, one of our three headmasters at Dulwich prep had died and there was to be a memorial service. Should we go? We went. It was a filthy rainy evening and as we drove down in Donald's car we talked, for the first time, about our friendship, how it had persevered through our professional partnership and its dissolution, through years when we had seen little of each other and, I finally managed to say, through those times when he had seemed to blow cold. He said rather sadly that he now saw, especially through the confessional couch, that such hot-cold, on-off relationships were, to use a cliché, the story of his life. It became clear that there are elements of what the professionals call the manic depressive in Donald's nature.

Another odd thing about Donald is his total lack of interest in nature. He does not even *see* nature. On our many trips many times I have pointed out this or that view or sight – a valley, a flock of birds, a river. Out of politeness he will look momentarily then turn back to the railway carriage interior. As a passenger in a car his eyes are always fixed on the road. It is almost impossible to divert him. Sometimes in the street I have waited for him by arrangement – he will pass by within two feet without seeing me. He is wrapped up in his own thoughts and simply does not see the world about him.

Donald is in some ways the clown who wants to play Hamlet – not that those lyrical tunes like 'The honeysuckle and the bindweed' are clownish, but I am sure that, perhaps like Sullivan, Donald wants to be known for his more serious music. And perhaps, unlike Sullivan, he may be one day. His music touches me a great deal, especially when he performs it himself. And Donald himself touches me. He is an original, and a good person. I love him. So does anyone who knows him.

(3)

E.M.G.

I was paid the vast sum of thirty-five shillings a week to sell records at E.M.G. Handmade Gramophones Ltd at 11 Grape Street. The shop was tucked away behind the Prince's Theatre, home of many musicals, the later *Hair* being the best known. I cannot remember any of the other firms and shops in this dark little street, squeezed between tall buildings, taking russet as its overall colour from the brick and stone of the theatre and the other neighbouring buildings. I knew the firm by repute. Its stock was heavily classical, and its speciality was a gramophone with a large papier-mâché horn, played with wooden needles. I guessed that by this time in the war – 1940 – they must be getting short of men.

I had already had my medical and was not sorry that my hearing had got me off military service. At that stage the authorities were still being fussy and, as they told me, if there was too much noise they might have to pay me a pension. 'We'll call you for factory work soon enough.' But they never did. Perhaps they thought my hearing was worse than it was. Certainly they didn't waste much time testing it, and equally certainly it tended to be not at its best when I was nervous. Certain again was the fact that I *was* nervous at that examination because I hated, always had, the idea of being regimented. Had I not managed to avoid being in the Officers' Training Corps at school?

E.M.G. asked me to come for an interview. I had said in my letter that I knew the gramophone catalogues backwards. I was tested and passed by Geoffrey Parsons, a fairly young man who had been left in charge of the managerial side of the firm. He did not know all that much about music (and, just in case there should be any doubt, neither was he an Australian pianist).

E.M.G.

What did the initials E.M.G. stand for? E. M. Ginn, the man who had started the firm. However, he had by this time been bought up or out by the brothers Davie, now high-ranking officers in the Army and Air Force. I saw the RAF one just once and he talked to me about an afternoon's leave with God and the Beethoven late quartets – simultaneously, I was led to understand.

Tom Fenton was in charge of the shop where I worked. The window of 11 Grape Street was completely plain, with no window dressing. Inside on the ground floor were two rooms to play records in, a counter and Fenton's little office. Fenton was a worried, lip-biting man with a high forehead, an angular nose and glasses. He came to work on a racy bicycle which he referred to as his 'cat'. He wore dark blue and purple shirts with dark ties which I thought were also rather racy. I overlapped with a tall, spiritual, heavy young man called Mason. He would very soon be going off to the war but for the moment he took me downstairs to a big underground listening room where there was the largest kind of horn machine – so large that customers were often said to buy one, put it in a field and then build a house round it.

I distinctly remember him playing to me that first morning a record that had just come out of Debussy's *La Mer* with Serge Koussevitzky conducting the Boston Symphony Orchestra. That rich music sounding so loud, combined with the smell of the polished wood of the case of that gramophone, plus the sophistication of those fat red triangular wooden needles, brought on a kind of ecstasy. As a child I had had similar feelings when listening to the record I had ordered at the local shop, Craven's, opposite the Odeon, West Norwood. In Craven's Ozzie Rose or his father played the new record – the one I can remember so well strangely enough was also Debussy, his *Fêtes* played by the Philadelphia under Stokowski – and on their radiogram it sounded much louder than it ever would at home. In my early teens my ambition had always been to work in a record shop and listen to lovely music swelling out to orgasmic loudness. And here I was in my late teens actually achieving that ambition.

La Mer over, Mason took me upstairs to the first floor where there were more listening rooms and the office. Higher up in the building were the workshops where the machines were made, or finished off, the horn jobs, and also frightfully superior radiograms or 'reproducers' as they were called. I was told not to mention the founder's name but to use, if asked what E.M.G. stood for, some phrase like 'Electrical and Mechanical Gramophones', 'Handmade' then becoming a post-noun adjective. Rum! Then we went downstairs to the shop and I met the other shop assistants.

The General was a diminutive personage in striped trousers, with his hair parted in the middle, compensating for his size, it seemed, by a serious and somewhat servile manner. Like others in the shop he had his speciality, in his case chamber music (as yet a closed book to me) and his melting point was Brahms, especially the piano quartets (a book I would rather keep closed, now that I know them).

Then there was the operatic expert, Quita Chavez, Spanish-looking, cockney-sounding, dumpy-looking, with spectacles continually pushed up a nose too small for the task. Tom Fenton himself was fairly expert on most music and he now had a hand in writing the excellent monthly newsletter which reviewed new records and compared them with any other versions, the best of which were then incorporated into a little book called *The Art of Record Buying*, a kind of gramophonic *Which?* before its time.

Those of us in the shop were expected to know the merits of the various recordings available or to know where to find the information. This was, of course, well before the days of long-playing discs. In those days the fragile records played at 78 rpm and the average length of a side was just over four minutes. The market was not yet flooded with duplications of certain works by innumerable companies, great and small. In a catalogue in front of me now there are no less than forty versions listed on record of the Fifth Symphony of Beethoven. In 1941 there were at the most four. We were expected not only to tell the customers about the respective merits but to warn them against the bad ones. Viz:

CUSTOMER: I want to buy records of Beethoven Five. I believe there's a Toscanini set. . . .
E.M.G. ASSISTANT: Yes, there is. With the NBC Orchestra on HMV and I must warn you that it has the worst faults of current American records – harsh strings, strident brass, drums that sound like biscuit boxes. It won't play with wooden needles and will sound its best, if you can call it best, on an American-type radiogram. On the other hand, please

listen to it and see what you think. (*Slight pause.*) Our recommended Beethoven Five, I might add, is the Columbia set, Weingartner conducting – not quite such a dynamic performance as Toscanini's, but very much in the German classical tradition, a good recording, no problem with fibre needles *and* it is eight shillings cheaper.

The assistant would then take the customer into a listening room, ensure that he or she knew how to clip the triangular fibres with our E.M.G. fibre-cutter and then the assistant would do what we called an FCR – First Chord and Run. The policy was that the shop was not only a market but a kind of club where you could drop in for a chat. Providing the customer was reasonably pleasant we didn't care if sometimes he didn't buy anything.

For the first fortnight I observed how it was all done but I didn't actually serve anyone. I was dreadfully shy and at that time I simply didn't have the nerve to go up to any human being, in a shop or not, and open the conversation. Then one morning I was sent downstairs for something and when I came up to the shop again there was no assistant in sight. They had all, on purpose, skedaddled so that I couldn't avoid dealing with the next customer who came in. When they came back from coffee twenty minutes later, grinning all over their faces, I was not only talking to a customer, I had correctly made out a bill and was actually doing up a parcel – never an easy matter for me. I had lost my commercial virginity. That was, by the way, the only virginity I had lost to date. I had no success with girls – too shy. But I reckon that serving in the shop was the first step towards losing some of my shyness.

This was the first period in my life that I spent any length of time in the centre of London. Up to 1939 my life was exclusively in South London. We had one family outing up to the West End every year, usually to Gennaro's Restaurant in Soho. Apart from that I don't suppose I was in London more than a dozen times – once to the Queen's Hall, once to a pantomime at the old Lyceum, once to Covent Garden. London usually made me feel ill, anyway. It was suffocating and hot. I was a suburban bumpkin in 1940.

My parents suggested that I had better take my lunches at the nearby Lyons Corner House on the junction of Tottenham Court Road and Oxford Street. Dutifully I went every day, Monday to

Friday, and had the one-and-threepenny lunch. My chief memories of that first fortnight are the dismal sound of the band and the yellow and green of the Russian salad. After two weeks I thought there must be something else better so I would go to a restaurant sometimes with one of the others from E.M.G. but usually by myself, at first to places recommended by them.

There was Oddi's where a lot of British Museum types came in – rather loud-voiced, grey-haired men and blue-stockinged women, my first sight of Bloomsbury. But gradually I tried out French, Italian, Greek, Hungarian restaurants. I discovered Mon Plaisir in Monmouth Street (where I still often eat). There was a first-class place in Dean Street – French, busy, noisy, and I thought myself a hell of a dog sitting next to someone who looked like a French admiral. It got blitzed, alas.

Every night I used to go home to Loudwater, near Rickmansworth, to the family. This was a safer part of London than where we had been living before and we had moved there a couple of days before war had been declared. The train fare took up a large part of my little salary. I gave Pops (my mother) something for the housekeeping but I couldn't have managed except by living at home.

When the raids started it was awful seeing what the bombings did to London – this street blocked off, that one a shambles, glass everywhere and buildings disappeared – but the English attitude of sang-froid prevailed. I was selfishly embedded in my new way of life, engrossed in the music I was discovering. And I was also discovering ways of communicating with people.

E.M.G. carried a stock that was entirely classical. The only exception was Benny Goodman playing *Bach Goes to Town*, the brilliant swing fugue by Alec Templeton. If jazz records were ordered we would get them for customers but jazz never made the shelves. The stock consisted of the best of the domestic catalogues plus certain imports, records available to special order and, amazingly, one or two German Telefunken records that E.M.G. pressed on special licence.

I was continuing my discovery of the colours of the orchestral palette and also delighting still in my own instrument, the piano. At this stage it was still the music itself, not its interpretation, that was foremost, although the Toscanini/Weingartner kinds of comparison soon took my education a stage further. The wishes of customers sometimes brought forth interesting items and, if the shop wasn't too crowded, I could always stay and listen to anything that took my fancy, instead of doing an FCR. The enthusiasm of Tom, Quita or the General also made me listen to things I might not have cottoned on to otherwise.

We were encouraged to take records home to familiarize our-selves with the stock to enable us to advise the customers better, and, one Easter I took home thirty records of Stravinsky. This was when Donald Swann and I were trying to see if we could make sense of works by the Master later than the three famous early ballets: *The Firebird*, *Petrushka* and *The Rite of Spring*, the latter two of which we also played in the composer's piano-duet version.

E.M.G. also sold miniature scores and I made it part of my job to cull them from the various music publishers, buying them at discount for the firm, but often buying additional copies for my own library, which was growing apace. There were still stocks of pre-war scores lying about in the dust if one could only get at them. We also sold books on music so that, all in all, E.M.G. was a valuable part of my education.

I was blissfully happy. The score hunts made me walk about the centre of London and I got to know the publishers. The walking kept me healthy – except that I also discovered interesting and exotic-looking restaurants. But I didn't put on too much weight at that stage because food was fairly short and the five-bob meal limit was statutory.

One event at a restaurant was a big marker in my life. A little worm popped its head out of a pea on my plate. I put it on one side of the plate and calmly finished the rest of the meal, without going pale and being put off my food. Insignificant you may think, but it was a first in my life. The other landmark was that I actually dared to call the waiter over and complain. I was growing up.

The knowledge that I was acquiring and the fact that I was at least being useful in the world, doing a job and getting paid for it, was very important to me. And I was making friends and acquain-tances, communicating. Otherwise I knew only one or two of my school mates and my parents' friends, and a few older people that I had met at the tennis club before the war. Really my only friends up to the age of eighteen were Donald Swann and, to a lesser extent, Colin Bryant from Dulwich College. I was a solitary. E.M.G. and

London changed all that. I became gregarious and, up to a point, adult.

I was beginning to go to concerts and theatres. I was reading like mad (the hour-long train journey morning and night connived in this) and taking part in amateur theatricals at the Mary Ward Settlement where my father had once acted. I was in Eliot's *A Family Reunion* (as one of the uncles), in Toller's *Masses and Man*, Synge's *The Playboy of the Western World* and *The Bear* of Chekhov.

Geoffrey Parsons and his boyfriend, the excellent light-music composer Berkeley Fase, took me under their wing, hoping to make me a political convert, taking me to see some good plays well performed at Unity Theatre, and their own Christmas revue there. I saw in the political persuasion something of the same sort of coercion that had been applied earlier, while I was at school, by the Crusaders. Just as I couldn't bring myself to come to Christ, so I couldn't come to Marx. Geoffrey gave me up, especially as I, quite innocently – I still didn't know really what homosexuality was – got on very well with Berkeley, whose tunes and company I found delightful.

At that time I think I must have been fairly sickeningly highbrow and snobbish artistically. A quarter of a century later Christopher Raeburn told me how toffee-nosed with him I had been in the shop when he asked me for some Lehar. On the other hand I was ever so 'umble with real artists, ready to learn and play second fiddle.

It was part of the E.M.G. euphoria that I was able to serve and talk to interesting people. A regular visitor was Sacheverell Sitwell, very knowledgeable about much more than Liszt and Scarlatti (about whom he had written biographies). In his elegant drawl he talked to me about Balakirev and many Russian composers, and about his friend Constant Lambert. When I said that I was stuck in my search for the complete *Façade* poems – neither the poems nor the music were available in print at that time – he gave me Edith's address and told me to write to her for the missing couple of poems. I said I wouldn't dare. He said she would be delighted to hear from me, and to tell her he had told me to write. I did and she replied immediately, sending me 'Scotch Rhapsody' copied out in her own hand but telling me that she neither could nor wanted to remember 'Tarantella'. I wrote to thank her for her extraordinary kindness and that was the start of a fascinating friendship, chequered of course, as I think nearly all her friendships were. Sachie, of course, looked every inch the celebrity.

It was only when writing down another customer's name on a bill that I realized he wasn't quite the business man that he appeared to be. 'No, only one "l" and one "t",' he corrected me. 'Not "T.S."?' I choked out. We talked several times when he came in and he actually asked my advice as to what to try next, for he found that he had by then obtained all the Beethoven string quartets. I suggested the second Bartók quartet, just then issued. He took it and came back some months later to say how much he was enjoying it. Was there anything else I could recommend? Sibelius Four? Mr Eliot tried it but I never found out whether he liked it or not.

The young Peter Ustinov came in and the impression that remains chiefly of him was his black inability to control his fountain pen, that dear old thing of the past – aptly named in Peter's case. Jessie Matthews I conned into buying my latest enthusiasm of the moment – Ravel's second *Daphnis and Chloé* suite. With Caryl Brahms I had the only row of my E.M.G. time and she gracefully admitted she was in the wrong and invited me to tea. We were on friendly terms ever after. Vivien Leigh came in to try to get Madeleine Grey's original recording of Canteloube's *Chants d'Auvergne* and thereby hangs a tale. Not long afterwards one of the tunes was included in the film score of Laurence Olivier's *Henry V* and William Walton was had up for cribbing Canteloube. He swore he hadn't but lost the case. Walter Legge brought in Maggie Teyte. Felix Aprahamian, then working with the London Philharmonic Orchestra, would also come in.

There was the lady whose son was sitting round a campfire in the jungle, she said, but had run out of records for his mark IX wind-up gramophone. Would I please choose two hundred pounds' worth of records. She didn't really know his tastes except for *Bolero* and the 'Unfinished' Symphony. I chose what I would have liked myself but avoided getting too esoteric. She came back a year later with . . . a shot-gun? No, a thank-you letter from the jungle.

There was the sad case of the boy my own age, seedy-looking and always wearing a dirty raincoat, under which, we came to suspect, he secreted a record when he went out. He never bought much but he always chose crowded days and good music to listen to. One day there was nobody in the shop and a twelve-inch square bulge under his mackintosh. (Don't misunderstand me.) I asked him tentatively if by any chance he had forgotten to bring back one of the records he had been listening to. At this he made for the door and I gave chase up Grape Street. As bad luck would have it, he cannoned into the midriff of a copper walking his beat.

There were funny moments too. The continuo player Thornton Lofthouse was known in the feline vernacular of E.M.G. as a 'kitten', i.e., a nuisance. We tried to avoid serving him and as the others were a bit sharper than I was I usually got landed with him. He was a dear old thing really but he fussed, hesitated and pernicketed, changing his mind constantly. After about five visits he eventually chose thirty odd records, paid for them but returned to us two hours later. He had gone to see Osborne Peasgood in the organ loft of Westminster Abbey and put down his records on the bench in front of the organ while they chatted. Absent-mindedly Peasgood put his capacious rump on the pile of records and broke the whole damn lot. The worst of it was that Thornton Lofthouse was now beginning to wonder if he had chosen the right records anyway, so that meant another couple of hours' dithering about at E.M.G.

Tom Fenton was called up for war work. So was Geoffrey Parsons. Shellac and therefore record stocks ran low. The workshops ran out of technicians – one of them got killed in a raid. And the General left. (His handwriting had become quite illegible and at one point he had been given the alternative of the sack or printing everything he wrote in capitals. Within a fortnight even his capital letters were unreadable.) In the General's place came Joyce Reah, friendly, capable and living up to her surname, although we unkindly called her Dumbo. The myopic Peggy Cochrane joined us. She was a friend of John Gielgud and he popped in now and then to see her.

Just as I hadn't twigged that getting on too well with Berkeley (who had done a stint in the shop but was whipped away quickly) got me in badly with Geoffrey, so now I failed to realize that being too friendly with Peggy was making trouble among certain ladies on the staff. Soon the ladies stayed in the back room as much as possible, reserving their attention only for a few favoured cus-

tomers. Unless they were in a very good mood the ordinary customers were greeted with a surly 'Yes?' or 'Well?' or sometimes that
silent upward toss of the head that was commonplace in that stage
of the war when demand exceeded supply.

Business dwindled but still orders came in by post and I had the
boring job of dealing with many of these, not for records but for
accessories. By now I was working in Fenton's office, facing the
door into the street. We were supposed to share the job of serving
the customers but as the girls were in the back room so much they
didn't even know or care when a customer came in. So muggins got
landed with more than his share of the customers. Moreover, I
think I was always polite and courteous to them and I hated to see
them treated badly. The result was that I got behind with my boring
accessories, so guess who got the push when E.M.G. found it
necessary to throw somebody to the wolves . . . ?

Never mind, I had learned a lot during my two years there —
about music, about people (not excluding myself), about restaurants, about the theatre, about living. Sometimes by myself, sometimes in conjunction with Tom Fenton, I had written quite a lot of
the monthly newsletter which was my introduction to setting down
thoughts on paper.

One of the customers had not only become a friend but he had
told me that any time I wanted I could have a job with the firm he
worked with, so I immediately went to see him on the third floor of
295 Regent Street and that will be the scene of the next chapter.

(4)

London Philharmonic Orchestra

'I wish you'd given me a little notice,' said Felix Aprahamian at
the office of the London Philharmonic Orchestra where he was
concerts manager. But he had said 'at any time' and, anyway,
E.M.G. had pushed me out very quickly, with only a week's notice.
Being sacked was a terrible blow to my pride and equilibrium. At
home I blamed it on the shortage of shellac without mentioning
that I had also got behind with my orders. It was important, then,
to be doing something and to be doing it in town.

I remembered a play that I had heard on the radio, *Youth at the
Helm*, in which a man had gone every day to a big bank, dressed in
striped trousers, his umbrella furled, a bowler hat on his head, in all
the right gear. He went up in the executive lift and made clever
remarks until everybody thought that he was staff but a robbery led
to an investigation – the man had been taking the contents of the
vaults home. Well, I didn't steal anything from the LPO except a
vocal score of Schoenberg's *Gurrelieder* that was in tatters anyway.
True, it was stamped THE PROPERTY OF SIR THOMAS BEECHAM but
it was the twentieth copy and I knew he would never include it in
his repertory. But I did, with Felix's connivance, infiltrate the LPO
without being on the staff. After three weeks, the managing director, Thomas Russell, called me in and asked me how much the LPO
was paying me. I didn't say 'I was afraid you'd never ask me'
because the phrase hadn't been invented then but it did lead to me
being put on the payroll at, I think, half a crown more than my final
weekly wage at E.M.G., which was half a crown more than I had
started at.

Soon, however, I was made secretary of the London Philharmonic Arts Club. Since Beecham was in America, the London Philharmonic Orchestra had decided to run itself, as most orchestras in the country eventually did. In 1942 the LPO was fighting for its life, as the rest of the country was. And they fought together, touring exhaustively and exhaustingly. At one time the directors of the LPO thought it would be a good idea to have a concert hall home a few miles away from the centre of London. Which was the most musical part of the metropolis? Why, it surely had to be Golders Green, with its large Jewish population and its large percentage of refugees, all starved of music. Would they not flock to the Orpheum, a large barn of a cinema about fifteen minutes' walk north of Golders Green towards Finchley? 'No' was the answer and the Orpheum combined for the LPO the functions of white elephant and millstone.

There were exceptions. I remember good audiences, for example, for a Boosey & Hawkes concert that included the British première of *El salón México*, with Constant Lambert sweating like mad over Copland's compound time signatures, and Mahler's *Das Lied von der Erde* with Peter Pears, newly arrived back from America, struggling, as the tenor usually has to in that piece, to be heard. I also remember that Michael Tippett conducted a Christmas concert with his Morley College Choir and the LPO. That evening was dreadfully badly attended but it brought me, through Felix, in touch with Tippett.

I would say meeting Felix (and through him, Tippett, and through Tippett, William Glock) was largely responsible for the way my life has turned out.

The London Philharmonic Arts Club was housed in the Orpheum up in the lounge on the dress circle level. The décor was not bad enough to be interesting and not good enough to be pleasing. I recall chiefly the green wicker chairs and glass-topped tables. It held 150 people, which was more than it usually needed to.

Up to then the secretary had been Denham Ford, now calling himself Denham V. Ford, although what the 'V.' stands for I don't know – not 'Vivacious', certainly. Denham was keen on music but he was a bit out of his depth at that time so I took over from him and he was supposed to help me. There was a committee of worthies and I remember its chairman giving a gramophone recital and translating the title of the last movement of Berlioz's *Sympho-*

nie fantastique, Songe d'une nuit du sabbat, 'Song of the night on Sunday'.

The stated object of the club was to promote the activities of the orchestra and to provide social links – a supporters' club, in fact. The trouble was that the LPO was desperately busy doing musical war work, bringing much needed concerts to factories, troops and music-halls, these last engagements often sponsored by the dance-band leader and impresario Jack Hylton. The programmes called for were popular – a couple of dozen war-horses, the best-known concertos, symphonies, overtures – so that there wasn't much scope for back-up talks at the club. And the orchestral players didn't really want to traipse up to the Orpheum on their free evenings. They wanted to be with their girlfriends/wives/families, or just catch up on sleep.

After some small-time stuff, then, I started to presume on some of the new friends I was making and some I had made at E.M.G. I got in some pianists and some chamber musicians and, since our name mentioned arts in the plural I put on one or two play readings and some poetry. The grandest was the Sitwell evening. Since she had sent me the *Façade* poem Edith Sitwell and I had corresponded. Greatly daring, I asked her if she would come and give us a poetry reading. She said yes, a date was fixed and lo! she appeared with brother Osbert. I didn't know until years later that the two of them rarely saw Sacheverell. He had let the side down by marrying, so I was lucky that she had even replied to my first letter.

They arrived in a large hired car at the Orpheum, were perfectly nice and friendly in a slightly royal way, and appeared not to mind the green wicker chairs. She read very well that night. She seemed genuinely pleased and touched and was very sweet to a very nervous and flustered young secretary, straightaway inviting him to tea at the Sesame Club.

I was still quite unused to dealing with such grandeur. I was getting better at dealing with people in ones and twos but I was not yet capable of talking easily in public. The responsibility of such public occasions, with the possibility that some or several things could go wrong, weighed on my mind and my gut. Even after I had stopped running the Arts Club some years later I still got a pain in the stomach just about the time of our evening meetings on those regular days of the week.

Yes, 'royal' is the word for the Sitwells. You paid court to them and they held it. And the courtiers were always losing favour for some imagined or, less often, real slight. Queen Edith's London palace was the Sesame, Lyceum and Imperial Pioneer Club at 49 Grosvenor Street. The other members seemed to be entirely elderly and nondescript. The only person I ever met there who wasn't a guest of Edith's was dear old Lionel Tertis, pioneer of the viola. Somehow the setting suited Edith and on 'her' days the other club members had to be tolerant. If they weren't they were immediately the subject of Edith's ridicule and the object of vendettas.

Edith claimed to be a Plantagenet and she certainly looked the part. Her hair was fine and difficult to manage so, quite sensibly, it was latterly always hidden in a snood and/or under a hat. Hats suited her, adding to the Plantagenet likeness, just as torques, crosses and vast rings became her. She believed that all these embellishments obscured what she wrongly thought, and had been encouraged by her parents to think, was her ugliness. In fact they enhanced her quite remarkable features.

After some years I could see that there was what's wrongly called protocol, a kind of hierarchy about the Sitwell entertaining. First you were invited to tea, just to make sure you were all right and didn't upset the other guests, who would be hangers-on, minor writers or other artists, translators, people, like myself, who had done some service or favour, perhaps a publisher or two, even a literary agent. Then, providing that you passed that test, hadn't slurped your tea or broken any crockery, you might graduate after a bit, as I did, to being invited to 'drinks'. Here there would be fewer old ladies, translators and so on, more and better-class poets, composers, publishers. The fry was definitely larger. The next stage was to be asked to tea and to stay *through* to drinks. If you were fortunate you might next be invited to lunch, where the party might be ten or twelve. Then came lunch and stay *through* to tea. Even on one occasion I was asked to lunch, *through* to tea and *through* to drinks. As I write this the awful thought strikes me that perhaps some favoured few stayed on to dinner. If so, then I missed out. But I wonder whether Edith's constitution would have stood such a long day. Formerly I had always thought that the supreme accolade would be invited to the family home, Renishaw. *Would* in my case.

As in the game of snakes and ladders there were penalties. Praising the wrong poet or someone that one hadn't realized was out of favour led to being struck off the list for a time, perhaps for ever. I was struck off once because, after climbing up the board to the luncheon echelon, so to speak, either Michael Tippett or our mutual poet friend Brean Douglas-Newton had put a foot wrong. Then, because later I became organizer of the Apollo Society, which put on programmes of verse and music and sometimes employed Edith as a reader, I was put back on the list. But – here's the rub – I was put back on the bottom rung again and had to work my way up all over again. That was the rule.

I was just getting up again to the luncheon stage when I was hurled into the pit. At this time Edith had been made a doctor of literature three times and it was made known that letters should be addressed to her, 'Dr Edith Sitwell, D. Litt., D. Litt., D. Litt.' I thought this was a bit much so one day in a hurry I put on the envelope 'Dr Edith Sitwell, D. Litt.[3]' Out in the cold once more!

But I got back again by having her invited to give a recital at the Edinburgh Festival. Instant luncheon! Only to fail yet again! Edith wrote to me to say that if the hall was of any considerable size she must have a suitable microphone. It would be a disaster otherwise because her voice was not strong enough. I passed on the request to the Director of the Festival. A few weeks later Edith wrote again. What was happening about the microphone? I again wrote to Edinburgh and was reassured that the matter was in hand. I warned the Director to expect big trouble if the amplification failed. He assured me that somebody was looking after it, so I conveyed the news to Edith and went down to Dartington to run my summer school secure in the knowledge that all would be well, even though I could not be in Edinburgh for the recital.

The next thing I knew was that a telegram of powerful invective arrived from Edith, the only telegram I have ever received that was so long that it ran to four pages. Edinburgh had mucked it and the papers were full of it. People in the audience had asked her to speak up. She had told them to get hearing aids and a bad time was had by all.

Osbert, by the way, was rarely seen at Edith's various bunfights. But after one of them I found myself with him leaving the Sesame. We talked and walked through Hyde Park together and most of the way to Carlyle Square. Among other things we talked about the latest volume of Ernest Newman's monumental *The Life of Richard Wagner* which had just appeared. Had I read it? No. Why on earth not? I hedged a bit and then confessed that I couldn't afford to buy such an expensive book. Then why not get it from your library? I had tried but for some reason it was not available yet. We parted. A few days later he sent me the book, suitably inscribed – a generous gift to someone he had met only twice.

That was the hallmark of the Sitwells, particularly Edith. Quirky, yes, but capable of great generosity. From what I read of her life in the biographies Edith couldn't really afford to give all these parties, but she did. The thing to do at these parties was to wait until she had received her guests and then get as near to where she seated herself as possible in order to hear her tell her stories. She was a witty raconteuse – spicy and not without malice. Some of the best were about the Chinese verse translator who had never been to China, Arthur Waley. Strange things always seemed to be happening to him, either at home with his lady, Beryl de Zoete, an expert on dancing, or at work at the Ministry of Information. These were essentially stories that depended on Arthur's quietness of voice which Edith mimicked perfectly.

One guest who *was* allowed to drop things and get away with it was Stephen Spender. It was Brean Douglas-Newton, known by his initials D. N., pronounced 'Den', who first drew my attention to the fact that not only did Stephen always knock something over or drop something – he is a very awkward person at the best of times – but that there seemed to be a sense of occasion to his clumsiness, a ratio between the importance of the party and the magnitude of his cack-handedness. At a tea party with only a few old ladies, faithful retainers, and a provincial publisher, say, Stephen would merely spill his tea or knock over a chair. If, however, at drinks, T. S. Eliot or John Piper were present, then Stephen would topple a vase of flowers or the like.

One day there was truly a grand affair. I think both Eliot and John Hayward were there, as well as William Plomer, Tambimuttu, John Lehmann, Cyril Connolly, Kenneth Clark, Constant Lambert and William Walton. It was a royal flush of an occasion and for once there was to be music. The old and frail Mrs Violet Gordon Woodhouse was to play her old and frail, rather small harpsichord;

everybody had to strain their ears, especially those in the far corner of the L-shaped room. Den and I happened to be quite near the tinkling instrument.

After the first item Den whispered in my ear, 'Where's Stephen?' Right on cue in the next slow, quiet Scarlatti sonata, Stephen came blundering in, bursting through a locked door and knocking over several trays of drinks which were stationed on little tables against the bolted door. Big Spender had struck again with his unique sense of occasion and timing.

When all this artistic glamour hit me, Sitwellismus and all these friendly musicians, the difficulty always was to descend to the humdrum, to get through the boring bits – sitting in the LPO office, checking on this, remembering to do that, writing the programmes, assembling the notes, correcting what needed to be corrected, answering the telephone, being interrupted a dozen times an hour.

Felix was in a superior position and in taking him as a kind of model – I say a kind of model because Felix was obviously *sui generis* – I tended to forget that Felix had the girls of the office doing quite a lot of his work. Cajoling and gently bullying, Felix was marvellous – for example, with Jocelyn Waterson. She was tall, eternally high-minded, a pretty grown-up schoolgirl it seemed to me, but she didn't appear to mind Felix snatching a kiss. Miriam Lewis seemed primmer, more schoolgirlish yet even less likely to object to Felix's flirtatiousness. Nor were the lads exempt.

He was everywhere, supremely volatile, outrageous, and yet courteous, flatteringly, exaggeratedly so – you felt flattered that he bothered to flatter. He was always involving me – introducing me to this person, taking me out to meals, providing free tickets for concerts, lending me scores, giving me scores, showing me where scores were to be bought, telling me who everybody was, what their stories were, who was related to who, who had been, sometimes who would be. He was a connoisseur not only of music but of people, and not only of people but of literature and food. He knew where all the best things were to be found and he shared his knowledge generously. And when he didn't know something, he made it up. Sometimes you knew he was wrong but he argued so well you could be convinced for a second that black was white. I remember thinking at the time that if Felix were put into a book his character would seem overwritten. No one could be at the same time like something out of Proust and something out of P. G. Wodehouse. But he was.

Of course Tom Russell and Adolf Borsdorf poured cold water on Felix's ideas all the time. They were more down to earth, and were trying to get the orchestra work and to get the show on the road. But Felix provided the touch of fantasy and the superior cultural range that was needed from time to time. Sometimes he dropped clangers out of sheer enthusiasm. Sometimes there were concerts with marvellous programmes and Felix sat in the front row of the dress circle with the scores of Bax or Ravel or whatever laid out in front of him. Alas, he was almost the only person there to enjoy these programmes, which were over-ambitious for the time.

Felix helped me greatly with the Arts Club and I was able to help him a little bit with various enterprises that he ran in a concert-organizing offshoot of the LPO. Chief of these was a series of concerts of French music, sponsored by the French government, channelled through the office of their cultural attaché, Toni Mayer.

At these concerts my love of French music was fostered by the business of getting the concerts on – attending rehearsals and playing through many of the works with Felix at his home: Debussy and Ravel to start with, then Fauré, Roussel, Satie, Duparc, Chausson, Berlioz, Poulenc, Milhaud, the rest of Les Six and so on. After the Liberation artists came from France: Pierre Bernac, Francis Poulenc, string quartets, pianists like the divinely attractive Monique Haas, Ginette Neveu, Irène Joachim, Yvonne Lefébure (like Mélisande grown old). There was also Maggie Teyte again and again with her extraordinary blend of passion distilled into an intoxicating cool liquid.

At Felix's house I was further intoxicated, not only by alcohol but by his library of books and music, and books on music, and by the artists and composers that I met, by the music that we made and that I learned. Added to which the food was always plentiful and marvellously cooked by Mrs Aprahamian, Felix's long-suffering mother, always referred to by him as his 'ancient and decrepit parent'. How much of the bullying and bantering was meant and how much just affectionate? Difficult to tell. She spoke with a very strong accent that I was to find later typical of Armenians.

Life with Felix was always a flurry and bustle, rushing from one place to another, or from one occupation to another about the house. He skittered a bit and sometimes he felt the need to butter his ego but these were small prices to pay for his generosity and what he taught me about music and the music profession. Felix had style.

Felix also introduced me to organ music, because that was his first enthusiasm. He was secretary, I think, to the Organ Music Society and it was via the organ that he had left Mincing Lane and the City to live a life totally in music. I speak of him in the past because it was in those days that I worked with him and saw such a lot of him. Nowadays his manner is less volatile and he is the revered critic, quasi number two, on *The Sunday Times*. We still meet, talk and have affectionate badinage. A constant incipit at concerts when we meet and have to introduce our respective companions is for whoever gets to speak first to say of the other, 'This is my father', to which the other has to reply, 'An ungrateful bastard.'

His home in Muswell Hill was always referred to as the 'House of Usher' (with Poe-faced humour) and it was stuffed with print. Felix at that time had two pianos in his sitting room which we pounded on my every visit except if there were visiting artists. One evening when the French pianist Monique Haas played to us I met the violinist Manoug Parikian. It was his first day in England for many years and he was to settle here permanently. He became one of my closest friends.

It is strange how I disobeyed the only parental advice I can ever remember receiving. Nothing about sex from my father but one day he did say, 'Now that you are going out to work, let me tell you this. Watch out for the Jews. They will rob you and cheat you. But worse than the Jews are the Greeks. Be very careful with Greeks. But worse than the Jews and the Greeks combined are the Armenians. If you meet anybody whose name ends with "ian", hop it.' So, what did I do? I married a Zorian, three of my closest friends were Felix Aprahamian, Manoug Parikian and Arda Mandikian.

Back to the House of Usher. Every room in the house, except the kitchen, was stacked to the ceiling with music or books. Felix must have spent a fortune on printed matter – not just books on music but a good library in the English and French languages, with a comprehensive Proust section. The books and music spread, growing upwards from the ground floor until the loft itself was converted into further library space, access being provided by means of a folding staircase. The last time I was *du côté de chez Félix*, the House of Usher looked likely indeed to collapse with an overweight top floor. (An architect predicted exactly this.) It would be a sorry waste if this vast library were to go to ruin, crashing down on sleeping inmates and the ever-watchful tropical fish on the ground floor.

Through my E.M.G. time I had lived at home and continued to do so at the beginning of my LPO time. But by 1942 there were more entertainments going on in the musical world and Felix and the LPO plus a horde of new friends meant that several times a week I found myself catching the midnight train from Baker Street. The journey to our nearest station, Rickmansworth, took some forty minutes, by which time, in the blackened out carriages, I was asleep. At Ricky the electric loco was taken off and a steam engine replaced it for the rest of the journey on through Metroland to Chesham and Amersham.

What often woke me up was the crunch as the steam engine was coupled after a stop of two minutes. But sometimes what woke me was the engine starting up, at which I would sleepily open the door and hurl myself from the train, occasionally restrained by some further-travelling old gentleman who, thinking I was attempting suicide, would shout, 'Don't do it, young man.' Only once did I actually get carried on to the next station, Chorley Wood, whence I had to walk, torchless, across the common in a black night, falling several times into ditches and tank traps.

My parents lived successively in three really quite good olde-worlde-type beamed houses. The mornings were fresh as I either walked to the station or piled into the Loudwater bus. The night walks were interesting, especially if the moon was absent. For some personal reason to have a torch would have been 'chicken' and I quite enjoyed walking as much as a hundred paces with my eyes closed, then finding out if the night was darker than closed eyes. Sometimes it was. But the lack of sleep began to catch up on me, so I decided to spend the week nights in town. Exciting to live away from home for the very first time, at the age of twenty!

Antony Hopkins at that time was about to go and live with his girlfriend, later wife, Alison, and was anxious to find somebody to take over his digs in Barons Court. These digs were very near the station in a row of houses. The landlady was Ma Coulton and the rent was twelve shillings and sixpence per week, including laundry, breakfast and the odd nightcap cup of cocoa. Ma was fat, greasy, sloppy and anguished-looking. As well she might be, for she had a lot of children, including one poor little wretch born when Ma was well over fifty. Her husband was an old and fairly useless night-watchman. Ma used to swear at least twice in every sentence.

After some weeks Tim Howatson, a young accountant from the LPO, joined me in a top-floor eyrie. First thing in the morning Ma called up, ''Ere, aren't you bleeders up yet? Yer bloody breakfast is waiting for yer, getting cold.' Ma had a heart of gold. The aggro was just a way of life. She gave us baked beans every morning on very greasy fried bread, with tea slopped into the saucer. She thought she was swindling us by charging so much and was always apologetic about taking the rent, which she doubtless spent entirely on the cigarettes that drooped perpetually from her lips.

One night Tim and I got home fairly late. 'I thought you buggers was lookin' peaky so I bought you some wine. Mind you 'ave a glass before you get into bloody bed, you bastards,' she said graciously. When we got upstairs there was a bottle of British wine on the table between the beds with a couple of glasses. I turned my nose up at the common stuff but agreed with Tim that it was sweet of her to take the trouble and think of us like that, especially as she probably couldn't afford it, so we downed a glass each. Not bad. Another. And another. . . . Next morning, ''Ere, I'm not buying you buggers no more bleedin' wine, I'm not. Singin' and shoutin' you was, keepin' the 'ole bloody 'ouse a-bleedin'-wake.'

Poor Ma Coulton. Not long after Tim and I had moved in, the bombs started in earnest in London and the effect on Ma was pathetic to behold. Not so much the bombs as what she called the 'sireens'. As soon as they started, Ma started shaking and she didn't stop until the all-clear went.

At first it wasn't too bad because it was just at night. Tim and I heard the nasties whistling by and if things got bad we would hurtle out of bed and leap downstairs a flight, maybe two, by the time the bang occurred. Then we went back to bed, feeling a mite foolish on our top floor. One night it got so bad that we went down to the shelter in the garden where Ma, Pa and the nipper were. The stench was so awful – they seemed to eat nothing but baked beans – that

Tim and I decided that death by aerial bombing would be preferable. Soon, however, the 'sireens' went on and the alerts would last all day. Ma's shaking and general condition got so bad that it was arranged that she should be evacuated out of town.

By this time Tim and I had moved to Sussex Gardens near Lancaster Gate and the LPO office was glad when the reverberation of the baked beans died down. Tim was a person of ups and downs. His energy on a new job or project was fantastic and he came to my rescue once or twice later on when I branched away from the LPO office and found that my accounts were getting behindhand. We had our own signature tune, the theme of the *Theme and Variations* from Tchaikovsky's Suite No. 3 in G which the LPO played a lot at that time. Every two or three years I will pick up a ringing phone and hear Tim whistling that tune. In those days we both heard it a lot, one or the other coming home at night, or meeting somewhere in a public place. Tim joined in the social life of the LPO. Sometimes Felix would arrange a 'symposium'. They were not particularly Platonic but nice pleasant binges, usually in a Chinese restaurant with the younger members of the LPO staff and the younger members of the orchestra itself: Malcolm Arnold and his violinist (first) wife Sheila, Richard Adeney and his wife, Michael Dobson and a few others.

My duties in the office of the LPO were those of a sort of general dogsbody, looking after the Arts Club fixtures, of which there were two or three a week, helping Felix and – my special task – looking after the printing of posters and programmes for the LPO concerts. There was a stock of programme notes that we re-used again and again so it was a matter of constant rehashing and getting new works written up, should the orchestra ever play anything new, which was pretty seldom. This however did happen in 1944 when Jack Hylton and the orchestra undertook a series of prestige concerts at the Adelphi Theatre in London. There were some new American works played, the odd Mahler symphony began to be heard, anticipating this composer's remarkable popularity later on when he almost began to replace Tchaikovsky at the Top of the Pops. Another work that was historically important was the first performance of Tippett's oratorio *A Child of Our Time* which Felix and I brought to the notice of Tom Russell and the LPO board.

At this time Anatole Fistoulari was appointed chief conductor of the orchestra. I found that the London orchestras behaved with conductors like fickle suitors. A new conductor would be welcomed like a new girlfriend. Flirtation led to an *affaire*. After a few months, disenchantment set in and then usually that conductor was Out with a capital O, and Out for all time. At one time Basil Cameron was all the rage with the LPO. By and by they couldn't stand him, said the concerts went best with him if there was no rehearsal, that it was his rehearsals that bored them to death.

Sir Malcolm Sargent they truly detested. When he was young, he was liked. Then he had got tuberculosis and the orchestra had had a generous whip-round for him. Then he had said in print something tactless, if true, about security of tenure of orchestral jobs being bad for standards of performance. His success with choirs and his success as a guest conductor all over the world made him conceited and his desire to be loved at home became acute. I think he developed a positive fear of the British professional orchestral musicians – he was marvellous with amateurs – and the more he wanted success, wanted to be loved, the more they disliked him. He could still be tactless because of his desire to shine. When he was knighted, on the day of the Honours List he tried to *rehearse* the orchestra in the morning singing 'For he's a jolly good fellow' in preparation for that evening's concert.

He positively wallowed in applause. I once saw him powdering and preening himself at Liverpool before going on stage. It was a nauseating sight. And after the concert, at which he had conducted the First Symphony of Michael Tippett extremely badly – he had prepared the score only in terms of beating it accurately, not understanding its idiom or content – his fury was apparent in the dressing room afterwards when, having got out his fountain pen and directed the attendant to let in the autograph hunters, the kids trooped in and went to the other end of the long table where Michael Tippett was sitting. There was a look of hatred directed at the composer, his former pupil at the Royal College of Music in London. Sargent never conducted another work of Tippett's. And yet Sargent, when not confronting his public and being thwarted of a chance to shine in front of it, was capable of great and often unobtrusive kindness, and he was a most entertaining companion.

Charles Hambourg was a frequent if not constant conductor of the LPO in those war years, a member of a distinguished family that produced the violist Hope and the pianists Mark and Michal. Charles was a major in the Army, obviously some division of it where nobody could tell him to get his hair cut, for it bulged and tumbled down beyond his hat. He was no doubt a good musician but not a brilliant conductor. He was never able to be punctual when accompanying concertos. Those awkward run-ups in Beethoven's Fourth or Khachaturian's only Piano Concertos invariably left the soloist either naked and embarrassed, or cut off in mid-scale.

One Saturday afternoon in a week when the orchestra and he had been doing the same programme over and over, he was bemoaning the fact that he was unable to start the Overture to Smetana's *The Bartered Bride* in such a way as to get the orchestra with him. He lunged, he dived, he brought his hand down, he held it high in the air, he tried both hands, he nodded, he twitched – all to no purpose. He could *not* get the orchestra moving together.

Charlie was at tea with some members of the orchestra that afternoon and one friendly player took a knife to the butter. 'Look, Charlie, do it like this,' and he flicked the knife in his hand to secure a small lump of the precious, rationed butter. Charlie said he'd tried everything else he could think of, so he said he would take the advice. At the evening performance he used his baton as an imaginary knife flicking at an imaginary pat of butter and the miracle occurred – the LPO began *The Bartered Bride* with a perfect attack. Charlie was so astonished that he stopped conducting and the orchestra fell apart once again, though this time because of laughing.

Lambert was a Constant, if a less frequent, conductor, of the LPO than Charlie, but that was partly because he was also Musical Director of Sadler's Wells Ballet and often busy with them. I quite often met and talked to Lambert, knowing that he was likely to be found in a pub called The George but nicknamed The Gluepot by Sir Henry Wood because so many of his musicians got stuck in it, it being the nearest pub to the Queen's Hall. Many of the BBC poets, writers and producers used this pub as well as musicians. One could often see Dylan Thomas, Louis MacNeice and W. R. Rodgers there, as well as composers Alan Rawsthorne, Elisabeth Lutyens and her husband Edward Clark, Denis ApIvor, music critic Ralph Hill, and music administrators Julian Herbage and his wife Anne Instone (both of *Music Magazine* fame).

Lambert was a fair old drinker, sometimes incapable even in the mornings, slug-white in the face and sweaty, limping his way unsteadily to the podium but safe once he got there. He also spoke in conversation, in my experience, as if he was addressing a roomful of people, which I took to be a sign of shyness. (I found the same with Beecham.) He was incredibly well read, well sighted, well noted, opinionated in the best sense of the word and (sorry) constantly witty.

Despite the fact that so many of his friends, especially in the ballet world, were homosexual, he had a rabid hatred of the two composers (Britten and Tippett) who became so well known during the war that they ousted Walton, Lambert, Rawsthorne and others from their perches of the thirties. In fact my very last conversation with Constant Lambert was terminated by his discovery that I was a friend of the 'enemy'. We were talking *à deux* in The Gluepot, where he always stood on the same spot, and, after about half an hour, he happened to flick open an Everyman volume of Dostoevsky that I had laid on the counter. By mistake, instead of opening the book at the title-page, he arrived at the endpapers and saw the signature of the person I had borrowed it from – Michael Tippett. He rapped the book shut, finished his drink in one gulp and bustled out of the pub without ever uttering another word to me.

Lambert, Rawsthorne and Tippett were all born in 1905 and were all at the Royal College of Music together. Something must surely have happened there to make for this later tension. One of the very few times that I have found Tippett being nasty to a colleague was when he and Rawsthorne were together at the summer school during one of our Bryanston years.

Except for those symposia of Felix's and concerts in or near town I didn't see very much of the members of the orchestra. I did come to know most of them, even so, and individually we overcame the suspicion and dislike that most players have for the members of the 'office', as they called us. The orchestra worked like beavers under conditions more like a dog's life and they had to be as strong as pack-horses to survive. They thought of the office as people who were parasites, sitting comfortably making mistakes. They had a point, too.

I certainly made mistakes. The printer we dealt with mostly was Vail and Co. of Farringdon. Old man Vail was a tartar, though golden-hearted in some ways. He had personally stumped up for concerts in his time, notably, I believe, to pay for a Berlin Philharmonic Orchestra tour in England. But he ate long-haired lads like me before breakfast. I couldn't resist trying to dent his bad temper but neither he nor the LPO directors were amused when a poster proof arrived one day with a work in the programme by Delius called *On Cooking the First Hero in Spring*.

I don't know if it was my bad jokes, or the noisy clouds caused by Ma Coulton's baked beans, or maybe because I was on Felix's side in artistic disputes, but when Tom Russell wanted to promote me to be Adolf Borsdorf's assistant in concert management, Adolf put his foot down and said he would resign. Adolf was an excellent business man and organizer, so from then on I continued with the Arts Club, removed when the Orpheum closed, to new premises, first in Fitzroy Square and then to the Fyvie Hall, part of the Regent Street Polytechnic, right next door to the LPO's offices above Boosey & Hawkes.

It was convenient having a music shop down below, both because of being able to buy books and music in our own building but also because Boosey & Hawkes ran at that time a most interesting series of contemporary music concerts – I have mentioned one of them already in this chapter – based largely but by no means entirely on their own composers. There was also a studio with two pianos on the premises and continuing opportunity to meet musicians passing through.

On one occasion I turned pages for Benjamin Britten as he rehearsed with Clifford Curzon his *Scottish Ballad, a jeu d'esprit* for two pianos and orchestra that Ben had written in America for Ethel Bartlett and Rae Robertson. Ben and Clifford were rehearsing the *Ballad* for a performance at the Proms. (It gave me a great kick to appear on the platform at the Royal Albert Hall, even though in so humble a capacity.) After shopping hours, the only way of getting out into the street was through the studio and suddenly in came John Ireland who had been talking to somebody upstairs. Dr John had been Britten's composition teacher at the Royal College and they hadn't got on too well together. Now they eyed each other with some suspicion, like a couple of dogs meeting on neutral ground. It could have been nasty but simultaneously they moved towards each other with friendly gestures – none too sincere, one could feel, but at least there was no hostility, much to the relief of Clifford and myself.

Boosey & Hawkes had taken over 'for the duration' not only the list of the Vienna-based firm Universal Edition, publishers of Mahler, Bartók, Kodály, some Delius and the whole of the Viennese atonalists Schoenberg, Berg and Webern, but also two of their staff turned refugees, Alfred Kalmus and Erwin Stein.

Kalmus was more or less in charge of the B. & H. concerts. He was said by many to be devious but he was always kind to me and pleasant. He looked like some Old Testament character, with his long grey beard, and one feared constantly that he would commit auto-arson, setting fire to his beard as he lit tiny portions of cigarettes, rationing himself because of the shortage. He had fascinating stories to tell of composers, including Mahler whom he had known in his youth.

Erwin was a little round bumbling absent-minded professor turned publisher, never with the right pair of spectacles on his nose. He was affectionately known to us all as 'Winkle'. He had been the writer-apologist for the Second Viennese School and had actually been a pupil of Schoenberg.

He conducted *Pierrot lunaire* for one of the B. & H. concerts, but he was so fanatical and impractical that he would never let the musicians have a preliminary runthrough of the piece to get a rough idea of the score, still unfamiliar at that time. No, as soon as anybody played a wrong note, he would shout at the player and go back to the beginning. Under these circumstances it is not surprising that thirty-seven rehearsals were necessary.

One of Erwin's editorial tasks at Boosey's was to see Britten's compositions through the press and the two of them established a great rapport. Erwin worshipped Ben and took Ben, and Peter, to the bosom of his family. Little Erwin, very Jewish, was married to a very tall, blonde, Christian lady called Sophie, an absolute sweetheart, who was considerably older than Erwin. Her son by a former marriage was still in Germany but she and Erwin, having married late, had nevertheless produced a child, an exceedingly beautiful girl called Marion, tall like her mother but possessing more of her father's colouring.

I used to visit them at their flat in Cornwall Gardens and sometimes Erwin would persuade Marion and me to play duets. I remember one time it was a Mahler symphony we had to play, probably the Fourth, arranged for one piano, four hands. Erwin would stand behind us, shouting in German from time to time something that neither Marion nor I could understand, so we would try playing faster and then, if the shouting continued, slower.

Marion was reserved in those days, lovely but cold, to me the typical child of elderly parents. She warmed somewhat after her first marriage, to George, Earl of Harewood, and even more after her second marriage, to Jeremy Thorpe. Marion has proved that she has not only beauty of feature but beauty of spirit. What a story she could write one day! I hope she does. What fantastic loyalty and incredible courage!

Further adventures at 295 Regent Street were the nights that I spent fire-watching, up and down, up on the roof sometimes, more often down in the basement playing table tennis and trying to get some sleep. This was a very different sort of night-watching from the ARP (Air Raid Precautions) work that I did out in the quasi-country of Loudwater.

After Adolf Borsdorf refused to have me as his assistant I continued with the Arts Club but divided the rest of my time into two yet further sections. Not for nothing was I born under the sign of Gemini whose creatures always tend, in poker terms, to split their openers. I don't think that I knew anything about zodiac signs at that time, nor had I realized that the pattern of my life was to spread my talents about perhaps too thinly. But then I had realized that my talent was thin, so perhaps the spreading of it was an unconscious attempt not to let that thinness become too apparent. I don't like change in the sense of wanting to move house but I do like to have variety in my life whether it is what I work at or play at or eat or drink or . . . but let's have a new chapter!

(5)

The National Gallery

During wartime the National Gallery sent all its pictures away and for a time music took over. The story is well documented of how the pianist Dame Myra Hess organized a series of lunchtime concerts, Monday to Friday, in a central gallery with a platform erected in the middle of four intersecting high rooms with curtains behind the platform and the fourth room, from which the artists entered, empty. This platform was big enough to seat a small choir or orchestra but the main fare was recitals and chamber music. The artists were paid a tiny nominal sum and the profits went to the Musicians' Benevolent Fund. Everybody was made happier by these concerts and at one time the Nat. Gall., as we called it, was the only place in London where you could hear live music of any distinction, quality and range.

Well, very nearly the only place. At that time there was no opera and the symphony orchestras soon gave up playing anything but twenty or thirty of the world's most popular classics. For really interesting music you had either to seek it out at Morley College where Tippett was in charge, or go to the ballet where Lambert was performing wonders, often with two pianos – himself at one – instead of orchestra; to Felix's French concerts, or to the Boosey & Hawkes series of contemporary music or – why not say it? – to my Philharmonic Arts Club sessions.

Myra Hess was delightful, rather like a Jewish Queen Mother. Polite, charming, gracious, very conservative in her tastes and behaviour, except that she had an unexpectedly rumbustious sense of humour. Her entourage on the feminine side frightened me, but at that time I didn't know what lesbian society or behaviour could be like. Her chief male adviser, friend, confidant, protégé and partner in the organization of the concerts and their programmes, was the composer Howard Ferguson, and it was through his kindness that I got the job of nannying the concerts.

My job was to make sure that everything was in order, the platform ready, the artists happy, push the artists on to the platform, often turn pages for the pianists, thank them afterwards – although Myra and Howard were there most days to do that – and then do the books, entering the amount of money taken, etc. Quite often I would go for a late lunch afterwards with Myra and Howard, and also probably with Beryl, Myra's niece/secretary, and sometimes the South African composer Arnold van Wyk, who became one of my closest and dearest friends.

We lunched sometimes at the Garrick Hotel at the back of the National Portrait Gallery, where we often stopped on our way out or in, by the statue of Garrick, to watch the crowd gathered round a Houdini-type. His mate would encase 'Houdini' in chains and ropes and would then deliver a spiel saying that 'Houdini' would in a moment escape miraculously from his bonds, meanwhile passing round the hat. All of a sudden there would be a cry from another mate: 'Watch aht, COPPER!' Whereupon 'Houdini' and his mates would all scarper with the takings without ever reaching the moment where he had to prove whether or not he could escape from his bonds. Certainly he was able to escape *in* his bonds. Lunches were full of fun and good stories. Myra called me 'Robert' because she thought she saw a likeness to Schumann – very flattering.

If there was no lunch afterwards I would eat at the public canteen quite happily because the open sandwiches and sweets were some of the best food in London at that time. Somehow Myra had organized a lot of society and other ladies to do their bit for the war by coming to make and serve food for the concert audiences.

There was one lady who fascinated me because I thought she was the visual equivalent of an amalgam of characters portrayed on the radio by Joyce Grenfell at that time in a series of very funny programmes. One day, of course, the inevitable happened. I was introduced to the lady and she *was* Joyce Grenfell. Not long after this I saw a man waiting at the bus stop several times whom I described to friends as being the epitome of Osbert Lancaster cartoons, then saw a photograph of the cartoonist . . . . Another 'comes to realize' – the expression so often used once upon a time in opera synopses. In fact 'comes to realize' describes many situations in classical tragedies, Verdi operas, etc.

I shared an office at the gallery just inside the front door on the left as you go in with the head keeper, Smith. I never knew his other name. He was a cheerful, helpful man with curly hair and an enormous conk of a nose. His assistant – I can't remember whether his name actually was Charlie or whether it was just that he was one – was often to be seen asleep standing up but the other uniformed men protected him affectionately.

I remember that one morning, quite soon after I arrived at the gallery, Charlie popped his head in the office door and said, 'It's in!'

At which Smith dropped what he was doing, reached for his cap, and said to me, 'Come on.'

'What's up?'

'Don't ask questions, get a move on, follow me, quick.'

So I upped and out with Smith. The attendants from all over the gallery, plus some of the non-uniformed staff, were converging on the front door, going out into Trafalgar Square, turning left, past St Martin-in-the-Fields and along the Strand until we got to Yates Wine Lodge.

I had been there before. It's a curious pub-like place with a street frontage of a mere ten or twelve feet but it stretches back quite a long way with a little parlour at the back. I had never seen such a scrimmage. How the word had got back so quickly to the gallery, I don't know, but what was 'in' was port. Port was very scarce during the war and a ship had obviously just managed to get through the blockade and a pipe or two of port had just been delivered to Yates. In twenty minutes every drop had been drunk, mostly, as far as I could see, by the staff of the National Gallery, and it was a happy, boozy lot that staggered back to work.

Sir Kenneth Clark, needless to say, was not among those present. The staff did not like its brilliant director very much, quite understandably, for in public he was a cold fish, quite unable to pass the time of day or indulge in small talk. Yet I went once with Irene Worth to dine with him and found him absolutely fascinating. The subject of staff relations came up at table and he said, 'Well, they say that I lack the common touch. (*Pause.*) And they're quite right. I do.' But like some others in high office, I'll bet he didn't ever try to do anything about it. (William Glock was the same.)

For me the National Gallery Concerts were a vital part of my education. I got to grips with the chamber music repertoire, in some ways the most rewarding music of all. Nothing speaks straight through to one's inner being more intimately than the string quartets of Haydn and Beethoven or the string quintets of Mozart. I heard for the first time the late quartets of Beethoven, played by the Menges String Quartet, and that was an overwhelming experience, enhanced because the cellist of the quartet, Ivor James, gave a short illustrated talk about each work before it was played.

'Jimmy' James was fairly old then but not so frail as Isolde Menges, already affected with the arthritis that eventually bent her double. As a result her playing was sometimes flat in pitch and sketchy in difficult technical passages but her sense of line and the pathos she drew from her violin gave the music the visionary grandeur inherent in the notes. Another Beethoven series that was similarly revealing was the complete violin and piano sonatas played by Max Rostal and Franz Osborn; they played better together than they ever did singly.

As well as encouraging young artists like Dennis Brain, Denis Matthews, the Zorian String Quartet and countless others, it was remarkable to hear some of the real old-timers perform. For example, the pianist Adela Verne. Like Isolde, Adela Verne was, or seemed, very old indeed, and her recitals were mostly sketchy and wayward, but occasionally the heavens opened and we had five or ten minutes of playing from another and grander world.

Then there was Elena Gerhardt. The very morning that I write this paragraph the BBC played some of the Hugo Wolf Society records that she made about 1930, and as usual I found that I got very little from them. But when she appeared at the Nat. Gall., even though she was getting on and her pitch problems had increased – her weight problem had too, so much so that one day she actually broke the stairs leading to the platform – yet, when you saw her as well as heard her singing, you were convinced by her. You were no longer conscious of her and you felt at one with the music – certainly helped by Myra Hess who was happy to turn accompanist when Elena came to sing.

Another quite remarkable, also large, singer was Engel Lund, the

Icelandic lady who sang folk songs of many lands. Engel was indeed an Angel, introducing each song in fractured sing-song speech to tell us what it was about, and then somehow penetrating to the very earth of each country to bring out its music, helped enormously by the accompaniment of her pianist, Ferdinand Rauter, nicknamed 'Loewe' ('Lion').

Once or twice I was able to suggest a programme that Howard Ferguson would accept – such as a visit by the choir of Canterbury Cathedral with solos sung by their first alto, the counter-tenor Alfred Deller. This was one of his first London public appearances, and mighty successful it was too. He sang the anthem 'This is the Record of John' by Orlando Gibbons.

I had been warned that the visits of the Harrison sisters' piano trio must not be missed but, strangely enough, Howard and Myra always did miss them. The first time one occurred I went along to the artists' room about half an hour before the recital was due to start, to see if they needed anything. I tapped on the door and was bidden to enter. I did so and nearly fell on my back through stepping on an apple. The entire floor seemed to be awash with fruit and vegetables. And the rest of the room was full of carrier bags, paper bags, hold-alls and, of course, the Harrisons.

The most famous was the cellist, Beatrice – she who used to play to the nightingales in her native woods, recorded oft-times by the BBC. Then there was May, the violinist, with her hair drawn back by a black ribbon into an apology for a bun. She looked like a French advocate, an effect enhanced by her pince-nez. There was also Margaret, the pianist. She was the easiest on the ear, partly because the piano doesn't suffer from intonation problems. This small room was full of these three old ladies, the accoutrements, the bags, the hairstyles – two frizzy, one straight – and, oh, the misapplied lipsticks! I'm certain there was a large looking-glass in the room but they were all wide of the target when it came to finding their mouths. (It reminded me of Myra telling me how, when she first made a success, she had photographers following her and she was so gauche that when they asked her to smile she couldn't remember where her mouth was.)

I cannot say that I got much out of the Harrisons' playing. I had the feeling that the grand manner was all they had left and that not much practising went on at home. But still, here was the cellist who had brought the Double Concerto and the Sonata of Delius into the world, recorded the Elgar Concerto with the composer conducting, and had a duo with Arnold Bax at one time. . . .

I also recall Vaughan Williams on another occasion, when his String Quartet was played, playing quiet havoc with the girls in that very room. Uncle Ralph was very sweet with the girls but he never seemed to have time to talk to young men like myself. To start with his deafness seemed to have difficulties with the frequency of my speaking voice whereas he could always understand what the girls said. Curious.

Other composers who came regularly to the concerts were Gerald Finzi, Arnold van Wyk, Edmund Rubbra and, of course, Howard Ferguson. Finzi's music always seemed to me so at variance with his nature. His music is mostly pastoral and placid, all 6/8 and 'Lisbie Browne', whereas his dark face was always fulminating with rage at some injustice, a sort of walking *Manchester Guardian*. Nevertheless, he was a dear man, sweet and kind and cultured.

The other side of the string quartet coin, so to speak, was the ensemble led by Sidney Griller. Their forte, I always thought, was not the classics, which they played quite well, but modern(ish) music. Their playing of Arthur Bliss's First Quartet was marvellous, eclipsed only by the extraordinary power and passion that they invested in Ernest Bloch's String Quartet No. 1, a long and steamy, erotic outburst of Hebraic passion.

The Grillers at this stage were in the RAF sitting on the back desks of the famous Uxbridge HQ Orchestra of the RAF. Later the Grillers went to the States, their stay there ending in stark tragedy when an internal homosexual fracas ended in denunciation to the police and sudden death, at which point the always happily married Sidney Griller came back to England.

The RAF Orchestra should be written up in a book of its own because it housed and contained most of the best solo, chamber music and orchestral talent in the country: Dennis Brain, Denis Matthews, Norman Del Mar, Gareth Morris, Harry Blech, the Grillers, Leonard Hirsch and dozens of others conducted by a Wing Commander whose gaffes were some of the best musical jokes of the war. One will have to suffice here: one day the Beethoven Violin Concerto was being rehearsed for a concert. The timpanist played the four D taps that begin the work. The Wingco stopped and said to him, 'Well, you can cut that first bar for a start. We don't need any drummer to give us the tempo.'

Occasionally a section of this RAF band was loaned to the Nat. Gall., notably for a series in which Myra played all twenty-seven Mozart piano concertos. I am sorry to say that my esteem and affection for Myra Hess rarely applied to her piano playing, which on the whole I found too pretty. But now and again she found depths that astonished her friends, even Howard Ferguson himself.

Both the times I recall were, significantly I think, unscheduled performances. One was when an artist had cancelled and Myra stepped in and played Beethoven's 'Appassionata' Sonata 'within an inch of her life', as somebody remarked. The same experience occurred one day when a film was being made about the Lunchtime Concerts. Myra was at the piano and something went wrong with the camera or lights and Ken Cameron, the director, asked Myra to play something for ten minutes or so while things were put right. Myra said, 'All right, I have a sudden yen to play a piece I haven't had in my repertoire for years – IF I can remember it. It's the first movement of Chopin's "Funeral March" Sonata in B flat minor.' She played like a woman possessed. It was great. It was magnificent. Now why could she not play like that when it was a programme of her own, one she had prepared?

Mind you, this happens not infrequently in the concert world. For years Gérard Souzay used to sing his encores much, much better than anything in the scheduled programme. And he is only one artist among many. I know that Myra Hess was extremely nervous and apprehensive before going on stage, 'Why do I ever say I will give a concert? I'm never going to appear in public again. Robert, remind me about this when I come off, will you?'

Towards the end of the series, there was a welcome though small influx of visitors from abroad. England was no longer just an island. Some artists would never have it so good again – when we had foreigners to remind us that our standards had lowered during the war. At the gallery I recall in particular the visits of Ginette Neveu, that fantastic violinist with a face like a French horse. What fire and finesse she showed! Then there was that wonderful singer of French song, Pierre Bernac, and, above all for me, the composer

Francis Poulenc, looking so much like the film-star comedian Fernandel.

Poulenc pinches so much from so many composers and yet makes it so deliciously his own, witty, winning – so like a child yet so adult. I find Poulenc's music never palls; he is one of the few composers that I still play on the gramophone. It was wonderful to meet him. One of the television programmes that I made that I think was worth while was about him. But that came a long time after his appearance at the dear old Nat. Gall.

Simultaneously with my time at the National Gallery I was very much engaged with the activities of Michael Tippett, as a friend, as a composer, and as Music Director of Morley College, which meant firstly, house concerts at the college and later, concerts organized by Michael and myself, and concerts in which the college choir was engaged. And that is the cue for another chapter . . . .

(6)

Up the Creek (or Fistula)

After the National Gallery job packed up I was rather on my uppers but at least I was living somewhere nice. On Linden Lea. But not the Linden Lea of the song. This was a road in Hampstead Garden Suburb, and the joke of it was that I am sure that only in two houses in that street were there people who would have known the tune that Vaughan Williams put into his famous song. For in Linden Lea lived the Abrahams, the Brainins, the Cohens, the Davidoffs *und so weiter*. Am I being anti-Semitic? No, merely making an ethno-musical point. The local tennis club was another matter. On applying to join that I was asked to come along for an audition – not so much to see how I played, but how I looked.

The houses on Linden Lea where they knew the difference between a floral arrangement and a Vaughan Williams one were 23, where Warwick Braithwaite, the conductor, and his wife Lorna and their two sons lived, and 14, where I lodged with Sheila Busch. I helped Rodrick Braithwaite with his music for his exams; he is now a diplomat. I didn't help Nicholas with his; he is now a conductor. This must prove something.

Sheila was the widow of William Busch, a composer that I had first met at Morley College. William knew Alan Bush, no relation, and that is how I think William's songs and his piano variations *Nicholas* came to be played at Morley. (Nicholas was his baby son; one-time chairman of the London Philharmonic Orchestra, and for many years now their marvellous first horn.) Apart from the songs, quite a lot of William's small output is violent, or seemed so at that time. Yet William himself was one of the gentlest creatures that I ever met – self-effacing to a fault, kind, highly intelligent, an adorable person. The violence in his music came, I suppose, from the frustration of not being able to step outside his innate gentleness except in his music. The cause may also have been rebellion against his rather Hunnish father.

The Busches had lived far away from civilization, certainly because of the war, and perhaps to get away from William's father. While Sheila was in hospital having her second child, Julia, William was on his own in their house in Woolacombe and a bad attack of flu or pneumonia coincided with a terrible cold spell. William failed to alert anybody to his condition and died. It was a tragedy, not least for his music which had not come to fruition in any quantity. Peter Pears sang and recorded some of his touching and exquisitely made songs but it is many years since either of his excellent sets of piano variations was played, or his Cello Concerto, or the fine Piano Quartet.

Returning from Devon, Sheila had set up in the good modern house where she and William had lived before the war. On the top floor was a music studio with a luscious Blüthner and William's library. Living as a friend/lodger I was able to enjoy all the facilities of a musical household, Sheila's superb cooking, the company of the children, and perhaps to help the beautiful Sheila to return to a normal life after the dreadful shock of William's death. At the best of those times she was shy, retiring and lacking in self-confidence – but she made an effort; we went to things together and she seemed to enjoy the company of the friends that I brought there. We had parties upstairs in the studio and I can remember clarinet quintets with Gervase de Peyer, then quite unknown, and the Amadeus String Quartet, then just starting to be known.

My only job for a short while was being London music critic of the *Scotsman* but after a time I took, with some misgivings, a job working for the London International Orchestra. You haven't heard of it, reader? Well, it didn't last very long; it didn't make any records, and it didn't ever broadcast or play for movies. That was part of the trouble. This symphony orchestra was thought up by Anatole Fistoulari and I don't think anybody else but 'Fisty' conducted it.

Poor Fisty had had a bad deal. The London Philharmonic Orchestra had taken him up in 1943–4 in a big way. It was the usual love affair that orchestras have, or had in those days during and just after the war, with conductors. Fisty was their principal conductor until the next conductor came along and then he was out – so much out that when the LPO had its fiftieth birthday it conveniently forgot even to mention him in its list of conductors. Nobody else seemed to want Fisty so he formed his own orchestra.

Now Fisty is a simple man, a likeable chap. He is not exactly an intellectual conductor. In two years' close collaboration and many railway journeys I never saw him read anything more highbrow than the *Daily Mirror*, let alone a book. I knew that finance and financing weren't Fisty's strongest points. He was naïve, incurably optimistic and he had been for some years touring with Russian ballet and opera companies. All this made me chary of having anything to do with the finances, except for paying the orchestra after concerts.

An orchestra can do well only if it has regular work, regular income, contracts. The London International had none of these essentials. All it had was one-night stands, single concerts. The orchestral situation in London at that time was fluid, in more senses than one. Many players were free-lancing; there were pick-up bands playing for films, records and concerts with orchestras of different names but similar personnel. For example, Dennis Brain, the great horn player, could be seen in at least half a dozen different chamber or symphony orchestras in London at that time.

Without a full-time fixer for dates, Fisty could not hope to keep his orchestra going for very long. Nor did he. Some of it was fun while it lasted, though; some rather pathetic. The first concert was quite good. To start with, Fisty can give good shows, without being a great conductor. He is a brilliant accompanist – he will stick to the most wayward soloist like a piece of chewing-gum to the heel of a shoe. I have also heard him make a seventh-rate orchestra play like a second-rate one, and that takes some doing! So the first concert contained quite a passable Brahms Symphony No. 4. Some of the Amadeus played in that first concert, and a lot of other excellent players.

The trouble was that Fisty's dates were neither regular nor prestigious. A concert on a Sunday afternoon at a cinema in Maidenhead perhaps, then a single concert at Newcastle, ten days later, with a Sunday evening a week later in the Royal Albert Hall. Another trouble was that Fisty didn't improve with repetition.

He learned his scores with the aid of a gramophone and a mirror. I visited his flat on Campden Hill too many times for him to keep that secret from me. (He was married at that time to, of all people, Mahler's daughter, Anna, the sculptress. Fisty, bless his heart, wasn't much of a sculp for her . . . .) And by the time he had done Brahms Four, and Tchaikovsky Four a few times, the orchestra knew Fisty's unvarying gestures by heart. They even knew which records he'd learned his scores by. Inspiration was absent and his repertoire was small – mainly out of necessity. One-night standers cannot programme Tippett or Szymanowski. Fisty's charm faded; he had a kind of desperate optimism; he blinked more than ever; the money sometimes ran out. . . .

My job was orchestral manager, that is, I had to get the orchestra together but, with things the way they were, I don't think we ever had the same orchestra twice, except for two short tours. Once we went to Belfast and Dublin, playing in cinemas. That was fun, especially the smuggling that went on. How popular some of the instrumentalists became! Kettledrums were stuffed with butter, bananas and chocolate; double-basses were full to the *f*-holes with stockings. This was the forties when things were still very short in the UK and Eire was awash with goodies. But there were disasters on this tour, like the local agent who had made a gigantic cock-up over the accommodation, and the final insult was when the roof of the cinema we were performing in leaked water on to the woodwind.

The orchestral world has been described as a rat race. At that time I knew it and developed a hatred of many of the players as a result. I spent most of my waking hours on the telephone, booking players. Certain players were not in demand so I could always get fiddles and violas and cellos though maybe not always good ones. But basses were difficult and so were most of the woodwind and brass.

Certain people I could rely on, and if they had to take a better job they would send me a reliable player. But some of them were villains. They would take a job over the road for half a crown more. That was bad enough. But sometimes they would do that and not tell me. I was lucky sometimes if I found out accidentally that they weren't going to play. Many's the time that I have been on the phone until two and three in the morning trying to get players for an out-of-town date the next day, entailing a 9.30 train. Oh, the chagrin of having to ring people at that time, getting wrong numbers, making a nuisance of myself, simply because of the villainy of some of these players!

Then I'd have to be up at 5.30 to go with a van to collect the heavier instruments; train to wherever it was; set up the orchestra, often no porter but me; try to explain to Fisty why there were only three double-basses or that the cor anglais was coming by car for the concert but would not be at the rehearsal; then explain to the orchestra why there was no ready money – 'Don't we get the candy on the counter?' was the euphemism that the north country brass players used – until later. Once I had to play an essential harp part on an upright piano (Boëllmann's *Symphonic Variations*) and another time I filled in the triangle part in Brahms Four and made the classic goof of grabbing the instrument by the metal instead of the string.

The first break I would get was when Fisty started yet again on a second half consisting of Brahms Four, Tchaikovsky Five or Beethoven Seven. Then I would escape and go out to see the second half of a crimi-movie. The more incomprehensible it was the more I laughed and liked it, and the more I got shouted at by those who had been there since the beginning. The trouble with this orchestra was that even old friends who played in it began to dislike me because I was on the management side of a dud organization.

Only once did I accept financial responsibility for a date. I was staying the weekend with the pianist Noel Mewton-Wood who lived at Renby Grange near Eridge in Nancy Eckersley's house. Nancy's husband, a former BBC Controller, was working at this time as Entertainments Manager for the Butlin holiday camps. Roger explained to me that Billy Butlin was just about to open a new holiday camp at Filey and that he wanted to have some kind of cultural splash, a grand opening to which he could invite all the mayors, all the local bigwigs and as many bishops and deans as could be found in the Ridings of Yorkshire.

Roger suggested that I might bring the London International Orchestra with Fistoulari. Roger would fix a soloist and would arrange the finances only with me – not with Fisty. There were to be three consecutive evening performances, with the same programme every night and the same orchestra, but different audiences, if they could find enough mayors and bishops. I asked Fisty if he would accept such terms. Providing he got his fee, the orchestra were paid and we agreed the programme, yes, it was OK with him. The first half was to be Beethoven, an overture followed by a piano concerto – for which Roger had engaged Solomon as soloist – followed by, I think, Tchaikovsky Five. The orchestra was intrigued by the idea, accommodation was provided and there would be no rehearsals after the first concert. Off we went. . . .

We had all expected to be dragooned by the famous redcoats at Butlin's but there was no 'wakey-wakey' in the morning. Everything worked well at the new camp. The beds were comfy and the grub was good, served piping hot and efficiently. There were only about a couple of hundred actual holiday campers, including a party of salty Glasgow cleaning ladies who got increasingly tiddly as the evenings wore on, and increasingly incomprehensible too. (Glasgow is the only town in the UK where I have had to leave a shop and try somewhere else to see if I could achieve linguistic compatibility.) Closing time in the camp was cunningly engineered because there was always an official surprise happening at one end of the room to coincide with closing the bars at the other. The orchestra played billiards, clock golf and took part in all kinds of events during the day and played their best at the concerts. It was the orchestra's finest hour.

The first concert was fascinating. The audience was quite noisy, what with all those mayoral chains, crucifixes and ladies' bracelets. Eventually all were seated and the overture was played. The orchestra was placed on a stage at one end of one of the camp's ballrooms. (This one was done up as a kind of White Horse Inn, only more vulgar.) After the overture the manager of the camp introduced the director of a lot of other camps who introduced Billy Butlin himself.

As the little guy himself came on so did all the spotlights the ballroom could muster. Mr Billy explained that Butlin's did not only stand for popular holidays but that he, Billy Butlin, was going to give them the best in entertainment and that was why this evening, for the first time at any holiday camp in the world, there was a symphony concert taking place. He reached his peroration – applause, applause – and came and sat down in the audience just in front of Roger Eckersley and myself, just as Fisty entered. Then the great pianist Solomon came on to take his place for the Piano Concerto No. 3 in C minor.

This particular Beethoven concerto has a very long opening orchestral tutti and Solomon sat there with folded arms. After a minute and a half of this Mr Butlin was shifting about in his seat and after another minute of the tutti he turned to Roger and myself and whispered, 'I suppose there's no trouble about Mr Solomon's fee, is there?'

There was no trouble about my fee either. Roger told me to send my account in for the orchestra and Fisty's fee and that I should add a generous fee for myself too. I was still very green and wet behind the ears about money matters. With great daring I put down £75 for myself. Roger told me not to be such an idiot. Why not add a nought? So I did. It was the only time in my life that I brought off a smart deal for myself. And even then I had to be pushed into it.

Seven hundred and fifty pounds was a lot of money in 1946 and for the first time in my life I was rich. But I wasn't for long because after I had paid my debts, bought a couple of suits, some shirts and presents for everybody I could think of, I was broke once again. The last of the money was spent on a holiday at Christmas time with a lot of de Peyers – Gervase, the clarinettist; his brother Adrian, the tenor; their glamorous actress sister, Deirdre. We all went to the Old Head Hotel at Louisburgh in County Mayo – and their mother came too! My last gift was to a beautiful flute player. She liked Mozart so I gave her the Köchel catalogue of his works with my last five pounds.

Fortune turned her wheel at this point. I was asked to go and work with a somewhat better orchestra than the London International Orchestra – Beecham's Royal Philharmonic. My shinning up the ladder coincided more or less with Fisty's orchestra going down the drain. . . .

(7)

Norman Del Mar

Orchestras call him the 'Mass of Life'. I shall never forget seeing him conduct his first professional public job at Drury Lane Theatre in 1947 during the famous Richard Strauss Festival organized by Sir Thomas Beecham. There was this tall young man (twenty-eight at that time), well built, a large wristwatch much in evidence. He did not conduct like Strauss, from the wrist, or as Beecham usually did, from the elbow, but from the shoulder, from *both* shoulders. In other words, Norman flung himself about quite a bit. (He has since moderated his style somewhat.) Old Man Strauss was present at Drury Lane but he did not say anything much to Norman – except once when Strauss was trying to get through the pass-door to the backstage area. The door would not open and Strauss cussed about the 'verdammte Tür'. Norman's assignments were the early tone poem *Macbeth* and a pot-pourri from, I think, *Die Frau ohne Schatten*. (Norman always pronounces the 't' in pot-pourri'.)

I first became aware of Norman as a presence in shops. While I was working at E.M.G. Handmade Gramophones I used to go on miniature score hunts round the various first- and second-hand music shops, at first for E.M.G., but very soon afterwards mainly for my own gain, as I had acquired the collecting habit. (I still love to follow at concerts with a vocal or miniature score. You get to know the work better this way and, after some time, you listen better, which stands you in good stead if you have to write about the performance, and if you are feeling tired it helps you maintain your concentration. And now that I have become a bit deaf, the score enables me to follow sounds I might otherwise miss.)

This presence loomed. I never spoke to it but observed it as it bought scores. Worse, it often had been the previous week and cleaned out the interesting scores for sale. You see, during the war there was quite a lot of music that would not be reprinted until after the war, music that came from obscure publishers abroad, music in formats never to be republished, music with pretty covers and so forth.

I remember, for example, nosing around behind the scenes at Novello's and discovering a dusty little parcel tied up with string. Opened up, it proved to be six miniature scores of Strauss's *Ein Heldenleben* in the Leuckardt printing. You won't see that format any more as the plates were bombed at Leipzig. I still have my copy, marked seven shillings and sixpence, and I believe Norman had one of the remaining five. It was one time I got in first.

Eventually I found that the presence's name was Norman Del Mar and connected it with a toothbrush merchant that my father used to chat to in the train. But for a long time I did not actually meet this presence. Sometimes I saw it in tweedy sportscoat, pullover and grey bags, very much the sort of gear I was wearing in those days, fairly standard stuff really for chaps from public schools, even though his Marlborough was a cut above my Dulwich . . . but at least we used to play them at cricket.

Then I started to see the presence playing in orchestras, sometimes in RAF blue, often sitting beside the great (but much smaller) Dennis Brain. Some physiological formation made Dennis look as though he was smiling while he played the horn – not so Norman nor, indeed, any other horn player I have ever seen. During the latter part of the war both hornists were in the RAF Central Band at Uxbridge. Somehow Norman became driver to the conductor of the orchestra, Wing Commander O'Donnell, and this, combined with his larger-than-life size and style, and his inability to perform certain very simple domestic tasks, made him something of a band butt.

Should you be wondering about those domestic tasks, let me give you an example from the late 1940s when Norman was thirty or so. One evening Norman and his wife Pauline came to Olive's and my flat in Holland Villas Road. Norman was in the kitchen with Olive who was cooking. She had an unlit cigarette in her mouth and said to Norman, 'Would you please light my cigarette for me? Both my hands are greasy.' To which Norman replied, 'I would really much rather not.'

OLIVE: Why on earth not, Norman?

NORMAN: Well, frankly, I'm not very good at lighting matches.

OLIVE: You're joking!

NORMAN: No, actually not. The fact is that I've only ever lit half-a-dozen matches in my whole life and they've all been dreadful failures.

OLIVE: (*Amused but slightly exasperated*) Oh, come on, Norman, don't be ridiculous. Please light my cigarette immediately.

Norman takes the matchbox, takes out a match, succeeds in lighting it but it flies out of his hands right across the room.

NORMAN: (*Triumphantly*) THERE, you see, that's the sort of thing that happens when I try to light matches.

I must also digress about the Wingco again because, to his credit, by forming that wartime Central Band Symphony Orchestra with most of the best chamber music and symphonic players in the country, he saved many musical lives and he also enabled these musicians to keep right on playing their instruments and developing their skill instead of either not playing or else playing soul-destroyingly inferior music. However, the Wingco was not really a symphony man and his gaffes were many and diverting.

For example, the flute player, Gareth Morris, was already in trouble with O'Donnell because his natural expression is frownladen and the Wingco thought that he was being rebellious. There had been a rift in the flute during a rehearsal of the Bach Suite in B minor when O'Donnell took the *Polonaise* at a great lick, causing Gareth breathlessly to ask if it could be slower as he couldn't play the solo part at that tempo. He started to mumble something about the polonaise in Bach's time being slower, only to be interrupted by his superior officer humming the well-known Chopin A major *Polonaise*. 'That's the speed of a polonaise, flute boy. Any more nonsense like this and we'll have you posted.' Poor Gareth was seated right in front of the Wingco in the rehearsal room at Uxbridge and it was not long before he was indeed posted . . . to Catterick or somewhere nasty.

This was the way discipline was enforced. There was no give-and-take at rehearsal. Dissenters were posted – some to the Orkneys merely for disagreeing over a tempo. Still, better Uxbridge and the Wingco than elsewhere. And for long periods of time, there would simply be a roll-call – Harry Blech used to be taken to Uxbridge by his wife in the car sometimes and, being an absent-minded soul, once appeared at roll-call wearing his Homburg – and then the lads would be free for the rest of the day, free to accept engagements in the orchestras of London.

This was why I would often see Norman, with Dennis Brain as like as not, playing in Walter Goehr's orchestra, in Alec Sherman's New London Orchestra, in Anthony Bernard's London Chamber Orchestra, in Sidney Beer's orchestras, in Edward Clark's orchestra and in many more of the little bands around London where the results were sometimes better than the conductors merited – had not the conductor's strongest asset been his cheque book. If he is paying you himself you are less likely to come in when he sells you a pup with a false entry.

Norman and I knew each other peripherally but were thrown into each other's company when I started working for Beecham and the Royal Philharmonic Orchestra.

At one point there was a cock-up in the booking of the players. This followed several other incidents that were clearly mistakes by the girl responsible for telephoning the players. Tommy decided that there must be a showdown in which it was to be apparent that the office was at fault and that he was on the side of the players.

Charles Cannon, the manager, Norman, as assistant conductor, and myself, as concert manager, were told to be at a rehearsal at St Pancras Town Hall. In the interval we were sent for and the orchestra, sensing that something was up, hung about. They had left their places and were standing at the back of the semi-circle of music stands, chairs and instruments. Norman was standing fear-fully at the exit door while Charles and I advanced to the podium where Sir Thomas stood.

He started to give us a dressing-down, working himself up in a simulated rage full of phrases beginning with words like 'I will not have . . . ' and 'In all my born days . . . .' He did not look us in the eye, partly out of habit – he very rarely did look anybody in the eye, except for special effect – partly because he knew as well as everybody else in the room that the sins were only in the last analysis to be laid at our door.

At one point Charles started to expostulate, 'But Sir Thomas . . . .'

I trod on his foot firmly, knowing that it was better to let the storm batter itself out. Sir Thomas reached a climax and then made a bee-line for the exit door. This entailed going segmentally through the chairs and stands knocking some of them out of his way·in his by now genuine rage, narrowly missing some cellos as he went. Just before going through the door, Sir Thomas looked up and saw Norman. He shook his fist at Norman and bellowed, somewhat inconsequentially, 'AND YOU TOO!' And he was gone.

Norman was much more upset than Charles or me. He always was more fearful for his position than we were, with some reason, for his future lay in conducting much more directly than our future careers did in our present jobs. After this episode we had to give Norman strong drink which he doesn't normally take.

'Episode', incidentally, is one of Norman's favourite words and that brings me to a consideration of one of Norman's most personal and endearing idiosyncrasies – his use of language. It is eccentric, to say the least. He will tell you that it stems from an aunt on Mum's side, who resided for many years, may do so still, in Florence.

So, to begin with 'episode'. Like many another word in the Del Mar vernacular, this has a connotation over and above the general meaning of the word. 'Episode' means an occasion fraught with drama, a 'scene', not nice. If you give Norman a present, he may well say that he is 'overwhelmed with touch'. To the question 'Were there a lot of people at the party, Norman?' the answer, 'The following', implies that there were quite a lot, people one knows moreover. However, no list will follow.

'The sort of thing' indicates complete Normanic approval. 'It doesn't do' implies the opposite, while the word 'sparse' is a danger sign of extreme frustration. If Norman says, 'Pauline, you're being sparse', she and anyone else who knows the private language will scuttle for cover before he loses his temper. 'Sparse', for some unexplained reason, means that a short fuse is alight. A 'footle' is a term of grave displeasure, though less severe than 'sparse'.

The Marriners (Neville and wife number one, Diana) once incurred something more than a 'footle' but less than 'sparse' for rebelling on holiday and wanting to do things in the wrong order and not *together*, at the same time as Norman and Pauline. 'It just doesn't do.' It is always advisable when you go to spend any time with Norman to do what he wants. It saves time, trouble and temper. He knows best, he really does. And he wants you to have a good time. His hospitality is lavish and generous.

If you go for a walk after lunch, there will be walking sticks provided. 'You really can't go for a walk without a walking stick. It just doesn't do. I think you'll find that a walk is actually *better* with a walking stick.' Lists are kept of many things. Green Line coaches and especially the garages from which buses and coaches emanate are the subject of great interest. The car once hurtled to a halt and there was much 'zz-zz'-ing and, 'Did you SEE that? A 435 from the *Catford* garage, not Beckenham!' It's all a bit like heightened Dornford Yates.

Putting two and two together becomes almost a mania in the Del Mar household. They spend hours doing king-sized jigsaw puzzles consisting mostly of sky. In order not to run out of sky they belong to a lending library of jigsaws. It is amazing that even a couple as energetic as this does not run out of hours, let alone sky. Once upon a time there was the building of Cologne Cathedral consisting of about a million small bricks especially imported from Germany. The thing was nearly four feet high. I haven't seen that cathedral about for some time, nor the manuscript scores which used to be kept and added to in the lavatory, actually composed on the (s)pot.

Works on the stocks at one time were a setting of *The Waste Land* and an opera based on *Hassan*. Knowing Norman's hatred of cutting or omissions it probably was not 'based on' but the *complete* text of Flecker. However, I do remember that it was heavily scored and that each new act contained yet another pair of horns. I never heard the sonata that Norman composed for Dennis Brain to play on his second instrument, the organ, but Felix Aprahamian still speaks well of it. I did hear, and enjoyed, the concerto that he wrote for Gareth Morris, the loudest flute concerto ever, a 'higgish' Straussian pot-pourri. ('Higgish' is another favourite word but, exceptionally, this comes not from the Florentine aunt's vernacular but from Pauline's family.)

Something of this linguistic exuberance transfers itself to his books which are 'enormously typical' of Norman. The three-volumed Richard Strauss biography has rightly become a classic; *The Anatomy of the Orchestra* will soon attain that status; fascinating, too, is the study of Mahler's Sixth Symphony.

On best form Norman's conducting rises to great heights:

performances that remain vividly in my memory are an early Walton Symphony No. 1 with the Royal Philharmonic Orchestra in Nottingham, a recent Elgar No. 2 with the Philharmonia in the Royal Festival Hall and, of course, the famous rehabilitating one of Tippett's *Midsummer Marriage* in the BBC's Maida Vale Studio. On a less exalted plane he will always give a well-considered performance with the nuts and bolts firmly in place; you always get a good idea of how the piece goes even though he may not plumb the depths. There is something of the virile efficiency of Sir Henry Wood about Norman; and he has the long arms necessary to keep a really slow tempo alive. If there is a tricky harmonic in an unfamiliar work you can depend upon it that Norman has spent time investigating the possibilities with a violinist (*not* one from the orchestra) so that at rehearsal, when the fiddlers are not sure how to find the note, he can then say, 'I think you'll find that if you touch the E string with the fourth finger . . . ' etc.

Norman is old-fashioned in that I think he firmly believes in the Divine Right of (not Kings but) Conductors; he is in charge and he likes to be right. It is just possible that he was happier in the old days when he conducted the Croydon and the Chelsea Symphony Orchestras in vast works like Liszt's *Faust Symphony* and Busoni's *Piano Concerto*; amateur players love a conductor who talks a lot, teaches a bit and explains things: how – 'as it might be' – 'd'Indy used to write his trumpet parts in E flat and when the original copyist wrote out the orchestral parts he transposed them by mistake . . . ' etc. The trouble is that, after a three-minute diversion of this sort, your average *professional* is inclined to ask, rather sourly, 'Do you want it loud or soft?'

It is a terrible waste that Norman Del Mar has never been given a major British orchestra of his own. Listen to his gramophone records and you will surely agree. Try Strauss's *Also sprach Zarathustra* or, even better, the *Enigma Variations* of Elgar. First class – 'higgish'.

(8)

Sir Thomas Beecham

Norman Del Mar brought me into the Beecham orbit. There was a job going on the staff of the Royal Philharmonic Orchestra and I was sent for by the Great Man. I was interviewed on 9 December 1947 by Sir Thomas Beecham himself and presumably not found wanting. But I was so terrified at meeting my absolute hero that I have no recollection whatsoever of the occasion or its whereabouts.

Previously I had seen Beecham only on the podium, never close to. His reputation was well known to me. He was something of a legend in his own lifetime – a legendary wit, a legendary conductor. His name was almost a music-hall joke, because of the money he had run through from the famous Beecham's Pills – the slogan 'Worth a guinea a box' was still current – and for the money that he owed to other people, debts that had landed him in the courts. The legends I knew then were of course augmented during the time that I worked for the London Philharmonic.

In 1946 Beecham had formed the new Royal Philharmonic Orchestra. There were two companies connected with the orchestra. 'Anglo-American' could accept engagements for the orchestra and was allowed to make a profit, while 'Royal Philharmonic Orchestra' controlled the prestigious side of the orchestra. It was officially a charity and could receive gifts and grants and sponsor its own concerts. It was non-profit-making or, more accurately, non-profit-distributing. (Not that there was any question of making a profit – Beecham's programmes would see to that.) Because of his bankruptcy Sir Thomas's name was not included in the list of directors. My official boss, if anybody, was the chairman of one or both of these companies. But there was never any doubt about who was running the show – or if there was, it was only because at times Lady Beecham the second, Betty Humby, seemed to be running Sir Thomas.

Within the orchestra there was a fairly powerless committee, headed by Gerald Jackson, the great flute player who had played with the BBC Symphony Orchestra for half a lifetime and was still a very good player and experienced in the ways of running an orchestra.

My position was that of concerts manager. I worked side by side with Charles Cannon who was my senior in that he controlled all the business side of the RPO, was responsible for seeing that the orchestra had enough engagements, how it worked and that it got paid. Naturally he deferred to Beecham's wishes at all times. He had a secretary, an accountant, an orchestral manager who booked the players, and me to look after the more artistic side of running the concerts and the printing of posters and programmes.

Charles, we eventually found out, was my junior in years. He knew little of music. He had come to the job because his father had been in some high-up job in Moss Empires, the theatre owners and entrepreneurs. Charles was out of the RAF but, we often felt, only just, because he was a complete Flying Officer Kite type, adorned with RAF moustache and spilling out all the slang like 'wizard prang' and 'all that flak'. The moustache amazingly concealed his extreme youth. If Beecham had known that Charles was in his early twenties I am sure he would never have taken him on. But all this was unsuspected until Charles was toppled from power.

One of my tasks was to extract from Sir Thomas the details of forthcoming programmes that he was going to conduct. For this purpose I would often go day after day to the 'House' as Sir Thomas's residence in Circus Road, St John's Wood, was called. I would get there at ten in the morning and wait, sometimes for twenty minutes, sometimes for two hours. Sir Thomas would make an entrance, sometimes in pyjamas and dressing gown, more often with dressing gown over shirt sleeves and waistcoat with the almost invariable morning trousers. He would be smoking what I imagined was his first cigar of the day. Wrong! I learned from the servants that Sir Thomas was one of those fortunate creatures who needed only three or four hours' sleep a night.

He woke at five and was usually studying his scores by half-past. At seven or so a cup of coffee would be brought to him and he would continue to work until breakfast, an hour or so later. It would be cigar of the day number four or five by the time he saw me. By now he was ready to talk a little to someone from the outside world, to discuss the news of the day, to talk about music in general, or his own work in particular. We would discuss the programme details that I had come to get but he never seemed to be in any great hurry.

We never got close to each other. I was frightened of him because, although he only once or twice showed me the temper that he used to lose so frequently in pre-war days, he preferred to keep all but a few intimate friends at bay. I think he was a very shy man and liked to hide behind formality. Thus I was never anything else in two years of often daily contact, frequently *à deux*, but 'Mister' Amis. Likewise his assistant conductor, Norman, was always 'Mister' Del Mar. (To this day Norman and I usually start our frequent telephone calls to each other with the ritual 'Mister Del Mar' and the response 'Mister Amis'.)

Sometimes Beecham would deliberately evade talking about the programmes. Often it could take six or seven visits to get one particular programme settled. On the rare occasions when a programme was settled in ten minutes, by the time I had returned to the office in Maddox Street there would be a message from the 'House' cancelling that programme and asking me to come again on the morrow for further discussion.

I soon discovered that there were certain names to be avoided when talking about music, or when proposing artists for programmes that Sir Thomas would not in any event be conducting himself. One day, for instance, an album of new Beecham records arrived in their American packaging. Included was an advertisement for an issue conducted by Toscanini. Beecham blew up. 'I will not have my records sullied with the name of that damned Italian lackey, that Milanese purveyor of spaghetti. Send a cable to New York . . . . ' (Toscanini had once labelled Beecham a dilettante, a rich amateur.)

At another time we had a dream morning planning a series of esoteric symphony concerts at Drury Lane, forgetting for the moment that there was no money for such a venture. Sir Thomas always lived well in advance of advanced royalties. He asked me who might be available to conduct one concert that he would not be available for. Stravinsky, I suggested? 'Yes, Igor's a good egg, why not? Igor, yes, well, why not? A good egg is Igor.'

Occasionally Beecham would play some unfamiliar piece to me on the piano. One such I recall was the aria 'Ruhe sanft' from Mozart's unfinished singspiel *Zaïde*. 'What, you don't know it?' he said. 'Why, it is one of Mōdesǎrt's (his pronunciation of the name – standard for Edwardians I have found) most wonderful and extended melodies. Come, I will play it for you.' His piano playing was the antithesis of his conducting: the sustaining pedal down most of the time, the right hand struck before the left, and the left hand made arpeggios of all the chords, while the singing voice was somewhere between a howl and a growl, a constant portamento between two notes, neither of them the right one.

This aria (printed, by the way, in Dent's book on the Mōdesǎrt operas) was one of Beecham's suggestions for a series of Mozart concerts that the BBC wanted to do. Many of the details, the choice of artists and so on, were left to me and Steuart Wilson, at that time Head of the BBC Music Department. Steuart, a former singer turned administrator – later at the Arts Council and Covent Garden – was a friend of the violinist Olive Zorian and we often dined with Steu and Mary, his wife, the feature of which was Steuart's excellent cooking. We needed soloists, among others, for the *Sinfonia concertante*, and I put forward Olive's name and that of Winifred Copperwheat, the viola player of Olive's quartet. Steuart agreed and, entirely on my recommendation, so did Sir Thomas.

When Olive and I decided to get married just before the performance, I felt rather guilty and broke the news to Sir Thomas. He cleared his throat rather more than usual, twitched his mouth round in that typical way of his and said, 'Oh well, it'll be all right, I suppose.' 'Which, Sir Thomas, the *concertante* or the marriage?' At which he laughed and hoped to God that both would be.

As it turned out the orchestra was very nice to Olive and Winnie – being girls helped. Because, apart from the harpist who didn't get much of a look in during a *Mozartfest* anyway, there was not a single gel in the RPO. If extra chaps had been brought in there would have been hell to pay from the leader and the first viola.

What was unusual in the preparation for the *Sinfonia* was that Tommy took it to bits at the rehearsals. His usual practice with a work, as he said at a big birthday lunch at the Dorchester once, was to play it through, get an idea what the piece was like, then play it through again, ironing out any little difficulties that might have presented themselves. 'By which time', said Sir Thomas, 'I know what the orchestra is going to do at the concert. But of course they have no idea what *I* am going to do.'

You may remember that Ned Sherrin and Caryl Brahms wrote a theatre piece, 'bio-doc' is the name of the species, that Timothy West Beechamed his way through most acceptably. The speech tempo was not right for the later years, although it was fine for earlier years, as was confirmed by watching the other day Beecham in a newsreel speech about the birth of the LPO in 1932. It was only in the later years that his speech became so measured. But the objection I had to the play was that it presented only the view of Beecham that Beecham himself showed to the world.

If Tommy was often seen as a dilettante – Toscanini was not the only one to voice that opinion – it was largely his own fault. He liked to give that impression, like the public schoolboy who never goes to nets, so he says, but makes a century in the big match. Beecham worked as hard as Furtwängler, or indeed as hard as 'any damned foreigner', but you would never find a German conductor maintaining that his art was a simple one that didn't need any hard work.

Of course Beecham worked hard, early in the morning as I have mentioned, and for the rest of the day too. He could never study his scores enough, paradoxically, provided they were works he knew well. His method was based on finding the tunes, finding the right tempo, finding the right balance, and putting it over to the public. The orchestral parts were littered with bowing and breathing marks. These were not the pithy instructions found in the scores of Sir Henry Wood, such as 'like a cavalry charge' (cellos and basses in the scherzo of Beethoven Five) or 'rushing onward to its doom' (towards the end of Tchaikovsky's *Romeo and Juliet* overture). Beecham's marks gave the shape of the music and were transferred into the parts of each player by that painstaking, hardworking, wonderfully faithful librarian, George Brownfoot, a typical Merchant Navy man, one of the best. Beecham would mime the implications.

These phrasing marks were constantly being changed. George told me that he spent most of Beecham's last Mozart concert in the Royal Festival Hall putting new phrasing marks into the parts of Symphony No. 40 because Tommy had had new thoughts about them *since* the morning rehearsal. Now the G minor Symphony was the one that he had conducted more than any other symphony in his whole repertoire. That was the thing about Tommy, as with all the other truly great conductors. He knew that the arch-enemy was routine.

I have a tape somewhere of Furtwängler talking about conducting, his only broadcast in English, and in it he says something absolutely true: 'Routine, with its loveless mediocrity, lies like hoar-frost on the surface of the world's greatest masterpieces.' And this absence of routine was one of the facets that made Tommy's performances so fresh and spontaneous. It also made his rehearsals fun and real music-making rather than seeming hard work. I sometimes think that Beecham's *joie de vivre musicale* was a bad influence on British musicians. If Beecham could make working such fun, why couldn't all the other conductors do so too?

Where dilettantism in Beecham became apparent was on those rare occasions when he had put down for performance, or let himself be persuaded to do so, a work with which he was not in sympathy. Then he would play the amateur, leaving that work until the last possible moment in the rehearsal schedule, by which time it was too late. He hadn't done his homework well and he was fallible.

He would lunge hopefully at the trombones in Brahms symphonies and they kept silent until one time he actually stopped and asked them why they didn't play. 'Sir Thomas, we don't play until the finale in Brahms Four.' 'I don't give a damn about that,' came the answer. 'If I bring you in, for God's sake play *something*, otherwise you make me look such a damn fool.'

The first performance in London of Rachmaninov's Symphony No. 3 under Tommy was a travesty. So was Bartók's *Music for Strings, Percussion and Celesta* – 'Gentlemen,' he said, as he looked at the slow movement with its lines indicating the glissandi of harp, celesta, piano and strings, 'we have here apparently some charts for deep-sea diving, but we will endeavour to swim our way through. . . .' So was his late performance of one of Ravel's *Daphnis and Chloe* suites. That nearly came to a stop and only the perseverance and tact of one flautist (good old Gerald Jackson) got Tommy out of a disaster.

One curious thing was that this master of rhythm – I mean *natural* sense of rhythm – was usually found wanting when it came to beating compound time. OK, the famous Tchaikovsky Symphony No. 6 movement in 5/4 time was all right, but anything else was hopeless. That is why he never conducted anything of his good friend Walton's – except for the relatively uncomplicated *Façade* suite. And oh! when Tommy tried to do Britten's *Four Sea Interludes* from *Peter Grimes* that was a shambles too. Again he left the rehearsal until the last possible moment. Then he tried to put off the performance by saying that he had lost his score. Felix Aprahamian trumped Tommy's ace by producing a duplicate score. Pity!

These excursions into unfamiliar contemporary music were marked by one curious habit. Nervousness showed itself by outward calm or a transference of fear. Sir Thomas's walk to the podium was usually fairly slow. But when he was nervous he came on twice as slowly. When he conducted Bloch's Violin Concerto for its London première with Joseph Szigeti, he was justifiably nervous, so just as he was about to give the upbeat to begin the piece he whirled round at the audience and, pointing a finger, shouted out, 'No smoking!' A woman was carried out fainting. When she came round in the first-aid room she said, 'Now I come to think about it, I *wasn't* smoking anyway.' By this diversion Beecham gained a little courage.

Most of the time, however, contemporary music was kept to simple stuff, or to the music of Sibelius and Delius that he knew so well and had championed. Shows of temper were few and far between and his old age would have been utterly serene if it had not been for the lady in the case.

When I told William Glock stories of how foully Betty Humby, Lady Beecham the second, behaved (I stress the hierarchy because Shirley, Sir Thomas's third wife, is a great friend and utterly adorable) he simply could not equate my estimation of her character with the pianist that he had known so well and intimately in the thirties. Certainly Betty had changed in looks – from a pretty curvaceous blonde girl of charm and wholesomeness into a thin woman of rather sinister, oily speech, dry hair and bony angularity, totally lacking in charm, jealous of Sir Thomas and vindictive. I don't think that a single person in the orchestra or its staff would contradict that grim evaluation.

Betty was responsible, it seemed to us all, for any storms or nastinesses that took place. She would come into the room where Sir Thomas and I were talking, and mention something that had happened or been reported. 'Well, what of it, my darling?' he would say, quite equably. And then she would start inciting him to action. I often saw the poor old boy worked up into a lather after twenty minutes of nagging, so that he would be breathing fire, sacking people and sending vituperative cables about the world. Sir Thomas was wonderfully loyal to her. Only once did he even comment, for example, on her execrable piano playing.

What had happened to the bonny buxom blonde? She had been ill for a long time and she had been put on drugs that hooked her, I believe. I once saw her bare upper arm and it looked like an old dartboard. I also believe that Sir Thomas's sleeping habits wore her out. He would keep her up chatting until the small hours, then wake her early the next morning. Fine for him, disastrous for her. She was also anti-Semitic and induced Sir Thomas to get rid of some of the Jewish members of the orchestra. Poor Leonard Rubens, a fine leader of the violas, was positively hounded out, for example.

It was bliss when she decided not to come on a tour to Northern Ireland and Eire with the orchestra, so that Norman and I had a happy time with the Maestro, going by train and boat first of all to Belfast.

The impresario for the three concerts in Belfast had made rather a hash of arrangements. I think he must have left it too late to book the usual concert hall and we had instead an unsuitable building. People were not used to going to it for concerts and the impresario's publicity had been minimal. Unexpectedly, Sir Thomas felt sorry for the impresario and decided to do his best – very sensibly, because if no one came there might be difficulty in getting paid.

So Tommy went into action at the press conference. He attacked the City Fathers, who had refused the late application for the usual hall, castigating them as intellectual thugs and, having telephoned Dublin to find out how the bookings were down there, whipped up a little rivalry between Belfast and Dublin. He thoroughly enjoyed this exercise in public relations and it worked to some effect.

At the rehearsal for the first concert there was an interesting and typical incident. At the end of the Overture to *Prince Igor* Sir Thomas, conducting without a score of course, had turned to Jim Bradshaw, master timpanist, obviously to bring him in with a drum roll on the last chord. Sir Thomas asked him why he didn't play. Jim said there was nothing in the part on the last chord. Sir Thomas told him it was an error and to put it in.

Now Jim was a most conscientious musician and he came to talk to Norman and myself in quite a state, saying Sir Thomas was conducting from memory, that he had clearly made a mistake, and what should he do? I knew that if one made a fuss about a point like this Sir Thomas would save his face and invent reasons for there being a drum roll on the last chord. He would say he had seen the original manuscript, et cetera. I counselled Jim to forget the drum roll except if Sir Thomas specifically turned to him to bring him in, in which case to avoid a barney and play a drum roll on that last chord. In the event Sir Thomas didn't look Jim's way at the crucial moment so the purity of the last chord of Borodin's overture (which, in any case, was written or at least orchestrated by Glazunov) remained unsmirched.

We moved on down to Dublin for two concerts which took place, as it happened, in the same cinema where the London International Orchestra had appeared previously. It rained and the roof still leaked on the flutes! I suggested to Norman that we should take Sir Thomas out to dinner on the one free evening of the tour and we went *à trois* to Jammet's, a remarkable restaurant with French cooking, the best meal you could get at that time in Europe off the Continent. Norman and I hogged it up, I remember, while Sir Thomas chose a frugal meal including brains.

I asked him about the events that led to the founding of the Irish Republic. He replied with a résumé that lasted about forty minutes, giving dates, quotations and other evidence that proved that he knew the history inside out. After about twenty minutes I was aware that the whole restaurant had gone quite silent as all the other diners listened attentively to what the great man was saying. The waiters crept about quietly, trying not to make a noise. I had found on other occasions that Sir Thomas's memory was astounding. Once we were discussing Milton, another time Macaulay, and on each occasion vast paragraphs or periods of poetry or prose rolled out to prove his point

Undoubtedly Sir Thomas had his weak side, sometimes the feet seemed not only gouty but made of clay, but we were all worshipping at those very same feet when next he conducted music that he was in sympathy with. And how much music there was that he conducted as well as anybody I have ever heard: Delius, Sibelius, Strauss; Berlioz, all the French repertoire up to Debussy; Handel but not

Bach; the even-numbered Beethoven symphonies and the 'Eroica' (with six extra horns kept back until the big tune in the finale when at last they joined the regular three); anything Russian; Italian opera – *plus* Schubert, Haydn and Mozart! What a man! He has certainly given me more musical pleasure than any other performer I have heard. Every concert was an event. Even if you had heard him conduct the same programme the night before, you never knew quite what you were in for.

How did he approach perfection so often? That's unanswerable. But it had something to do with that avoidance of 'the hoar-frost of routine', with a natural sense of rhythm, the way a phrase breathes, with music's ebb and flow, with the selection of the tune of the moment, its relation to any other important or less important strands, the relation of detail to the whole, the choice and gearing of tempi, when the music should sing, when it should dance, *how* it should sing, *how* it should dance; how to make a natural accelerando that quickens the blood as well as the tempo. Experience tells, naturally, but if it isn't in the imagination and the blood, no amount of learning will help.

Towards the end of certain pieces Beecham would make a slight quickening or holding back. There is very often nothing in the score to indicate these fluctuations. If there were they would as like as not be grossly exaggerated. But most conductors would not dream of making these minute fluctuations – 'dream' or 'imagine' being the operative words. Listen to Beecham's records of Chabrier's *España*. Notice a million things about the performance, but consider the last two chords. He ever so slightly anticipates the last chord. What a risk to take! I am willing to bet he did not rehearse that and yet the whole orchestra is with him. ESP? No wonder that Beecham himself used to refer to conducting as 'a mysterious craft'.

(9)

Gerard Hoffnung

Donald Swann rang me up one day in 1951, and told me I must go to a certain gallery in Piccadilly – unknown chap there got an exhibition of drawings and cartoons, a lot of them about music, funny, name of Hoffnung, Gerard. I went. Paid my half-crown to the only other person in the gallery, the bloke behind the table. I vaguely took in a baldish, oldish, stoutish, tweedish man, then set off to look at the cartoons, starting on the left of this not very large square room. Imagine seeing several dozen Hoffnungs for the first time in your life! Enchanting.

As I went round I gradually became aware that my progress was being observed by the bloke at the table. If I laughed, there was a muffled echo of a laugh from him. The third or fourth time I swung round quickly just in time to see him adopt a pose of looking intently at a book in front of him. I tried to catch him out a few cartoons further on. It became a game, like grandmother's footsteps. When I reached the end of the second side of the square I made a diagonal across to the man at the table and accused him of being Gerard Hoffnung.

He admitted the soft impeachment; I introduced myself and a friendship ensued. We went round the rest of the drawings together and had a long chat afterwards until it was time to close the gallery – nobody else had interrupted us – at which point, typically, he invited me to join him in some food. Anybody else would have said come and have a *drink*. Gerard did not really like 'rotting grapes', as he referred to the demon.

At this time Gerard was in his late twenties – so was I – but he had the appearance and manner of an old man – assumed of course, but while he was alive it never occurred to me to ask why. A lot of Gerard's life was putting on an act and it was only after his death at the age of thirty-four that I began to wonder.

One day many years later I was with his widow Annetta and we were looking through the family album and I saw the infant Gerard, the little boy in Berlin (where one of his playmates was André Prewine, better known now without the 'e' at the end of his surname and a 'v' instead of a 'w') the adolescent and the young man, slim and hirsute, up to the age of about twenty-four. So what had happened to that young man? His parents died; he was alone, give or take an aunt or two, and he started to lose his hair.

My theory, which Annetta does not entirely discount, is that losing his hair was the last straw, having lost so much else, and that he decided that being bald would make him look like an old man. On the principle that if you can't lick 'em, join 'em, he decided to play the part of an old man. Which he did very successfully.

Gerard was the sort of person who tried to yank life out of the ordinary and put it one notch higher. Thus, when I first used to visit him, the arrangements to go to his house were done not just on a 'Well, I'll come to your place next Thursday at 7.30' basis, but much more dramatically than that. There would be several telephone calls or one of his notes with drawings all over it, funny letters addressing me as 'Dear Kassler Rippchen' and so forth. Phone calls would follow. 'Are you still coming next Thursday? Look, make it 7 not 7.30 because I've got a lot of things to show you/something special.'

Everything was heightened. When you arrived at the house in Hampstead Garden Suburb the welcome was massive. 'Come IN. Come IN.' There were large pieces of furniture – too large for the small suburban house with its flimsy wooden doors – furniture from Berlin for sure, lovely stuff almost right for *Rosenkavalier*.

These were early days before he met and married Annetta. He lived alone in the house with a troll called Marie. She truly looked like a Hoffnung creation with distended nose – descended from Bosch and Busch (or Peake translated into German) – like Alberich's daughter who had lived in a cave all her life. But she cooked hare with red cabbage and dumplings like a mistress of her art – though, alas, always served from cold dishes on to cold plates.

Music was the great bond between Gerard and myself, needless to say. Humour and music. I speak just enough German to savour certain ridiculous names. And broken German/English had always been a family joke, something my father shared with his brothers. Gerard and I liked the same noisy romantic twentieth-century music. For example, I must have been one of the few other people in England who knew, let alone liked, Honegger's music. I also savoured the way Gerard rolled French titles round his mouth with a strong German accentuation. (Ustinov and I used to do this too.)

We both loved Stravinsky too – *Le* SACre *du Prin*TEMPs was his accentuation – and Respighi's tone poems, Milhaud's *Suite provençale* and all the great Walton pieces. On the telephone after one of us had heard some Walton there would be a repeat performance there and then by the two of us, shouting, singing, whistling, grunting, imitating the instruments, burping out the percussion bits, roaring with laughter, above all *enjoying* our creation of the scherzo from Walton's Symphony No. 1 – the one marked *con malizia* – or the same composer's overture *Scapino* or, a great favourite of Hoff's, the *Colas Breugnon* overture of Kabalevsky.

During dinner, between courses, Gerard would reach for one of his ocarinas, which he played most beautifully. Later, perhaps, he might draw something and give it to me. Soon after we first met he fell in love with the tuba and bought one, gradually teaching himself to play it. At this stage he did not read music.

Nearly always on these visits he would try out his latest spoken set piece, which might be something out of his own experience, like working in the bottle-washing department of an Express Dairies factory, or might be something that he had seen in the paper, like the letter in the *Manchester Guardian* from the Jamaican bricklayer – this last he made particularly his own, so that people thought he had made it up.

Part of the one-notch-higher meant that a new idea in Hoff's nut could not be wasted on anything as ordinary as a telephone call, although phone calls with Gerard were never ordinary – they rarely lasted less than forty minutes for a start. No, ideas had to be presented at the right psychological moment over a table heavily laden with food. One day we found ourselves at the Chinese restaurant called Ley-On's, then on the corner of Wardour and Brewer Streets. His idea was to organize a concert that would be an aural equivalent of some of his musical cartoons. What did I think of the idea, what could we do, who could we commission to write some pieces, would anybody back it, and would I please manage it? I said I thought the whole idea was absolutely crazy. Let's do it! All sorts of ideas then spilled out. We finished the meal, went and sat on a bench in the open air nearby in the bombed-out site of St Anne's Church.

By this time several of us had persuaded Hoff that his tuba playing was by now good enough to let him satisfy his heart-felt wish to play in a symphony orchestra. But he would have to learn to read music and submit to the discipline. To his eternal credit he buckled to and did both, and joined the Morley College Symphony Orchestra conducted by mutual chum Lawrence Leonard. Therefore it was natural, indeed economically indispensable, to use the Morley Orchestra which, being amateur, would play for nothing at our proposed concert.

We asked around and eventually Ernest Bean, the manager of the Royal Festival Hall, persuaded the London County Council to back the concert on 13 November 1956. We all wondered whether there would be any bookings because there was no real precedent in London for a crazy concert. There had been a few April Fool affairs. I had even taken part in one or two of them. There had been some good ideas but they were practically lost in a welter of overlength of event plus overkill of jokes plus amateurish presentation and performances.

One calendar month before the concert the booking opened and there was a queue round the Festival Hall. We broke the record for a sell-out, held up to that time by Liberace, with every seat gone by lunchtime.

Perhaps the most thrilling moment of all was not the first concert itself but the first rehearsal, with the Morley Orchestra, of the big commissioned piece for the concert, Malcolm Arnold's *A Grand Grand Overture*. At the concert the orchestra was joined by Dennis Brain playing his second instrument, the organ, and the players of the concertante parts for three vacuum cleaners and a floor-polisher (Jean Stewart, viola player and dedicatee of Vaughan Williams's String Quartet; Pauline Del Mar, wife to the conductor Norman, herself a viola player too; Annetta Hoffnung, the only possible wife for Hoff because she had been trained as a children's nurse, and violinist Olive Zorian, my wife), and four rifle players.

That first rehearsal saw the unveiling of Malcolm's funny overture with that marvellous lyrical tune, slightly ironical of course but so emotional that we were all caught up in a surge of joy and tears. It is one thing to write a symphony but another matter entirely to write a great tune, a gift that should be cherished but is all too often sneered at these days.

I think Ernest Bean occasionally regretted having unleashed Hoffnung on his hall. Gerard was all over the building making a nuisance of himself. For him there was no other concert going on, only his. He harried the staff. He plagued. Gerard could not understand their reluctance to drop everything they were doing and just attend to his requirements and his jokes.

It was the same when he was planning later concerts. He wanted to do the bit near the beginning of *The Rite of Spring* where Stravinsky has the eight horns bouncing out the same crunchy chord umpteen times with socking great accents off the beat here and there. Gerard wanted not only eight horns but also eight musicians wielding those machines that you see in the road stamping down asphalt. The London County Council – 'Could you believe it?' said Gerard incredulously – did not want to have eight stamping machines on their parquet platform.

And again, when *Let's Fake an Opera* was being planned, Gerard was almost mortally offended because the LCC wouldn't permit the Valkyries to ride on between the front stalls and the orchestra platform on eight Vespa scooters. 'Why not? Confounded red tape. Just because it hasn't been done before. . . . '

Gerard constantly hounded me during the organizing of that first Hoffnung Festival in 1954. He had persuaded Boosey & Hawkes to lend us from their museum a monstrous bass drum that had been constructed especially for pre-war performances by Toscanini of the Verdi Requiem (*Dies Irae*, bar 11). Hoff kept on ringing me up: 'Johannes, my little Windbeutel, supposing that drum won't go through the doors in the Festival Hall?' 'Now, Gerardus, my little Schinkensalat, Boosey's have measured it, the backstage staff at the hall have checked, the transport people have checked it and double-checked since last you asked. Please leave it to the experts like them and me. That drum will get in.' Damn it, it didn't! So often Gerard nagged about something. And he was right, nine times out of ten.

I was glad to hand over the managerial side of the next Festival two years later to Harold Holt's agency. That meant that I could help more on the artistic side. The think-tank committee meetings were great fun. We went to them in a spirit of resignation – all except Gerard – feeling utterly drained of ideas. Suddenly ideas sparked and flashed around. Malcolm Arnold would have a notion. Ernest Bean would improve on it. Lawrence Leonard would chip in. Eric Thompson would modify and all the time Gerard would interrupt and amplify.

These meetings were sometimes in Ernest Bean's office. Later there was one outside the vulture house of the Zoo. There was also one planned up in a balloon – but Gerard spoiled that idea by dying too soon. The result of meeting together was a profusion of ideas. I said, for example, that the first *Fest* had been good simple stuff, was it not time to have one rather more esoteric item, something Third-Programmish, a tilt at contemporary music perhaps?

Gerard perked up at that, said he had been listening to some German station, Cologne maybe, with two musicologists analysing at inordinate length a twelve-tone piece which was then played and took only three minutes. Why don't you write something, he asked me, and then we will make up as two German professors. But we must play the piece. Would you like to compose something, Humphrey Searle, or is that too near to the sort of music you compose anyway? Humphrey, bless his cotton socks, stammered out that he would be delighted to have a go. 'Just send me your analysis of the work when you've written it, John,' he said, 'and I'll, for once, compose the work *after* the programme note.' Great idea. And it worked out.

I retired for a holiday on the beach at Antibes just by Gérard Souzay's villa and cobbled together a script using all the corny old jokes about modern music plus one or two new ones – like not writing with thirteen tones instead of twelve as the French were doing, as that would be the baker's dozen, the Nadir of Boulanger. My girlfriend, Angela, who was with me at Antibes, suggested one gag which got the biggest laugh of all, calling it not a tuning fork but a forking tune. I shaved most of my hair off in order to get the right Cherman look and *Punkt Kontrapunkt* was a hit. (Later both Henze and Karajan said it was their favourite record.) Gerard, of course, looked fine and Cherman as he was.

The title was a straight translation from Aldous Huxley and our supposed composer was called Bruno Heinz Jaja. Terrible to have to explain jokes, but in the fifties Bruno Maderna, (Karl)heinz Stockhausen and Luigi Nono were big flowers in the avant-garden. My favourite adaptation of an old joke was taking the mythical Webern *pensando* marking – you don't play that note, you just *think* it – a couple of stages further (German development section) by making it a bottom B flat beyond the range of the viola, and having the centre point of the palindromic form of the piece – Humphrey followed the analysis through thick and thin – a silent bar in 3/4 time 'thus giving the whole work a quasi-Viennese flavour'.

Hoffnung was used to an audience and his timing, the way he gaffed the audience, was brilliant. It is something you cannot rehearse, that timing, and I was relieved that I was able to pick it up and enjoy it too. It's a quite intoxicating feeling, having hundreds of people hanging on your words, and riding over the ebbing laughter with the next speech. Gerard was a most unselfish colleague and performer.

It was in the third Festival that he scintillated even more in the *Concerto for Conductor and Orchestra* that Francis Chagrin concocted so cleverly for him. In a repeat performance I played the part of the pianist who tries to thwart the conductor. We had a duel, Gerard using his baton as a weapon, me seizing the lead cellist's bow, and both of us eventually sparring up and down the aisles of the stalls.

In the same festival I sang a duet with Owen Brannigan. This was another turn in the avant-garden, a skit on the splintered vocal techniques then in vogue, and it took its cue from the criticism that you could express horror and tragedy in music without harmony but that it was difficult to imagine a comic opera in the dodecaphonic idiom. We proved it and guyed it in a scene from an opera called *The Barber of Darmstadt*, based on the text, 'Who was that lady I saw you with last night? That was no lady. That was my brother. He always walks like that.' Translated into German, of course. Moderately funny, music again by Humphrey Searle.

The Hoffnung Festivals were at their best in Hoffnung's own inspired foolery and in the works that we commissioned: Malcolm Arnold's overture in the first; the United Nations piece in the second with several military bands marching and counter-marching, all playing their own national tunes in an Ivesian jumble; and his Beethoven *Leonora No. 4* in which the climax was firstly silent when the offstage trumpets failed to come in on time, and then secondly very noisy indeed when the offstage trumpets sprouted up disastrously all round the hall to Del Mar's dismay; Joseph Horovitz's brilliant parody on the 'Sleep sweeter, Bournvita' commercial in the style of Verdi, Schoenberg, Stravinsky *et al.*; the little Dolmetsches playing Elizabeth Poston's rehash of the big moments in Tchaikovsky arranged for a broken consort of recorders, viols, portative organ and medieval percussion; Franz Reizenstein's *Let's Fake an Opera* and his wedding of all the popular piano concertos wittily divorced between pianist Yvonne Arnaud and conductor Del Mar. There were many other fine moments such as Sir William Walton coming on to conduct an excerpt from his *Belshazzar's Feast* which turned out to be just the famous shouted-not-sung word, 'Slain'. William improvised one extra touch at the performance, substituting for his baton a fly-swatter.

On holiday in September 1959 I bought a copy of *The Times* in Geneva echoing to my friends, as I turned to the hatch, match and despatch columns, C. M. Bowra's words, 'Any amusing deaths today?' And then being stunned by the announcement that Gerard had died suddenly at the age of thirty-four. It seemed that Death had taken Hoffnung's old-man act seriously. A tragedy. The amazing thing is how much he left behind him professionally after such a short space of working as a comic artist. What would he have got up to next? Would he have pursued perhaps the more serious side of his art, like the ravishingly beautiful illustrations for Ravel's opera *L'Enfant et les sortilèges*? Stage design? Films? Telly?

Hoff was lovable and life-enhancing. He was intolerant where wrongs were concerned. It could be very embarrassing to be with him sometimes. One day he argued at Schmidt's restaurant that a Kassler Rippchen was not the rib it purported to be. A slanging contest became a shouting match in the restaurant and we were finally dragged into the kitchen where meat was slapped about and cleavers were waved in our faces. I didn't understand half the German but I had the feeling that Gerard was wrong, although I tried to back him up, using that great standby word, 'doch'.

Hoff could also be quite ununderstanding on those mornings

when I didn't have time to spend forty minutes taking part in an impromptu re-creation without orchestra of the scherzo from Roussel's Symphony No. 3 in G minor, for the simple reason that I was already late leaving for a BBC broadcast.

He was larger than life, committed to his act. As we sometimes said, 'An evening with Gerard Hoffnung was a Gerard Hoffnung evening.' But the world would have been a poorer place without his brief meteoric career.

(10)

Summer School

The summer schools of music, at Bryanston, 1948–52, and at Dartington, 1953–81, absorbed an average of a quarter of my year from the age of twenty-six to fifty-nine, a big chunk of my life, the longest commitment to a single cause or organization.

It started like this: Artur Schnabel went to the Edinburgh Festival in 1947 and said things to Gwynn Jones that made Mr Jones start the summer school. Schnabel had held summer schools himself, notably at Tremezzo just after the war. They were small affairs, masterclasses for the Master's pupils. Festivals before the war were rare, Bayreuth and Salzburg being the two best known. Edinburgh was the first post-war festival of any size in the United Kingdom – although Aldeburgh also started the same year. Schnabel probably said something on the lines that it would be a good idea to combine the idea of masterclasses with a festival, i.e., concerts and teaching.

I do not presume to know the extent of the friendship between Artur Schnabel and Gwynn Jones but I got the impression, partly from seeing the two together, that Gwynn Jones (GJ from now on) was a fan, a worshipper at the Schnabel shrine, and that GJ's idea of heaven would be for Schnabel to play every day and occasionally to pat GJ on the head.

When Schnabel suggested this idea of a summer school of music – I call it SSoM rather than SS, for obvious reasons – GJ said, 'I'll do it somewhere in the UK, will you come and preside?' 'No,' said the Master, 'I haven't time.' 'Who will preside then?' And, lo, it came to pass that the Master bethought himself of his pupils from the UK and came up with the name of William Glock. William was not only a pianist and a musician but a critic on the *Observer* and also known as organizer of and participator in a series of Mozart concerts given immediately before the war at the Cambridge Theatre in London.

That is how it came about that William was appointed. Venues were sought and eventually Bryanston was chosen and hired for a month. It stands in beautiful Dorset countryside and within one big building some 400 people could be accommodated. A secretary for the organization was hired in the person of Noel Hughes and also what amounted to a bursar, Beatrice Musson, a handsome girl from Northern Ireland. She had been a schoolteacher but had been reduced to working in a wheelchair because of an attack of polio.

Noel Hughes had little experience of concert management or handling artists so William suggested that I come in and look after that side of things. The suggestion came at a good time for me because I had fallen foul of Betty Humby, the second Lady Beecham, and I therefore succumbed to the blandishments of G. Jones. (Ironically Betty Humby had been William Glock's collaborator in the Cambridge Theatre Mozart concerts.) GJ offered me not only an interesting job at the SSoM but also an all-year-round job putting on concerts here, there and everywhere, in the provinces and London. I was experienced enough to know that to succeed in such a venture was unlikely but GJ was silver-tongued. In fact, silver-tonguing was GJ's job. He was a professional strike-breaker and his task was to go and address meetings of miners or whoever and persuade them that black was white. Despite his unprepossessing appearance – he was short and of his face one can recall only that he had spectacles and a moustache on a long upper lip – GJ had the gift of the gab.

On one occasion William and I went to see him at his flat opposite Westminster Cathedral ('that vast dissenting tabernacle', as GJ quoted), determined to talk about a certain feature, something to do with the finances. We arrived, talked for forty-five minutes and left. And when we had walked about a hundred yards away we turned to each other because we had suddenly come out of GJ's spell and realized that we had not even broached the subject we had gone to discuss. Rum.

On another occasion I was working at the office in Cavendish Square. On the desk was an envelope containing a cheque addressed, I think, to the pianist Denis Matthews but which GJ said must not be posted until some more money was in the bank. The telephone rang. It was Denis Matthews obviously asking why he had not received his cheque. GJ said he could not understand it. It had been posted. Quack, quack from the phone. 'But I know it was posted. I posted it myself in the postbox in the square. The postman came to collect it as I was standing there, he said to me . . . . ' After a few minutes of more conversation, quack quack, followed by GJ's ever more convincing arguments, I became convinced, just as Denis no doubt was, that GJ *had* posted the letter. And yet there it was in front of me on the desk. I have never experienced a similar case of such an amazing gift of the gab.

I still have somewhere a letter, or a copy of it, that GJ wrote to Thorold Coade, a sympathetic man, the brilliant headmaster of Bryanston, explaining that, by dint of private income, GJ had some £2000 per annum to spend on music for the summer school. As things turned out it seemed that this was a figment of GJ's imagination. It later transpired that he did not have any spare money, and the finances of the SSoM were in a mess by half-way through the actual session at Bryanston.

Some fees were arranged by GJ in the most haphazard way. I believe that the Amadeus Quartet and other artists were given blank cheques. Others were booked by letter through their agents. Some of those who played early during the month at Bryanston were paid. Others were kept waiting weeks, months, years even, before they got their money – or a percentage of it. I don't say that he was dishonest – I believe that settlements were made with all the teachers and artists – but he certainly behaved in unwise and strange ways, putting off the evil day. Even so he did start the school and his family and he himself must have suffered to pay for it. Yet it was obvious that the SSoM could not continue with GJ at the helm. And it was also obvious that the SSoM *must* continue, because it was worthwhile and it was needed.

Why was it needed? Are there not summer schools of music all over the country and do not the colleges and academies in the big cities provide adequate teaching with visiting professors and teaching artists from other countries? The answer is that it was needed because in 1948 there were very few summer schools. There was nothing on our scale and not one providing a festival as well as teaching. There was nowhere in the country at that time where students could attend a course held by a Hindemith or a Nadia Boulanger, which is what we provided during the first years at Bryanston.

The regular colleges had got extremely conservative and insular during the war and were making no efforts to get less stuffy. Julian Bream being forbidden to take his guitar inside the Royal College was one instance. Anthony Milner offering to lend a Hindemith sonata to a piano student and receiving the reply, 'I say, Milner, we are not here to waste our time, you know' was another. It was necessary to provide somewhere for students to receive their further education, to show them that there was something over their limited horizons, to give them a taste of teachers from abroad. We found it rewarding to hear that, because of attending their courses at Bryanston, students had gone for further study with Georges Enesco or Nadia Boulanger in Paris, or Boris Blacher in Berlin. That was the aim of the SSoM on the highest level.

We also realized – I must stop writing 'we' because at the beginning nearly all these important decisions were made by William Glock (although I did even then make suggestions, like engaging Enesco, but William's decision was final if we did not agree) – *William* realized that the small composition or instrumental master-classes would not pay their way, nor was it likely at the start that we could get sufficient good students. That was why we needed large numbers of audience to fill up the school.

Some were just audience but others could join in at different levels. We soon provided for all sorts of levels of musical competence and incompetence. We formed a chorus each week to rehearse every day with a view to performing in a choral work at the end of the week. We got coaches who would take what came in the way of chamber music players. Preference was given to preformed ensembles but others were put together on the spot. We had classes in musical appreciation, lectures that most intelligent listeners could comprehend. There were auditions for masterclasses, but otherwise cash would secure a place. There was something going on most hours of the day, often two simultaneous events, on higher or lower levels, with a concert every evening after supper and often one or even two during the day itself.

We would also have classes, not every week or every year, in subjects like figured bass, singing, teaching. In the early years we had some rather starry non-music lecturers like E. M. Forster, Elias Canetti, Stanley Spencer, C. E. M. Joad. Some of the best lectures in the early years came from Imogen Holst who could talk about the basic elements, 'Rhythm' or 'Melody', in such a way as not only to instruct but to touch you by her exposition of the simple facts of musical life. I have seen Paul Hindemith and Artur Schnabel in Imogen's audience jingling pennies in their handkerchiefs to imitate percussion instruments and loving it.

I thought that those early years at Bryanston, especially the novelty of the very first month in 1948, were some kind of heaven. To have all that music going on, all those famous musicians, the opportunity to talk music all day and all night . . . all right, the food was pretty awful and sparse – we still had ration cards in those days – and the accommodation was literally back to school with little boys' beds in big dormitories, no mirrors, no hanging space, collective washrooms with rows of baths. There were no single or double rooms except for artists and teachers. (A few we put up at the local hotel in Blandford.) There were very few visitors at the concerts and with the vast majority of people eating and sleeping together under one roof there was a great communal spirit. At my age I loved it, but there were many, especially older people, who found it too spartan.

Bee Musson turned out to be invaluable that first year, and right through until she retired thirty-four summer schools later. Being in a wheelchair, she could not get away from the customers, and it always seemed to the customers that she did not want to get away. She was always interested in their problems, amazingly helpful with young people and patient with the old. She remembered them all, and their names, sorted out the accommodation and, eventually, the finances. In fact I think she, and I too, and our 'trogs', made the atmosphere friendly and sympathetic.

After the 1948 summer school was over there were a number of autumn concerts organized by GJ with the help, I think, of Noel Hughes. GJ's main interest was in pianists, and in Schnabel's pupils, family and colleagues in particular. Paul Baumgartner was the best of these and I remember looking after several recitals that he gave in places like Gloucester and Winchester. Other pianists engaged were Rita MacIntyre, Maria Donska, and Schnabel's son, Karl Ulrich.

There were also some concerts in which the Amadeus Quartet played a string quartet in the middle and, with William Glock, the two Mozart piano quartets at the beginning and end. I recall one of these at Bexhill in the De La Warr Pavilion. I don't remember how many hundreds or thousands that hall holds, but I do remember that there were not many more in the audience than there were on the platform. I turned pages, as usual, for William and the main concern of all six of us was to get the music over – it rattled ridiculously round that large empty hall – so that we could get back to an important session of pontoon in the artists' room.

Needless to say, GJ's concert scheme fizzled out and so did his tempting offer to me of a year-round job. The main concern of William and myself was how to keep the SSoM going in the face of artists and tradespeople not, so far at any rate, receiving their money.

We started a new organization to arise phoenix-like out of the ashes of the old. I knew the Earl of Harewood and he sportingly became chairman of a limited company that we formed – now I can use the 'we' because from 1949 onwards all the business and many of the artistic decisions were shared – under a new title, and with T. F. Coade, of Bryanston, and Edric Cundell, Principal of the Guildhall School of Music and Drama, as additional directors. I fought against the word 'Bryanston' in our company title, because I already foresaw the possibility that we might want to move house in the future.

We floated our company and managed to keep it above water. But only just. Neither William nor I had any money. Bee Musson threw in her lot with us. According to our articles of association we were entitled to a reasonable salary but for years we kept to the same pittance simply because we knew that there was no money in the kitty. Even after thirty years the salary that Bee, William and I received had only gone up to a nominal £1000 each – and this in the late seventies – so we were subsidizing the school quite considerably. (After I left, Dartington itself took over the school of music and paid my successor eight times what I got for all those years.)

For several years the venture was dicey. We could not spend much on advertising, had to rely more on word of mouth. Amateurs came and came again but it was difficult to get good students and young professionals for most of the masterclasses. We booked teachers and artists in advance in order to sell the school for that year. But then if we did not get enough bookings, we sometimes had to ask the artists to come for cut fees. They usually did, thank God – and them! A rich young man called Tony Hubbard bailed us out one year when we were up to our ears. The anxiety while we waited for bookings to come in was acute. They were lean years. But the school prospered artistically. We gave good value: £9 a week, all in, in 1948.

The Amadeus came that same year, the first of their public existence, and regularly for many years afterwards. Even later on they came back occasionally. I remember in the seventies they reduced their charge so as to come one more year. William announced to me one day – typically, he loves numbers and fractions – 'The Am. Quartet are coming for eleven-twentieths of their usual fee.'

Although T. F. Coade was always sympathetic and pleasant, the rest of the Bryanston staff made the summer school an uphill ride. Presumably up to that time there had been no necessity for the public school to think of earning extra money by letting the premises during holiday times, so our music summer school seemed an intrusion and an invasion into their holiday privacy, and we were made to feel this. We began to think of going elsewhere. Dartington was the obvious place but, despite Imogen Holst being Music Director at the College of Arts there, we could gain no entry. Then William did an adjudication tour in Canada in the company of John Clements, formerly Choir Master at the BBC. John was appointed to succeed Imogen when she left. William had helped John to get the job. John helped us to get Dartington.

We moved house in 1953. It was as if we were now at our university after our schooldays were over. Instead of dormitories being the rule at Dartington, they were the exception. Single and double rooms were the order of the day. Baths could be taken solo and the women (and the men) now had mirrors to gaze in and wardrobes to hang their clothes in. So far so good.

The cost went up, though. And the average age went up too – by about fifteen years, all of a sudden, from twenty-five to forty. And the spirit went down. This was partly because, instead of being housed in one large building we were now accommodated in three different venues. And where you slept you ate. The only time that everybody was together under one roof was in the evening at the concert in the Banqueting Hall. Most of the staff – artists, teachers, organization members – ate in the same place as the customers in the poshest accommodation – which usually meant the older people.

There were many improvements, however, at Dartington. There was not much to choose maybe between the countrysides, with Devon's contours more dramatic than Dorset's, but Dartington's grounds were better kept, with sensationally beautiful trees and really fine gardens. Then there were the buildings round the fifteenth-century courtyard and the lovely lawn – until we wore it down with walking on it and villains tossed their cigarette stubs on it. Another great advantage was that Dartington was more geared to visitors, and that the catering and domestic staff were friendly and courteous, more than ready to meet us half-way with our requirements.

With some of the Dartington personnel and inhabitants the initial welcome wore off. I saw their point of view. For eleven months of the year Dartington belonged to them and there was room for them to walk about in comfort and go to any cultural event – except now for August when the place was crammed with the summer-school people. They lost their identity somewhat and they had to ask for tickets for concerts and even pay for them on occasions. Worst of all, the summer school got a good press and often if Dartington was mentioned at all in print it was because of the SSoM. An attitude of love-hate built up over the years, sometimes stronger, sometimes weaker.

Dorothy and Leonard Elmhirst, Dartington's founders, were good to us, but even they treated us like naughty schoolchildren occasionally. And, of course, sometimes our students got wild and did silly things. But it was a treat to have a decent bed, a good meal and lovely surroundings. The Gothic Banqueting Hall, stone and wood, with its wood floors and hammer roof, was ideal for chamber music. And chamber music was really the basis for the concerts. Two evenings a week we would have string quartets or quintets: Haydn, Mozart, Beethoven, Schubert, Bartók.

Here's a day or two in the life of the summer school at Dartington, starting at the beginning of one, say in the sixties.

Thursday, two days before we open, I arrive about five o'clock in the evening, go to my room, unpack, see how green the lawn is, how gorgeous the swamp tree in the courtyard is, go across to the office in the courtyard, dump my files and scores. Have the telephone engineers put in our phone yet? No, of course they haven't. Start making list of things to do.

Bee arrives with her sister in their heavily laden wagon. She has a typewriter and umpteen files with details of all the accommodation sheets, financial books, etc. On the journey down Bee and I have no doubt been doing the same annual task of searching our memories to make sure we remember the names of all the Dartington folk, especially the cleaners, the kitchen staff, the secretaries and so on. She is better at this than I am; amazing how you forget the names of people you only see for one month of the year.

A few of the trogs begin to arrive, more as we have supper. A small group gathers in the large dining room – in medieval days the kitchen, with its enormous cowl, a contraption that prevented the smoke from smothering everything in the room – where stone predominates. ('Jeez, it's AD 1410', as a member of the Hollywood Quartet wrote on postcard after postcard.) Trogs = troglodytes = the fancy name that George Malcolm gave to the body of helpers that we need every year to run the summer school.

These trogs are handpicked because it is their efficiency, tact, good humour, patience, conscientiousness and pleasant behaviour that help to make the SSoM fun, pleasant and unusual, regardless of the artistic or academic success. They are needed to move chairs and pianos, fix the music stands and electrics, keep the public moving, ring bells, run errands, help in the office, do the typing and duplicating, help with the tickets, look after Bee, answer the telephone, help the customers with their travel arrangements and laundry and answer questions about where to buy stamps, music, pottery, cream teas, where to telephone – or just have a chat or tell them where the next event is. It takes about thirty-six hours to know where things are – it's a large place. Cosseting artists was another endeavour: seeing that they had a boiled egg or a hot-water bottle or whatever and the right meals at the right time on concert days.

I found early on that the seemingly obvious people to be good trogs, i.e., music students, are not so in practice because they are too interested in attending events rather than marshalling them. Likewise lovers get preoccupied, and having a mate on the staff is not a good idea. Nevertheless from time to time musicians did work for me. Composers Hugh Wood, Gordon Crosse and Donald Swann did their stints at the SSoM before fame claimed them. But the good old faithfuls have been Jeremy Wilson, surgeon; Jeremy Barker, schoolmaster and even one year mayor of Sherborne, and people of that ilk – architects, Freudian scholars, etc.

On Friday morning we start in earnest. We organize the office physically, shopping for ping-pong balls, pens, pencils, paper, etc. We start labelling things and places, visit every practice room, check the pianos, the classrooms, the stage, move chairs, make sure there are chalk and dusters in the lecture rooms, install tape recorders, gramophone record playing equipment. I co-ordinate the private bus schedules picking up those travelling by train from Totnes station, have a word with my favourite Dartington man Horace Davis about the films that he is going to show for us on Sunday evenings – Jacques Tati or the Marx Brothers are the best for relaxation – and then with my head trog I begin to work out the timetable for the week – our most complicated job – to see which class can go where and to make sure that the overlaps are not going to matter. Then Joan Goldsborough will be demanding details so that she can print the Proper and the Ordinary (again named by George Malcolm, our dearest friend and most hardy of annual artists, and also Hon. President of the trogs – the Ordinary being the general information sheet for the whole month and the Proper being the particular details of any given week).

Although the SSoM lasts for a month each week is self-contained, with the exception of some classes – composition and maybe one or two string masterclasses – that last for two. The Proper contains not only class lists, but also the evening concert details, including the movements of works, a few dates and notes, where the interval occurs and so forth. The day goes by and we scarcely stop. William Glock and his wife Anne arrive sometime during the late afternoon. Supper and early bed after a pint in the pub. New trogs have been shown round. Old trogs have caught up with gossip.

Saturday morning sees more of the preparations and we have a meeting with the Dartington helpers. These are year-round students at Dartington who stay on to work in the kitchens and bars, and/or act as ushers for the evening concerts.

After lunch two or three hundred students/customers arrive. A fine day is important for those who haven't ever been before. On a dark, filthy, rainy day the place steams with wet gear and seems inhospitable. Maybe I can persuade William to welcome the students before the first item of the evening concert. More likely I will have to do it myself.

Sunday is the crucial first full day. After breakfast the choir meets at 9.15 for the first time. Will there be enough tenors? Will the altos be too heavy and too many? (No and yes are the usual answers.) I seat the singers according to the conductor's wishes, introduce him to the pianist and to the choir, leave him to it, go back to the office, making sure that the Sunday papers are on sale, a trog at the ready and with enough change. Some classes will be beginning at 9.30.

Then, also at 9.30, there will be auditions for one of the master-classes. Those on bursaries will be presumed to have passed but will attend to tell us what they want to play and how soon in the week with this or that work, to be introduced to a pianist if they need accompanying, to say a word to the professor – except if he or she is not wanting to make decisions him- or herself – in which case I and an expert in that subject will do the auditioning.

Coffee break at 10.45, a chance for people to meet and a chance for us on the staff to find anybody we need or to chat over arrangements with a teacher or artist. At 11.15 a lecture, maybe. I probably won't hear much of it as I need to sift out the names of those who have passed the audition and make out a programme for the rest of the week for that particular class. Lunch.

In the afternoon more of the same, another masterclass, maybe two, to sort out, programme and put the results on the noticeboard. Dinner. Concert, maybe turn pages for William or another pianist. (I like turning pages, it focuses the mind, stops me thinking about other details and leaves me free to do the pushing on and off of the artist(s).) Make sure the artist is happy in the interval, get his drink or whatever, go out on the lawn, talk to trogs, friends, customers, artists, the Elmhirsts, William.

After the concert we control backstage traffic, eventually get the artist(s) wined and either dined or sandwiched, attended by a greater or lesser group of friends, fellow artists, William maybe, trogs pouring drinks and finishing off the sandwiches. Artists need to unwind so we hang around until near midnight most evenings. A good chance to get to know them better.

By Monday, choir, classes, lectures, coaching sessions and concerts are in full swing. Time to go dipping into these events. The concerts are of course different every night and so are the lectures and lecturers. (At a public lecture after some minutes of Sir Isaiah Berlin's habitually incredibly fast speech a woman holds up her hand and says, 'Please can you talk a bit slower?' 'No,' he answers, 'certainly not. I'm like an aircraft – if I go too slow, I crash.')

In the office until Thursday we shall have 'all hands on deck' until lunchtime, then only two or three trogs on duty for the afternoon. Tennis, swimming, Dartmoor a few miles one way, the sea – as a German trog once put it – 'nearly'.

Fridays are different, being the last complete day of this week's course. The choral rehearsal will take all the morning. After coffee there will be a complete run-through with whatever the work might need in the way of soloists, orchestra or two pianos. The Banqueting Hall can hold about 200 comfortably on separate seats, but there is a lot of bench accommodation and on crowded nights, by dint of packing and squeezing a bit, we have occasionally got over 400 in. If the weather is at all humid – par for the course in August in Devon! – then it's trying for string players and the piano keys sometimes have to be wiped down with neat gin. If there is an orchestra we have to take the front rows of the audience out and we have the pleasant situation of 150 performers and 150 listeners.

On Friday afternoons the students show what they can do. The student composers let us hear what they have been writing during the week. The amateur orchestra plays down in the dance hall for half an hour and then the audience moves up to the Banqueting Hall to hear solo items and chamber music. Then comes the evening meal, while Richard Gardner tunes one, maybe two pianos, or a harpsichord, in preparation for that Friday evening choral concert after which there is a party and we all go to bed late.

Saturday morning quite a few will depart and we prepare for the next intake of two or three hundred guests/customers/students in the afternoon. And so it goes on.

And so it went on at Dartington from 1953 onwards. William Glock left first. He did his last SSoM in 1979. He behaved in a curious manner. Presuming that when he went I would want to take over from him – correct – he made sure that the succession of Music Director went to the person of *his* choice, Peter Maxwell Davies. He told no one of his plan but called a meeting of the directors of the company without me, its secretary. He invited the Earl of Harewood, Peter Cox and George Malcolm, as directors, to lunch and told them what he wanted to do. It was hoped that I would stay on to see PMD in.

I agreed to do so but when I discussed the matter with PMD I warned him that there might be difficulty because, with my hand on my heart, I could not say that I enjoyed more than two or three of his works. He said that would not matter.

And so Bee and I continued to work for the SSoM. After seeing PMD in, I announced my intention of retiring from the scene after the 1981 session. To make that final I arranged to go immediately after the session to New Zealand on a lecture and broadcasting tour. However, during the 1981 school PMD asked me not to announce my retirement but to continue for one more year looking after the musical management side while someone else would do the business management side.

I agreed but when I came back from New Zealand there was utter silence from PMD and I found out from others that plans had fallen through with the man who was going to do the business side and that somebody else entirely had been appointed to look after both the business and the musical ends. In other words PMD had replaced me altogether without advising or consulting me. Sad.

William's reason for retiring was that he had done it long enough but, more than that, he felt that the SSoM was standing still and that it needed someone to give it new life. In that he was right and that is why I continued with the school – to give PMD some help in his task. There is less reason for such a summer school any more because tuition, courses and masterclasses are available elsewhere more conveniently for the serious student – notably at the Royal College of Music in Manchester.

You can have an entirely amateur summer school, no doubt, but the SSoM has always had its life blood in the masterclasses for young professionals or would-be professionals. It was only after some ten years or more that we started giving bursaries to students to make the masterclasses work. And nowadays students won't come without bursaries. They expect them, and they need them. Otherwise, and alternatively, many students need to earn money in the long summer vacation by taking jobs. The amateurs tend to get older and older and so did the regular SSoM attenders. It was touching one year to find, in a sweet little thatched summerhouse a few yards from the main courtyard at Dartington, a string quartet whose ages totalled 300 years scraping away – but it also showed the way things were going. No wonder the biggest choir we ever had was when we did *The Dream of Gerontius*.

Bee Musson left after the 1982 session, much loved by thousands of summer-school folk. So that is the end of that. But it is not the end of the SSoM which – I write in 1984 – continues. But already there are signs of cracks. My successor will soon have left, likewise Peter Maxwell Davies, and I hear that Gavin Henderson is taking over. Gavin will do the job well, I think . . .

(11)

Sir William Glock

I first saw William on the platform of the Wigmore Hall in London. Peter Pears was to sing the *Seven Sonnets of Michelangelo* by Benjamin Britten but the composer was ill and therefore unable to play the piano so William came on as a substitute, wearing Air Force blue. At that time William was constantly writing about contemporary music in the columns of the *Observer*, but this was one of the few occasions I can recall when he played any of it in public. This was late in the war and William was leading a double life: music critic and RAF officer.

William was then in his thirties and was almost the only critic of a national newspaper in the United Kingdom who liked contemporary music. This was partly due to the fact that he was young and that his senior colleagues were very senior. (More information about them in chapter 13.) William was a lone enthusiastic voice on the *Observer*, writing much of the time about the new music of Britten, Tippett, Berkeley and others from this country as well as the works trickling through of the 'Great Modern Four' – strange now to think that Hindemith was considered then in the same breath as Stravinsky, Schoenberg and Bartók. At Morley College Concerts, thanks to the enthusiasm of Tippett, we heard as much if not more of Hindemith than we did of the other three – partly because the pianist Noel Mewton-Wood was also keen to play such works as the Hindemith piano sonatas and *Ludus Tonalis*, which was then considered a masterpiece, although it is scarcely ever heard nowadays. William Glock wrote so repeatedly and passionately about contemporary music that he was warned by his editor, Ivor Brown, to desist or be fired. William got fired.

I actually met William at one of the Morley College 'house' concerts. These were held on Saturday nights in the Holst room, packed with 150 hot and sweaty people, with the trams noisily roaring round the corner. It was an exciting atmosphere and the programmes were often introduced by Michael Tippett himself. The audience consisted of Swiss Cottagers, i.e., the refugee musicians, and oh, Arthur Waley, John Craxton, Paul Dienes (the Hungarian mathematician) and among the musicians there might be Mátyás Seiber, Priaulx Rainier, Antony Hopkins, Peter Racine Fricker, William Busch.

William G. was usually present in RAF blue, with cap and gloves. He was tall, handsome, shy but quick to laugh, somewhat magisterial. Somebody once told me – I thought it was William or one of his sisters – that the Glocks were of recent German descent and that the name had originally been Gluck. I was delighted with the information because if you imagine a long peruke round William's features he would look very like old Christoph Willibald. Alas, William later denied any such connection. But the resemblance remains, although others have said that 'Dresden policeman' is more like it.

A friendship struck up between me and William and his first wife, Clement. We were often at the same concerts, at anything interesting in that rather unenterprising wartime cultural desert. We had meals together and I was in the happy position at that time of having for musical mentors Michael Tippett and William. With Michael it was usually discussion and talk; with William often music-making.

Weekends at Clement's house in Marshfield contained long bouts of four hands at one piano – the great Mozart and Schubert literature, very rarely heard then in public, on the air or records, or *three* hands at one piano playing through most of the big Bach organ pieces, he playing the manual bits, me doing the pedal parts. (Did you know that there is a volume in the British Library with, added to the inscription 'Bach's Organ Works', a lower line reading 'and so does mine'?)

I was more than happy to sit at the feet of these two master musicians and learn from them. They formed the basis of my musical education, those two, plus what I picked up from books, records, radio and public performances. William was a natural teacher and he was generous with his time, and he lent me books and scores.

His own potential was not realized fully for a long time until, as a complete outsider, he got the job of Music Controller, boss of the Proms and renovator and innovator at the BBC. But in the days when I met him first he was, as I have said, critic/RAF. He had behind him also many concerts as a pianist although entirely, I think, as a chamber music and concerto player rather than as a solo pianist. He had attended Artur Schnabel's masterclasses and his name was reasonably well known for having organized many Mozart concerts at the Cambridge Theatre. Indeed Ernest Newman once suggested that the Cambridge should be renamed the Glockenspiel.

William's greatest asset as a pianist was his sound – or touch, to use an old-fashioned word. This touch, together with his supreme musicianship, his real insight into what the music was about in terms of style, shape, phrase, made him a joy to listen to, a performer who positively illuminated what he was playing. That is, when everything went right with the technique – and it quite often did. But, by 1945 it was not reliable and it was limited. There were places in works like the scherzo of the Shostakovich Quintet, or the finale of Beethoven's 'Archduke' Trio that exposed inadequacies. Also there would be sudden lacunae; a crucial note in a chord would fail to sound, or he would completely botch a very simple tune.

Ears used to the so-called perfections of gramophone records could not fail to notice such lapses and also were put off by William's constant groanings. These would sometimes disappear if there were microphones about but not always. (This groaning was a feature of many of Schnabel's pupils – Clifford Curzon, for example.) But, despite these imperfections, fairly natural concomitants for somebody who gave at most half-a-dozen concerts a year, the joys of William's playing for me and many others were many. He simply could not make a harsh or unloving sound.

He knew his limitations and when helping to plan the SSoM programmes I had to tease and cajole him into including his own performances. He *wanted* to play but needed the encouragement I was wholeheartedly able to give him. His playing of the Haydn trios was outstanding nearly always, and also often of the Mozart piano quartets and trios, the Beethoven trios – Op. 70 No. 2 in E flat was a favourite – and latterly of the Schumann Quintet, occasionally of the 'Trout' – simple things like the trio of the

Scherzo were like flashes of the sun through trees – and of course the two big Schubert trios.

Various violinists and cellists came and went in the various piano trios, in favour for a year or two. Then there would be shrugged shoulders at planning time and they would fade away. At the beginning there were many concerts with the Amadeus and latterly duos with Sándor Végh. William could be impatient at some rehearsals – I have known him get sick of bowing discussions and march out in a huff – but inspiring at others. He had theories about sound. Several years at the beginning of the SSoM we had to have a screen to throw out the sound. There were other years when he insisted on having the piano wide open, ignoring protests of colleagues and audience.

There was never any French music in William's repertoire. His technique and temperament would not have survived the Ravel Trio, for example. Perhaps some of the finest flashes of inspiration came in song-cycles, particularly in Schubert with Flora Nielsen in the early days at Bryanston, with Dietrich Fischer-Dieskau a couple of years in the sixties, and with John Shirley-Quirk.

William is not a smooth person, nor easy, nor tactful nor, in some respects, the most faithful of friends. Having helped Tippett and Britten so much in the *Observer* he quarrelled or cooled with both of them as the result of adverse comments about their works. He went off them and wrote frankly what he thought. And, nearer home than that, he antagonized the Zorian String Quartet.

His articles were so concerned with the actual music that he barely mentioned that the Zorians had played the premières of works like the Tippett Second, First (revised version) and Third Quartets and the Britten Second. In conversation he said he would put this right in the future. But the only time he mentioned more than their mere participation in a performance it was to say that they 'made a hash of it'. Despite this Olive and William got on well, even played at the Dartington summer school and elsewhere in sonatas and piano trios.

The summer school did not start until 1948 and the period between leaving the RAF and the *Observer* and beginning the school was a fallow one for him.

At this time William lived in a large house in Well Walk, near Hampstead Heath. It was rather austerely furnished, with pictures on the walls by Clement, his wife, or by painter friends like John Craxton. There was a fine Steinway Grand and for me, living a shortish walk away in Swiss Cottage, a treasure trove of books and scores, which were generously lent. When I was working for Beecham I sometimes got William to write programme notes, and later when planning for the first summer schools at Bryanston, conversations about music or business about music were constantly interrupted by William telephoning his bookmakers. His preoccupation at this time was betting. He had little else to do and he made, he used to say, about £600 a year, quite a tidy sum in those days. He used to pore over the articles on form and the day's lists of runners, prices and so on. But he also allowed himself to be swayed by the idea of what he called 'spiritual' bets. There was, for example, a horse called Schubert that unfortunately produced fewer masterpieces than the composer.

It seemed to me awful that a musician of such talents should not have a proper channel for them, and should be kicking his heels. Inactivity bred inactivity and when William was to give a lecture or write programme notes, everything was done at the last minute and sometimes not delivered. Several times I had to improvise programme notes at the printers because WG had failed to deliver. The really sad thing was that what he *did* produce was of such superlative quality. (This made my improvisations seem even worse.) Some notes he wrote for Beecham's Glyndebourne concerts of music by Mozart, Haydn and Schubert were very good, as were his lectures on the same composers.

I remember once talking to William about his senior colleague on the *Daily Telegraph* in the thirties, Richard Capell. William said that Capell loved helping young people but that when they began to stand on their own feet Capell went off them, possibly because of jealousy. I began to wonder whether this was not the case with William and myself. No doubt my own shortcomings were partly a cause that our relationship became later one of love-hate on my side, on-off on his. As with Tippett, I looked on William as a kind of musical father figure and so I was disappointed when, as I thought, he let me down.

The worst of it with William was that he so often failed to support me at Bryanston. He would change plans and schedules without consulting me or go against arrangements that I had made.

Running a complicated plan of lectures, teaching, concerts and domestic affairs means that if you alter one piece on the board you must bear in mind all the consequences arising from it. William would change things on the spur of the moment, partly because he thought it was a good idea but partly also to show he was the boss. The plans and my confidence and pride were thus undermined. I may have been tiresome, too keen to make jokes, but I always treated William with deference, and always had respect and reverence for the musicians, especially him.

William lacks the common touch. He cannot chat easily, if at all, to people he does not know. Sometimes he can be plain rude and bloodyminded. But once the ice is broken he is tremendous fun, although you have to remember that he is old-fashioned in his relations with people in many ways and very reserved. There are many things you just cannot talk to him about – sex, for example. He is prudish. Our relations were not helped by the fact that we tended to like the same girls.

What is especially interesting about his two wives is their disparity. Clement was an English intellectual – tall, blonde, handsome in a rather boyish way – a dull private painter but a brilliant public one. The ones hanging at home showed her hang-ups; the public ones were done in her capacity as scene-painter at Covent Garden where she was, until her sudden death from a brain tumour, in charge of the paint room. (André Derain was once so delighted with her realization of his sketch into a backdrop that he asked Clement's permission to sign the finished work.)

Clement had previously been married to the critic and writer John Davenport. She had a man's brain. She could cook but had no interest in other feminine pursuits. She liked having babies but showed no interest in them after they were born. I visited her in Charing Cross Hospital after her and William's daughter Oriel was born. I walked through a ward full of twenty-three ladies lying back in bed in their flouncy nightdresses. At the end of the ward was Clement sitting cross-legged on the bed in pyjamas.

William was proud to be a parent but hardly able to converse with Oriel until she was in her teens, let alone look after her or deal with any of the wants or needs of a child. With such parents, Oriel was an individual if awkward child, well able to express herself. Once several of us had gone from Bryanston up a hill from whose top there was a magnificent panorama. We all cooed with expressions of amazement and approval only to have Oriel put in the child's point of view: 'I think views are soppy.'

In adult life, Oriel, like the three children of Anne's first marriage, tended to put considerable distances between herself and the parental home. Unfortunately while Oriel was in Brazil she picked up some bug which caused illness and complications which resulted in her early death. William was desolate with grief, partly I guess because he had seen so little of his daughter. Oriel was a clever, jolly, even rumbustious girl and she inspired loyal friendship. When she was on her deathbed a group of her intimates kept a twenty-four-hour vigil round her bedside.

Often a second wife will be a carbon copy or a younger version of the original. Not so in William's case. Anne is French, small, beautiful in a quite different way from Clement, a good cook, skilled in dressmaking, feminine, sharp where Clement was blunt, gracious in movement and a musician. Anne is a good singer, from a family of famous French musicians, a minor Dolmetsch-like group called Geoffroy-Dechaume, with eleven or twelve brothers and sisters. Above all, Anne was ambitious and made William so.

One day at Dartington I received the news that Clement had died and had to pass it on to William. But long before this there had been a divorce and I went to the second wedding and was entrusted with the ring as a sort of best man. We walked to the wedding all together and, very typically French, Anne broke line to go and see about buying some onions from a Breton on a bicycle.

In many ways William changed with the marriages and his fortunes changed too. William the First, for example, betted, liked playing cricket – typically, his best shot was a late cut – and drove incredibly fast. William the Second did not bet, gave up cricket and began to drive more and more slowly, until by his sixties he really drove like an old aunt. William I never used the first person singular in his writings; William II did so more and more. William I would always *discuss* music, especially contemporary things; William II would not – single epithets only.

I was in charge of the International Musicians' Association Club in South Audley Street for a year. It was set up by a Mrs Hubbard, a rich American lady, to try and contain her son Tony, a friend of William's and mine at one time. It cost many thousands of pounds to run and Mrs Hubbard shut it up when her son stopped visiting the place. William had a similar period in office. My title was Secretary; William immediately called himself Secretary-General. The same sort of thing happened at the BBC later. Most titles like Head of This, Director of That were downgraded so that William's title sounded superior. Everybody else was called Assistant.

Incidentally it was the I.M.A. Club that was responsible for William's elevation to the BBC job. It was the secretary's task to get musicians interested in joining, so many of them were invited to visit the club, have a meal and a look round. I invited William and Anne one day and also Richard Howgill, then BBC Controller of Music. There was also at that time a Director of Music at the Beeb, Maurice Johnstone, who had no time for William.

Anyway Howgill came to lunch and although the conversation was comic – Howgill, I remember, put forward his view that the finest contemporary work for years was Moeran's Violin Concerto, at which William and I nearly choked on our vichyssoise – Mrs Howgill and Anne got on well together. I think it was Anne's hints on clothes to Mrs Howgill that formed a greater social tie than the common interest in music of Mr Howgill and William. Not so long afterwards it was Howgill's advocacy that brought William to the BBC job, fame, success, fulfilment and a knighthood.

William's is a fine musical mind. He has an ability to think at speed and order his thoughts. With people that he knows well he is tremendous fun and stimulating company. He likes to be in charge and he is inordinately proud. I don't think he ever tried to conquer his shyness because he is too proud to think of the difficulties caused by his aloofness. Once at Dartington I chided him because a well-known string quartet had been at the school for four days, eating in the same dining room, and he had not yet said hello to them. 'But you haven't introduced them to me. . . . '

At other times I have known him look out of the window surreptitiously and go away without opening the door to me although he was expecting me. Challenged, he said that someone else was supposed to be opening the door. The worst he could say about an accompanist was, 'He plays like a lackey.'

One evening Olive and I were in his flat, saying that we were considering which kind of record-playing equipment to buy. 'Ah,' said William, 'there's a chap living in one of the rooms upstairs. He has made some equipment himself. We'll go and hear it.' 'Er, it's rather late. Don't you think we'd better make sure he's still up?' 'Nonsense. He'll be delighted to let you hear it.' And off we went. William knocked and went straight in. The chap was on the bed with a girl. 'We've come to hear your gramophone,' says William, while the girl wraps a dressing gown around herself.

The strange thing is that William's authority is such that the poor chap put on a record and we all sat there listening to it, four of us in great embarrassment and showing it, William with his head in the air taking no notice of anybody, pretending that all was normal. Referring to the incident later, William replied, 'I didn't notice anything.' He *never* saw what he didn't want to. I have never seen his emotions crack in forty years.

It doesn't need a psychiatrist to see what a love-hate attitude I have towards William. He helped me a great deal; taught me a great deal. And he has hurt me a great deal. For many years he and Anne lived at Faringdon in the country but not once was I ever invited to the house, although during that time William has several times been my guest in London. And I still feel keenly my disappointment that, knowing my worship of Stravinsky, I was never invited to dine *chez* Glock when the great Igor was present.

Another bone: that although I was for a score of years responsible for half, sometimes more, of the summer school planning, choice of artists, teachers and programmes, William never acknowledged this. When he made his 'end of term' speeches it was always something like, 'And I must also thank John Amis for all the hard work he has put in', whereas most years it was Bee Musson and I who did 80 per cent of the hard work. Mind you, that 20 per cent of his was inspiring.

'Inspiring' is perhaps the key word to use about William. If you didn't get on well with him, didn't get beyond the cold outer circle, you could have no idea of the bright flame of his personality. That flame may not have always been warming but it made you brighter, sharpened your susceptibilities and sensibilities, inspired you. In olden times he might have been a great headmaster, vice-chancellor or master of a college. As it was he had his thirteen years in charge of BBC Music when he changed the face of the musical scene in this country – mostly but not always for the better – and brought our standards and our repertoire up to date.

(12)

Apollo

For several years I was embroiled in the Apollo Society. This had been started in wartime jointly by Peggy Ashcroft and Natasha Litvin. Natasha had been a pupil of Artur Schnabel but her career as a pianist was hampered partly by marriage, to Stephen Spender, and partly by the fact that she rarely played as well in public as she could in private. Latterly she has interested herself in the psychology of music, taking a degree and writing excellent articles on subjects like perfect pitch, absolute pitch, memory and psychology in the *New Grove*.

Peggy and Natasha started the Apollo to put on programmes of poetry and music – not, I hasten to add, poetry accompanied by music, but the two arts displayed audibly side by side, the music complementing and supplementing the poetry. Thus you could devise a group of poems about spring preceded by either a piece of music called 'Spring' or some piece of Bach, Beethoven, Schumann or whoever, the mood of which coincided either with the group as a whole or, in particular, the first poem succeeding the music.

The Society at first had a bias towards Cambridge, having done many shows at the Arts Theatre, and at least three of the directors were Cambridge men: Norman Higgins of the Arts Theatre, J. T. Sheppard, and G. H. W. Rylands, known as 'Dadie', who was perpetually chairman.

A great friend of mine, the Australian pianist Noel Mewton-Wood, was on the committee at one time and pushed me into the job of secretary at a time when a new one was needed. It was a part-time job and even though I found that I couldn't really do this and all my other jobs properly I could at least do all the more interesting side of it. And there lies the rub! I would usually neglect the more humdrum side of the business. I would get the show on the road, yes, organize the events quite well but at the expense of answering correspondence promptly or keeping the books up to date. That I was bad at. However . . . .

I took the job on. It was not arduous as the Society never seemed to put on more than twenty or thirty shows a year. Many of the dates were engagements – that is to say, we were hired to provide (usually) two readers and a musician. When I joined, that musician was always a pianist. The committee would consider the date, suggest artists, usually waving across the table, 'Darling, wouldn't you like to go to Winchester?' Of course, often Darling wasn't free so the secretary had a list of the members and he went home and got busy on the blower. The fee was usually ten pounds a go – not much money even in the fifties.

The list included poets Eliot (by that time he didn't want to appear); Dylan Thomas (who never answered telegrams, let alone letters). I once bearded him at the Royal Albert Hall just before he went on to recite Edith Sitwell's 'Gold Coast Customs' set to music by Humphrey Searle. He was affable, explained he couldn't do the date, invited me to have a drink and while I sipped one small brandy, he downed five quadruples. In the performance he was as sober as ever I saw him; Louis MacNeice (who once or twice arranged programmes but didn't take part in readings); Laurie Lee (utterly beguiling, read several times, a gently naughty man); Christopher Hassall (sneered at as a poet – 'My dear, he wrote Ivor Novello's lyrics! – but one of the best readers we had; we also became good friends), and Cecil Day Lewis (now somewhat debunked as a poet and a person, but a marvellous reader, and, alas, so heavily protected by his wife Jill Balcon that it was difficult to get through to him). There was also Edith Sitwell, D. Litt., D. Litt., D. Litt., and Dame.

The readers were either actors or poets. The stage readers ranged from Edith Evans, Peggy herself, Sybil Thorndike and Margaret Rutherford through to some younger ones like Claire Bloom and Dorothy Tutin; from John Gielgud and Paul Scofield through to a few younger ones like Derek Hart.

What I found interesting was to discover those who could prepare a reading for themselves and those who hadn't the foggiest idea how to read a poem without a producer to direct him or her. I didn't presume to do any directing at the beginning but later on I did, out of sheer necessity. But of course with readers like Peggy, Flora Robson (one of the few who hit top form during the first minute), Irene Worth, Jill Balcon, Sybil Thorndike and Margaret Rutherford, there was no difficulty, nor with the poets, nor with one or two readers on the lighter fringe like the mercurial Max Adrian or Joyce Grenfell. But it surprised me to find that an 'intellectual' actor like Paul Scofield seemed lost without a producer, and even Gielgud needed time to work himself into a good performance. The first time he did *The Seven Ages of Man* with Julian Bream playing the guitar/lute numbers was a pale shadow of the solo show he finally did.

I would sometimes go with a team to nanny the programme, show willing and have a good time. One day we set off to Abingdon in a car with Jill Balcon and her husband, whom Julian Bream, also with us, used to call C. Night Lewis. One of Jill's little protectivenesses was that the poet was always to be called C. Day Lewis, never Cecil. Mind you, when Jill was in a good mood she was adorable, tremendous fun and always an excellent reader, although inclined to come on a bit 'heavy' if faced with a big star – the reason being compensatory, I suppose, because it seemed to me that Jill felt, quite wrongly, inferior with actresses who had made it big in the theatre. (This kind of tension was very noticeable at committee meetings or the annual general meetings.)

Cecil (sorry, Jill) made a funny on the way. We passed by a large estate in which there were little chapels and we wondered what on earth the place could be until we passed the main gate with the sign 'St Godric's Theological College'. 'Ah,' said Cecil, 'now I see what those chapels were: practice rooms.'

We arrived at the hall and they rehearsed, but during the recital the readers and musician found themselves swamped by a peal of bells in the very next building so loud that the jangling noise seemed to be in one's very head. I rushed up to the organizer as soon as the bells started to see if they couldn't be stopped. 'What bells?' he asked, being so used to the sound. After about fifteen minutes of this holy purgatory Jill was reading a sonnet by Sir Thomas Wyatt with the phrase repeated, 'Is it possible?' Never has Jill coloured her words so heavily.

Margaret Rutherford was a strange, lonely person, I felt, in spite of the fact that she had married, after a long single life, an elderly actor who played small parts, mostly butlers I believe. There were also sad stories of her infatuations with hopelessly queer young men, after her for her money. On journeys one saw her trying to overcome her shyness to say something to a stranger and thereby making those irresistibly comic faces.

It was the same when she read for the Apollo. The way she began, for example, a poem like Walter de la Mare's 'Is there anybody there, said the traveller?' seemed to me to indicate that she had to make gestures in order to spur herself on to start, to break the silence and break through her shyness. Rather like Beecham beginning something like the *Meistersinger* overture, Rutherford would let the upbeat surge upwards from the feet and knees. The body would convulse. The arms would wave. The mouth and face would contort and then suddenly she had broken through the sound barrier.

One Sunday afternoon I was in a hired car going to an Apollo with Christopher Hassall and Margaret. Christopher was the perfect Apollo man not only because he read well, but because he had a vast knowledge of poetry, could put programmes together, could gently hint to the other reader(s) how to get more of the meaning across, and was courteous and helpful with the great ladies of the stage – Evans and Rutherford in particular, who were nervous and unsure of themselves because every poetry reading was like a first night without the protection of a director or the distancing footlights. He could act as a squire and a lover on his best behaviour: 'Oh, Margaret, you look lovely in that dress. Your hair? Perfect. Yes, you read those sonnets marvellously at rehearsal. Of course you can be heard at the back. No, don't worry, *I'll* carry your books on. Yes, I've opened them all at the page. That's right, I'll come on first holding you by the hand . . . .'

On the journey there Christopher suddenly became a tiny temperamental dictator: 'John, I simply must have a whipped cream walnut or a Cadbury milk flake, I can't go another minute without sweets of some sort.' So we stopped the car at the next village and found a little old-fashioned sweet shop. Margaret and Christopher went quietly berserk, to the delight of the old biddy behind the counter who had recognized Margaret. 'Oh, *acid* drops, must have some of those. Coconut *ice*, yum, gosh, *liquorice* in bars, coffee *chocolate* drops. . . .'

The time of the Coronation brought a vogue in programmes about the two Elizabeths, with first half stuffed with Shakespeare and sonnets, Donne, Dowland, 'The Carman's Whistle', Campion, Bream on the lute, 'My Lady Hunsdon's Puffe', *Lachrymae*, and so forth, and second half back to the guitar or piano and all the modern poets. One of these brought with it the saga of 'Walthamstow and the Silent Bulging Upper Arms'.

The South-West Essex Arts Club, or whatever it was called, engaged the Apollo to do such a programme. Claire Bloom and Christopher Hassall were the readers and Kathleen Long was to play keyboards. 'Fine,' said she. 'I'll bring my clavichord for the Elizabethan half.'

'OK, Kathleen, but we'll need amplification in that case otherwise the clavichord will never be heard. In a large room it'll sound like a pin dropping, won't it?'

'Nonsense, I've given recitals for S. W. Essex for the last three years. I know the hall. We positively won't need amplification.'

Along we went in the car, with the tiny, beautiful Tom Goff clavichord easily stowable in the boot. We get – note the historic present – to the hall, go in and are met by the bearded secretary of the club. Kathleen immediately goes on to the platform, opens the piano and plays a chord or two. 'Ah, I thought you'd be pleased with the Steinway. We had it tuned only last week.'

A brief rehearsal to try out the acoustic and the seating arrangements, coming on, going off. It proves not at all easy to hear the clavichord which Kathleen tries out for a minute or two. I say this to her. 'Nonsense,' says she. 'You need to accustom your ears, you should know that.' I do but doubts remain, and there is nothing we can do because we haven't brought any microphones.

Cup of tea. The artists change. Time passes. The audience comes in. I wish the artists luck, push them on and go to sit well up in the audience, fourth row, so that I can hear the clavichord – she's chosen some good pieces. Christopher stands up to read the first introductory poem, evoking the first Elizabethan age, then sits down with Claire as Kathleen starts playing her first piece.

But has she started? Her hands are moving about on the keys and we can see the bulging muscles on her rather hefty arms rippling up and down. (Why will keyboard players wear sleeveless dresses?) But, of course, the clavichord does make a small sound, you *do* have to concentrate like mad, and focus your hearing on the sound. The instrument was never intended for any but small rooms.

After a few minutes, as I remember from hearing Thurston Dart playing at Bryanston at early summer schools, your ears do adjust – providing of course, there is silence. But here at Walthamstow there is not silence. In the bicycle shed just outside students are locking and unlocking their bicycle chains. They are saying hello and goodbye. Others are starting up their motor cycles. But sometimes there is nobody doing anything in the bicycle shed, which is the point at which the ears become aware that on the side of the concert hall opposite the bicycle shed there is a canteen where cutlery makes a music of its own, where there are washing-up machines that sometimes drown the sounds of the cutlery and almost obliterate the sound of the kitchen staff trying to make themselves heard above the din.

Meanwhile there is Kathleen Long at her clavichord, upper arms bulging and her fingers indulging in the vibrato called 'Bebung' that can be applied when playing this delicate instrument. But there is not a sound to be heard and the Bebungs look positively ridiculous. Claire and Christopher are trying not to look at each other – a bad sign. It will not be long before they start giggling. But now I hear whispering around me: 'Is she really playing that thing? I can't hear a sound.'

Three minutes of bulging arms and vibrato fingers accompanied by clanking revving engines, dish washing and distant shouts come to an end. Something has to be done, O representative of Apollo! Exceptionally I get up from my place in the audience and go up to the platform. I approach Kathleen and say, 'I'm terribly sorry to interrupt, but we can't hear a thing.'

'Nonsense,' she says. 'Go and sit down. There's nothing I can do about it anyway.' Nor there is. I glance despairingly at Claire and Christopher and move back to my seat.

Claire gets up to read her first poem. After the first group of poems is over the pantomime begins again, like television with the sound off. The audience gets more and more fidgety and giggly. Claire and Christopher have to get their handkerchiefs out to hide their laughing. Somebody in the row behind mentions the story about the emperor's new clothes. Meanwhile Kathleen continues with her part in the first half, not cutting a single moment of her fifteen minutes' playing. Some of the audience depart at half-time. But the second half is balm. Never have I enjoyed Kathleen's piano playing so much.

The annual general meetings of the Apollo Society were fun except for my anxieties that someone would say the minutes were wrong. Dadie Rylands in the chair, usually smelling of TCP, the only inelegance in this lovely exquisite, sometimes called the 'Queen of King's' by his irreverent Cambridge students. He had a fine light tenor speaking voice. Beecham used him several times for the main speaking part in Schumann's *Manfred*. He was good until he forced his tone because the hall was large. Dadie also produced complete recordings of Shakespeare plays by the Marlowe Society with unnamed actors – a few stars, the rest amateurs from King's where Dadie gave lectures to whole generations of undergraduates. He dispensed good sense and suave bitchery in equal proportions.

The cast would have been expensive if assembled on the stage: Peggy Ashcroft, all sweetness and earnestness, Diana Wynyard, Margaretta Scott, still very beautiful, Rachel Kempson, Dorothy Tutin, Claire Bloom, Irene Worth, Margaret Rawlings (why were they all so nasty to her?), Jill Balcon, Flora Robson, Constance Cummings, Barbara Jefford, Edith Evans, Natasha Spender, some boa-ed boring pianists and a rather less star-studded male cast but sometimes Marius Goring plus cigar, Laurie Lee and John Carroll (for some reason known as 'Willie Wet-Leg').

Dame Edith would appear to be slumbering gently but all of a sudden would trumpet forth in a voice that nearly shattered the chandeliers in the Arts Council's boardroom. 'We must provide SANDWICHES for the WORKERS', apropos some lunchtime recitals at Stratford, was her slogan one year. Another time she woke up when we were considering the possibility of an American tour. 'Our Secretary must write personally to EVERY' – Edith spoke this word with three syllables, of course, not the usual two – 'School, College and UnivARsity in the United States. EVERY one.'

After a fairly disastrous Apollo on television in which the director had run amok with waving corn and lapping water, Dorothy Tutin took the floor at an AGM to give us a blueprint for the next TV recital, should there be one. 'The lighting must be very subdued, movement kept to a minimum. The reader seated at a desk, perhaps just one candle. No,' said Dorothy, warming to her task and thinking on her feet, 'not even a candle, just the voice alone, with the screen blank.' There was a silence at the AGM as Dorothy's next words were eagerly awaited: 'No,' she said, 'that's radio, isn't it?' The round of applause woke Dame Edith up. 'What's the dear gel saying?'

At the end of one AGM I went to lunch with Natasha Litvin. Fortnum & Mason's was fairly full that day and we were put at a table where there were two ladies having a nice chatty lunch, up in town for the day. However Natasha has a commanding voice and the ladies grew silent as I was given a compelling account of how Stephen Spender had come to realize that CIA money was at the back of *Encounter* magazine, which he was then co-editing. It was a lengthy blow-by-blow story with a cast of big names and at the end of the saga the two ladies got up to pay their bill and leave but after they had gone two steps they turned round and in one voice said, in Natasha's direction, 'Thank you very much.'

Most institutions that enjoy the benefits of an Arts Council grant, as the Apollo did, have a member of the Council staff appointed as an 'assessor'. Ours was Eric Walter White. I had met him at Morley College concerts first, then once by chance, on the Scilly Islands. I was with Michael Tippett and Priaulx Rainier and Eric was with his wife Dodo.

Eric had first met Michael in Berlin, I fancy, when Eric had been composing film music for the director of early silhouette films, Lotte Reiniger. However he had given up composition and had the job of Assistant Secretary to the Arts Council, acting also as their Literary Director, in charge of the Poetry Panel. In his spare time he was a most hard-working writer, of poetry for distribution among his friends, and also prose for publication: books on English opera, the operas of Benjamin Britten and several excellent volumes on Stravinsky.

At the Arts Council he was a trifle disconcerting until you realized that beneath the formal, indeed pompous, exterior there dwelt a creature of great sense, sensibility, wit and fun. Most of the time, being in a position that dealt with a deal of formality, not to say red tape, Eric played formal. 'Madam Chairman', he would call Peggy Ashcroft and would outline the best way to play the formal game. In the end his suggestions would be seen to be the quickest and most sensible way of toeing the line in such a fashion that we got the best out of our association with the Council.

Eric recommended that the Apollo Society should become a limited company and he, I, the Secretary-General of the Council and its legal adviser had a meeting. Eric pompously laid down the division of labour at this meeting of four people. We elected Eric chairman. I was to take the minutes and Eric asked MacRobert to 'put us in the legal picture'. A five-minute speech full of bewildering terms soon had me lost. At the end of this speech Eric nodded solemnly and then leant over and dug me in the ribs, saying in his campest voice, 'My dear, isn't he SWEET?' Collapse of all four.

I did three things during my Apollo days that were of some benefit. Up to this point the musician members who played in the recitals were all pianists and of these only Noel Mewton-Wood had succeeded in making a big career. The musician's role in the Apollo was not easy, in that he or she usually had to start and had to create the mood in a three- or four-minute piece. Too many of our pianists were unable to start with a head of steam. They needed time to get going and could not strike the mood. Therefore the music scarcely did anything for the poetry that followed.

I wondered if it was partly the nature of the instrument itself. At that time in other places, Dartington in particular, I was working with Julian Bream and Osian Ellis and I had observed how a chord of D major on the guitar or G minor on the lute, or a few notes on the harp, played by masters like these two at any rate, seemed to draw its listeners into an immediate response. I got Osian and Julian into Apollo recitals and the enhancement was magical. Compared with these more intimate instruments, the piano seemed to distance artists and audience alike. The readers were so delighted by both artists and instruments that they performed much better. In fact everybody was pleased – except of course the poor pianists who had previously done so much hard work for Apollo.

The second thing I did for Apollo was to initiate regular recitals in the Recital Room in the Royal Festival Hall. It is called something else now. Mind you, we called it something else too. It was a curious shape, L-shaped so that readers had to operate what Peggy Ashcroft called the 'lighthouse gaze' and its acoustic was not very good for music, so we dubbed it the 'airing-room cupboard'. But it was a useful, intimate size and the fact that it was part of the South Bank complex meant that our recitals needed little extra publicity beyond the large mailing list of the Festival Hall diary.

I organized more than fifty recitals and towards the end of that time I grew bolder, devising programmes myself sometimes and even swotting up the programme and directing the readers if they asked for 'notes'. Betjeman evenings were always fun because John tried to keep the recitals informal and we had a regular 'dialogue' with him pretending that I was really Kingsley Amis. From my seat at the back of the hall we had little chats about the interval, whether you could get a drink at the Festival Hall and so forth.

Benjamin Britten had once been gently shocked that I had read only the novels of Thomas Hardy and strongly recommended that I read the poems. I had become eventually so fond of the poems that I arranged more than one programme almost entirely of Hardy. Another idea of mine was to have the *Four Quartets* of Eliot interspersed with a Bartók string quartet. (I was sorry that my old customer from E.M.G. was no longer alive to come and hear himself and Bartók in tandem.) The readers were Peggy, Jill, Cecil (Night) and Dadie. I was present one evening when the four had a readthrough. It was one of the most inspiring evenings I have spent for Dadie 'produced' and proved to have an incredible knowledge, not only of the meaning and background of the poems but how to bring all this out in performance.

For the fiftieth programme in the series I had the notion of reading Max Beerbohm's 'Savonarola Brown' from *Seven Men*. We had a large cast of men, including the co-opted Manager of the Festival Hall, Ernest Bean, reading the part of Second Murderer, Lewis Casson, William Squires and Christopher Hassall, while for the only female part I got Margaret Rawlings to read Lucrezia Borgia and even managed to convince her for one rehearsal to read the rank blank verse quite straight.

Margaret and I once went as official representatives of Apollo to the Argentinian Embassy in London where we were stuck in the front row for a recital given by a celebrated copper-haired *diseuse* whose name I have quite forgot. Towards the end of her recital, all in Argentinian argot as you might say, she turned to us — we seemed to be the only two English there — and said, this time in Engleesh, that as a compliment to the two distinguished visitors she would now speak poem by Keepling translated into her native tong. When the refrain returned as something like 'Botos, botos' for the seventh time and we realized which poem of Keepling she had chosen, we got the giggles in a bad way and nearly got the bloomin' boot ourselves.

My third innovation was to get some good festival dates for the Apollo and to get good festival fees when we went, say, to Edinburgh or King's Lynn. This proved very popular with members of the Society, glad to add a nought to the sort of fees they got when they took part in our own self-presented recitals. That Edith Sitwell spent most of her extra fee sending the secretary a long abusive telegram is another story, told elsewhere in this book.

Working for the Apollo was yet another part of my education – not only the poetry but the experience of working with and meeting actors, poets and readers that I would not have encountered otherwise. Even some of the most successful actors and actresses do seem to live much more like gypsies than musicians. The poor/rich dears do not know what they are doing in two months' time. The only 'safe period' when Apollo could rely on having intercourse with them was on a Sunday if he or she was in a play running in London. Otherwise they could say yes to a date but then if they were asked to do a film or a telly or a play they would have to go off and do it. Musicians I could book months, even years ahead, and non-actors like Hassall or Dadie, but not a Bloom or a Worth or an Evans. So, life was quite interesting and eventful. But God help me if my telephone were out of order.

Except for Claire Bloom and Irene Worth, friends that I made with actors mostly turned out to be 'when present' friends. In other words, when you didn't see them or work with them nothing happened – unlike musicians, in my experience. And of course some of them died. Noel Mewton-Wood committed suicide during those times; Christopher Hassall died one day in the train and Martita Hunt died more slowly.

Martita never actually got as far as doing an Apollo but she was on my list of members, so one day I rang her up. We talked for three hours on the phone and were friends from that moment until she died. She was impossible, temperamental, volatile, outrageous, witty, *jolie laide* and even slightly crippled. She knew all the best things in life. That she didn't have any money, had quarrelled with practically everybody in the business and had talked herself out of most jobs and companies did not stop her from being madly generous towards those few that she still loved. I was thinking then of being a singer, so she took me in hand and tried to make sure that I would at least come on to the stage properly, stand still and straight.

The few times I saw her on the stage were utterly memorable. With the limitation of that husky voice and the body that needed the utmost attention if nobody were to realize that her back wasn't straight, she was something of a genius of mind over matter. Despite outstanding performances by Irene Worth, Duggie Byng and Alec Guinness in *Hotel Paradiso* I thought Martita absolutely stole the show.

Martita had a boyfriend whom I thought unpleasant, and one or two evenings spent with the two of them were fairly horrendous because they brought out the cruel side of Martita. She encouraged her friend to bait waiters and others who couldn't answer back. So I retreated from her company, being too cowardly to protest openly since I was her guest.

I have mentioned how some readers had worked everything out without needing direction, how others needed it desperately. There was a third sort of which I had experience only once. Louis MacNeice arranged a programme for a big show in the Royal Festival Hall itself and on the morning Louis and I sat at the back of the stalls as Michael Hordern read through some poems by Gerard Manley Hopkins.

Michael read with such beauty and such blinding sense that Louis and I found ourselves speechless, tears coursing down our cheeks. We went down to the platform where Michael looked up at us, not realizing the effect he had had on us, and said angrily, 'Will you kindly tell me what those bloody poems are about? I haven't the slightest idea.'

(13)

Critics

During the year (1953) that I was secretary of the International Musicians' Association Club in South Audley Street, Mayfair, I organized a luncheon to celebrate the eighty-fifth birthday of Ernest Newman, the doyen of English music critics. The elders of the profession turned up to honour their colleague. The only trouble was the seating. 'Don't put me next to Cardus,' said Eric Blom. 'I won't sit next to Frank Howes,' said Neville Cardus. And so on. An hour before the affair started there was a telegram from Richard Capell saying he had to go to a funeral. These five in fact were the big names in music criticism at that time in England.

Ernest Newman wrote for *The Sunday Times* for thirty-eight years and everybody's grumble was that at least each second article of his was about Wagner. That was not quite true, but what was true is that his biography about 'Old Richie' (as Beecham used to call him) is one of the best biogs about anybody, a model of clarity and probity. Nobody should hold off because of their lack of enthusiasm for music. It is an astonishing story and Newman can make completely non-musical parts of the books enthralling – like a chapter on Wagner's finances.

Bernard Roberts, as he had been born, lived from 1868 until 1959 and started as a bank clerk. (Perhaps that is why he wrote so well about Old Richie's finaglings.) When, in his spare time, he turned from writing about philosophy and literature he saw the importance of being a 'new man in earnest' and therefore adopted the pseudonym that became so well known. (Strangely enough Newman also wrote about sport, being an addict of boxing and wrestling matches.)

He changed his mind about many composers, having at first hated Mozart. He gradually came to hate Liszt as a person, and handled him brutally and inaccurately in his biography. 'Hate' was not too strong a word to describe his attitude towards some colleagues that he disliked – for example, Paul Henry Lang – saying something like, 'I would as soon take critical notice of Lang's comments as I would the slaverings of a mad dog.'

Newman was exceedingly old by the time I came to see him. He was little in stature and had a curiously mottled bald head like an old foxed billiard ball, a large cigar in his mouth, and a very useful habit at Covent Garden, which I follow to this day, of handing his coat in at the cloakroom with a tip and saying to the attendant, 'Put me out with the cat, will you, please?' At the end of the opera one's coat will be neatly laid out on a nearby banquette, and there is no need to queue for ten minutes with one's girlfriend and one's belly rumbling.

By the post-war period Newman rarely attended musical events, being content to leave that to a younger man, contenting himself with writing about a book or a current subject – or, as people grumbled, a recurring one.

Newman's opposite number on the *Observer*, when I first became aware of critics, in the early forties, was A. H. Fox Strangways, but I knew only his successor William Glock. During the forties and fifties Glock was the only critic that I felt made sense, the only one who was not either old and academic, or old and Establishment. Glock got to grips with the music I was interested in – Britten, Tippett, Stravinsky, Bartók and Hindemith, the music of the day – whereas the others were mostly tired of music and were trying to keep Britain free of the moderns, free for Elgar, the Three Choirs Festival, England and St. George.

After Glock on the *Observer* came Eric Blom (1888–1959), who spoke in the back of his throat, was small, bespectacled, had a hump on his back and quite a lot of chips on his shoulder. The hump one never mentioned, nor the fact that he was not English – Danish, Jewish? He was in fact Swiss-born. He complained continually about misfortunes and he even suffered a posthumous prank of fate at his cremation.

After the committal to the flames the organ broke into Offenbach's Barcarolle from *The Tales of Hoffmann* and those present had a hard job not to break into giggles. Blom's son-in-law, Paul Jennings, marched out, red in the face. The organ ground to a halt. Angry words ensued and then the organ started up again in a Bach chorale. Bach chorale/Barcarolle, ah! yes, a telephone misunderstanding.

Blom wrote fairly and decently, if somewhat middle-of-the-road. A pianist once asked me how to get a good notice from Blom and I advised him to play something esoteric, not recorded, out of print. Busoni and van Dieren got him a rave review.

Despite his labours on the fifth edition of *Grove*, which he edited, Blom did not get a good press because he allowed his prejudices to influence him. Composers like Strauss and Rachmaninov, for example, got very short shrift and it was rumoured that he would even edit other people's opinions to suit his own. In his adoring book on Mozart Blom permitted himself to say the Piano Concerto in C (K. 503) was a rather mediocre piece. I got to know it because Glock played it to me and made me see how grandly Olympian and ravishing it was. I put the point to Blom who said that, it not being a work he knew very well and him not wanting to seem over-enthusiastic about *every* Mozart opus, he had not given K. 503 the benefit of his doubts.

Frank Howes (1891–1974) became senior music critic of *The Times* in 1943 and retired in 1960 and, for most of that time, had only the by-line, 'Our Music Critic'. Very respectable, professorial, wearing tweeds whenever possible and even occasionally – only out of London, of course – the sandals that betrayed his love of folksong and folk dancing. English for the English wherever possible – I am sure that if he had been consulted (and he well may have been) he would have supported the Director of the Royal College of Music in saying no to the suggestion that refugee Arnold Schoenberg should be allowed to enter England to teach composition.

Howes tried very hard to keep back the tide of modernism. Stravinsky, the Second Viennese school, *et al.* were all judged against Elgar and Vaughan Williams and found wanting. Herbert Howells, E. J. Moeran and Edmund Rubbra were the ones for Howes. He lived, alas, to see the Gone to Earth of the British Symphony at the Cheltenham Festivals in the fifties, and the Rise and Fall of the British Comedy Overture.

Tippett had, true, used folksong but was fairly suspect, whereas Britten – before *Peter Grimes* – was considered too clever for his own good. I can remember walking through Hyde Park towards Bayswater from the Royal Albert Hall one evening after the London première of Britten's *Scottish Ballad*; I came across Uncle Frank and we walked side by side in silence because I could see that he was beside himself with rage about something. At last he turned to me. 'That fellow Britten, he's just not serious, is he? He *can't* be serious.'

Nevertheless I was fond of Frank and one day met him at the aforementioned cloakroom at Covent Garden. It was a couple of years after his retirement and so I said, quite genuinely, 'Frank, it's very good to see you. We miss you.'

'Ah,' he said, with absolutely no twinkle in the eyes, 'but I'll bet you don't miss my opinions.'

Contemporary music aside, he was a very fair man, Establishment but good, and he could always be relied on to say the right thing when, as so often, he chaired a meeting or had to make a speech. His writings were well organized, although he amused, to say the least, Walton and Vaughan Williams with the motivations he ascribed to their works – writing, for instance, that RVW's Symphony No. 6 heralded the next war or the atomic age or something like that.

Edwin Evans (1871–1945) on the *Daily Mail* was also an elder figure, a friend of all the great modern figures of this century, and he had grown fat on his memories. He came to talk to the Philharmonic Arts Club one evening and was so portly that when he got up the chair got up with him and we had to peel it off him.

This great champion of the new was now a spent force, writing little reports for his newspaper and churning out programme notes, the worst of which were those for the Boosey & Hawkes concerts of contemporary music at the Wigmore Hall. Alas, Evans's notes were out of touch, perfunctory and sometimes downright wrong – as when he described the fugal second movement of Tippett's String Quartet No. 2 as being 'based on a cantus firmus'.

Scott Goddard (1895–1965) looked like a queenly version of Don Quixote and indeed he not only was quixotic where his own sex was concerned but he also once gave a masterly broadcast commentary with records on Strauss's tone poem of that name. He also gave good service to Britten and Tippett in particular. His scripts and timing made for perfect broadcasting and I would like to think that I learned something from him, especially in not spelling out everything to the listening public – also in differentiating between a script to be read aloud and one to be read.

Scott was touchy and flighty but well worth it if one could get beyond his elaborate minefields of nervousness and *noli-me-tangere-ness*. He actually shook and quavered most of the time. All that disappeared when he broadcasted – as far as his voice was concerned. But I do remember taking part in one of the Third Programme (i.e., pre-Radio 3) Christmas quizzes in which the producer found that Scott hadn't answered a single question and hadn't recognized a single piece of music. So he was quietly edited out of the programme in advance and even his name did not appear in the *Radio Times*.

Richard Capell (1885–1954) was a war correspondent for the *Daily Telegraph* during the war but resumed as its music critic afterwards. He had a very high forehead with his straight hair brushed back over it. His face was lopsided, as if he had once had a stroke. His apt nickname was 'Mad Caesar'. His book on the songs of Schubert remains a classic but I think he got bored with journalism and his notices were quite often perfunctory – he wanted to get back to the bridge table which latterly took his days and such of the evenings as music spared him. He was averse to most music of the twentieth century and he once perverted William Glock's notice from Berlin of Stravinsky's *Symphony of Psalms*, the first performance in Europe, by inserting a negative into each assertion of praise or enthusiasm.

This kind of last-ditch stand against modernism is very much at variance with critics in the eighties who fall over backwards in their desire to praise the latest piece of rubbish. Innocent readers must be bewildered to read the paeans accorded to recent works of Iannis Xenakis, Stockhausen, Peter Maxwell Davies and so on. It would appear that the pieces are attractive, bound to be classics, and yet soon the more discerning reader must become aware that there are double standards being applied. Works of composers like Malcolm Arnold or David Del Tredici that have obvious tunes are castigated, while other works are praised if a single feature of an interval or facet of instrumentation can be singled out.

Two obvious features of the new music are consistently ignored by those critics jumping on the bandwagon and wishing to point out that the new in art is always hated by the old in heart. The first of these features is that the banishment of tonal centre means that the listener is required to learn a new language with nearly every piece, rather as the reader was with *Finnegans Wake*. Just occasionally a genius may make this work. The second feature is that, in music, this kind of anarchy has the effect of 'white noise', i.e., all notes sounded at once make an impenetrable blanket of sound. On the other hand there is in musical sound a kind of law of gravity – higher notes will be anchored by the lowest note sounding, and this may easily give a feeling of tonality, providing there is not so much going on that the effect of 'white noise' is attained.

My own entry into music criticism, albeit a humble one, was towards the end of the forties, when the 'last ditchers' were in the majority among the critics, and ended when the 'first ditchers' were beginning to shout 'rah-rah' at every trashcan that made a noise in the concert hall – just so long as it wasn't tonal.

My actual entry to music criticism took place one day when I was standing on a street corner in Hampstead. William Glock came up to me and said, 'Are you doing anything this evening, Amis?'

'No, not much.'

'Well, now you are. You're going to *Tosca* at Sadler's Wells and you're writing 350 words about it as "Our London Music Critic" of the *Scotsman*. No "mister"s and don't be facetious.'

I knew that William had this job, which paid practically nothing, but was useful for getting free tickets, just in case he wanted to go to something. This, in effect, was only about twice a year, because he was jaded about concerts and operas. If somebody Scottish was making or doing something important then the London office would ask him to make a personal appearance, otherwise they were content to let him run what we called the syndicate. This consisted of several friends who would be asked, 'Doing anything tonight?' It was risky but it worked.

I went to my local library, got out a vocal score of *Tosca* and refreshed my memory. At this stage (1947) I had become rather snobbish about Puccini – and Rachmaninov and composers that I considered sybaritic – but of course I was fairly bowled over that evening, despite my funk.

My experience of attending opera was limited. I went alone to *Tosca*. At the end of the first act the attendant lady who had showed me to my seat accosted me and said '*Manchester Guardian?*'

'No,' I said with an assumed Scots accent. 'The *Scotsman*.'

'In 'ere, then,' said she, and pushed me through a door. And Scotch

19 With Andrew Lloyd Webber, 1979.

16 *Gerard Hoffnung and myself as two German musicologists in 'Punkt Kontrapunkt', Royal Festival Hall, 1958.*

17 *Myself in oil (although in the Louvre labelled as a self-portrait by Chardin).*

18 *Cartoon by Hoffnung, c.1952.*

14 With Alan Bush.

15 Norman Del Mar, Jascha Heifetz, David Bicknell (EMI manager and husband of
the violinist Gioconda da Vito) and Sir Thomas Beecham at EMI Studios,
London, 19

12 *Julian Bream and John Williams playing to a provincial audience of*
bullocks between recording sessions for their album, Together, *July 1971.*

13 *Sir Thomas Beecham with the 17 year-old Noel Mewton-Wood at the latter's*
London début, Queen's Hall, 1940.

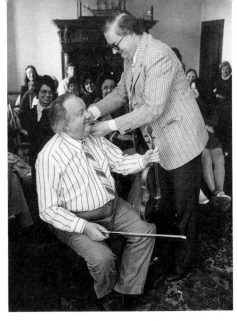

8 Benjamin Britten and George Malcolm at Dartington on the occasion of 'A Boy was Born', 1959, with, left to right, Mini, Ginger, Bobbitt and Bullers.

9 Adjusting a microphone for the Hungarian violinist Sándor Végh at the International Musicians Seminar at Prussia Cove, Cornwall, 1978.

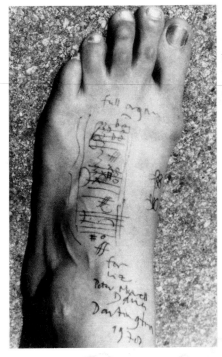

10 Caught with our bells in our hands: John Amis with Manoug Parikian (left) and John Warrack.

11 An unpublished pedal composition by Peter Maxwell Davies, Dartington.

6 *With Peter Maxwell Davies and William Glock at Dartington, 1979.*

7 *Line-up of organizers and trogs at Dartington, 1979. William Glock is at left, with myself behind at the foot of the stairs, Bee Musson, our invaluable Registrar, in wheelchair at the front, and Peter Maxwell Davies at the right.*

3 *With William Glock (later Sir William) at one of the early summer schools of music which were held at Bryanston School, 1948–52.*

4 *Donald Swann, Michael Flanders, and friend at Dartington Hall.*

5 *With my father at Dartington, c.1955.*

1 *Steve Race warming up the 'My Music' team. Left to right, Frank Muir, Denis Norden, John Amis, Ian Wallace.*

2 *On the waterfront, 1983, Chicago.*

it was, neat, a tumblerful of it, thrust into my hand by some PR person. (They boozed up the critics in those days. Nobody had warned me. I think I should have been told!) I downed the spirits quickly and nervously but I was not used to such stuff. And I was so unused to it that, to clear my head, I did the worst thing possible. I went out to get some fresh air.

I saw the second act in a trance, somehow got through the third and went to 63 Fleet Street to the *Scotsman*'s London office to write my notice. God knows what I wrote but the sub-editors were kind. One of them said, 'Oh, we'll soon take the pith out of that.'

William never looked at the paper though he asked me how I had got on. There were no complaints from the office so William gave me more tickets and more jobs. It was easier for him to let me do the jobs than to ring up other friends so after a few weeks I took on the whole job and the syndicate lapsed. I was thrilled to see my words in print. I was scared every time but somehow I survived.

I took it all very seriously. I started going to the Reading Room of the British Museum, enjoyed the business of looking up the items, waiting for the books, the thumping great echo, getting to know the regulars. These included the Superintendent, Angus Wilson, and Arthur Waley, the sinologist who had never been to China, and some curious research workers – one bearded man in a raincoat that had large holes in it and an elderly woman who wore shorts even in winter. In the summer you could smell the holey raincoat man thirty yards off; in cold weather, about ten. He always sat in the same seat in the same row, which was given a miss by other regulars. The story about the lady in shorts was that she and a female friend had both been in love with the Director of the British Museum but that the friend had pipped her to the post in some way that had literally driven the shorts lady mad.

Most days for three or four years I went to the Reading Room and studied the scores of those works that I would be covering. At home I would use records to familiarize myself further, or printed music that I possessed myself, or would borrow from libraries. In later years I was able to use the BBC libraries for such purposes. I read voraciously books about music and went wherever possible to rehearsals where new works were concerned, sometimes badgering publishers for a score not yet printed but available in manuscript or some kind of interim copy.

Curiously enough, there were very few critics encountered at such concert rehearsals. Either they were cleverer than me, or less conscientious, or both. Those I did meet at rehearsals were Peter Heyworth, John Warrack and Desmond Shawe-Taylor, never any of the old brigade. Indeed Frank Howes made a point of not going to such things on the grounds that he thought the critic should record his first reactions about new music, which puts him in the same position as any, dare one say, intelligent member of the public.

At the beginning of the season the first notice made me horribly nervous. Would my brain react, would thoughts come, panic, panic? I don't think I was a particularly good critic but I was conscientious and I did always try to keep in mind the difficulties of the performers and the realities of music-making – the cost of productions, rehearsals and so on. I tried not to make cheap gibes and not to injure the feelings of performers – especially young and inexperienced ones.

Most of my colleagues were, I thought, insensitive on many counts. Some were good at writing about music; few had any feeling for performance. On those occasions when I could test their reactions, when they had to use their ears because facts were withheld, they seemed like beginners. If an encore was played without the title being announced, most of my colleagues had no idea what it was.

One time at the Aldeburgh Festival six composers wrote a variation each on the 'Sellinger's Round' tune. We critics knew that the six were Lennox Berkeley, Arthur Oldham, Humphrey Searle, Benjamin Britten, William Walton and Michael Tippett. For fun I wrote out score cards, handed them out to my colleagues and collected them with their guesses. To me such musical detective work was easy but not one of them got anywhere near. Admittedly the Oldham was Brittenish but the others were highly characteristic. The Britten expert thought that Walton's was the Britten and a great Tippett fan thought that Tippett's was the Britten. . . .

Martin Cooper on the *Daily Telegraph* was a delightful man, older than most of us, a former schoolmaster and a brilliant linguist. He was rather dapper and wore a trilby and pepper-and-salt mixture suits. He was a better *feuilletoniste* than an on-the-night critic and ended up most conversational sentences with

'What, what?' usually shot through with an incipient laugh. He wrote an excellent book on French music and that was his taste. He was anti-rehearsal-attending, anti-fraternizing with artists. It was poetic justice that his attractive, lovable daughter Imogen became a performer, a first-rate pianist. Martin and I always talked so much in the *Music Magazine* studio when awaiting our turn that Anna Instone would throw us out.

Colin Mason (1924–1971) had a rather niggly way of talking which belied his good brain and charm of manner. Slight in build, he was a hard worker and wrote very well on Bartók and other special subjects. I always enjoyed his company. We several times went on hikes, usually to Paradise – a nearby village – from the Cheltenham Festival. Colin wrote too little, for he died much too young.

Neville Cardus was fairly aloof from us younger ones and didn't seem to like the elders much either. They would sometimes refer to him as 'that cricket correspondent' and point out that he had had no academic training. I find that an academic training does not necessarily teach people how to listen or write. In my experience Neville Cardus listened and wrote better than most. He was also almost alone in giving you, in his notice, an idea of what you had missed – no small matter considering that a concert is ephemeral compared with a play that has a run ahead of it. Cardus conveyed a sense of occasion and excitement and, above all, enjoyment – how many critics can do that or feel that? I think Cardus didn't see too well close to, and also I think he felt antagonism from most of the 'down South' lot.

I used to sit with him sometimes at Lord's and found him good company, although in old age he wasn't much of a listener to other folk's conversation. I would play a game sometimes with him of attempting to stop the flow – no effect whatsoever. He would just continue from where he had left off. I noted once that I managed to get a word in edgeways while he was saying something about Strauss's opera *Der Rosen——* and at this point I interrupted him and went on talking for at least a minute. He waited patiently until I drew breath and then continued: *——kavalier*, and went on in his rich and fruity, slightly gravelly voice. Writing a notice during cricket was pleasant, especially when the fast bowlers were on – plenty of time to scribble while they walked their long way to their marks.

The *Scotsman* had the prestige of being a national daily. On the other hand its sales in London were very small. Therefore I never had any importance as a critic. I had no place in the pecking order of the London critics – which certainly existed – and, although I was on friendly terms with them all, they never saw what I wrote and neither did the artists, except if their press-cutting agent was particularly busy. However, I wanted to go to concerts, operas and festivals and this was a way of getting to them free, and writing about them was a fine way of clearing the mind and finding out what I thought.

Sometimes I was pleased with myself. For example, I was the only critic at the time of the première in 1955 of Tippett's opera *The Midsummer Marriage* to declare that it was a masterpiece, an opinion that took twenty years to percolate through to the other critics. However, at about the same time I wrote a notice after the première of Britten's Hardy song-cycle *Winter Words* that still makes me squirm for its stupidity and lack of perception.

I soldiered on as a critic partly because I thought the general standard of perception was so low. Some artists and composers seemed to be considered sacred and it was with satisfaction even that I wrote unfavourable reviews of their work. As Virgil Thomson once said of the recipients of such reviews, 'The higher they fly the louder they squawk.' I believe that Jascha Heifetz or his agent complained of a notice in which I observed that the lollipop encores seemed nearer to the performer's heart and art than the Bach, Mozart and Brahms major works on the programme.

Kathleen Ferrier did not complain about some of my notices late in her all-too-short career, but lots of her admirers did. Did I not realize that this artist was a dying woman? Yes, I did, but I would not insult a great artist by failing to discriminate between her good performances and her less good ones. Kathleen understood that perfectly well herself, as I found when I visited her during her last spell in hospital. She had worked quite a bit with Olive and she had come to our wedding party. Olive and I went to the hospital wondering how on earth we could cheer up Kath. There was no problem. Kath cheered *us* up.

Was there a problem writing criticism while knowing so many performing artists, even being married to one? Not a very serious one. I never wrote notices about Olive or her Zorian String Quartet. And apart from very 'high flyers' I rarely wrote 'stinkers' about artists, only about composers.

Things did get a little sticky with Antony Hopkins, who, in the late forties and fifties, did more composing than he does now. And once on a plane from the Edinburgh Festival I did quickly stop reading my anti-Ormandy notice when I realized that the man who had just taken the next seat to me was the conductor himself.

On the other hand it was also at Edinburgh, after I had written that Guido Cantelli's performance with the New York Phil., although superbly virtuosic, sounded more like drill than music-making, that I was accosted by some members of the orchestra in Princes Street. 'Are you the guy that wrote that notice?' they asked in a seemingly belligerent manner.

'Yes, I did,' I said nervously.

'Great! May we take you out to lunch? We've been wanting someone to say that for years.'

During my fifteen years or so on the *Scotsman*, for about half the time I was 'Our London Music Critic'; the other half I was given a by-line. Likewise about half the time I wrote notices on the night; the other half a weekly column. Quite often I would go up to the Edinburgh Festival to give a hand to Christopher Grier, at that time 'Our Music Critic', i.e., the resident critic up there. I found 'on the night' reviews more tiring but the excitement made for better writing.

Without employing anything like Glock's syndicate I occasionally needed a substitute and sometimes got Felix Aprahamian, Harold Rosenthal and, his first newspaper work, John Warrack, to write. I also got Malcolm Rayment his London job on the *Glasgow Herald* and, before we both got by-lines, we used to write each other's columns when the other was on holiday. This entailed writing two weekly columns for rival newspapers about the same week's musical events, an interesting exercise in tackling the same events from different angles.

Felix did quite a lot for the *Scotsman* when I started going to Switzerland for two months at a time, but eventually even the *Scotsman* began to realize that their man in London was never there for long. By which time writing about contemporary music had become quite a chore. The sixties, in particular, were a time when going to rehearsals of new works was pointless, because (a) scores became impossible to read, especially those that had written introductions and sign legends as long and complicated as the pieces and (b) because some composers stated openly that they would be disappointed if they heard what they had written – that is, if they could hear what they had written anyhow.

Of course there was good music being written, there still is – but damned little of it. And there is so much partisanship where modern music is concerned – more than ever there has been. So many critics employ one standard for, say, Beethoven and another for Maxwell Davies. And then there is the matter of the *Zeitgeist*. My father could dance a samba but he could not play one on the piano from written notes. Likewise it is more than likely that someone thirty years younger than me hears Maxwell Davies *et al.* differently. At least I sincerely hope so.

(14)

Composing Mortals

'Love me, love my music.' Or, rather, 'If you want me to like you, you must like my music.' That has been my experience with composers. I am sure that it was my not liking Peter Maxwell Davies's music that led to my leaving the Dartington summer school. Harrison Birtwistle had been a regular at the school for several years, but it was only after I had finally liked a piece of Harry's (his *Cantata*) and said so, that we became friends. Some composers I became friends with, however, before the question of liking their music or not became possible, i.e., they had had no performances of their works that I could have attended.

When I first met him in 1941, Michael Tippett was almost totally unknown. He was earning a tiny income as Musical Director of Morley College, the working men's evening-class establishment in Lambeth. He was thirty-six then, although he looked younger. He has always looked younger than he is. Now that he is rising eighty he looks like a well preserved sixty-five – Dorian Gray without all that nastiness!

Michael was a late starter and developer: schoolmastering, conducting evening-class choirs and labour pageants, amateur orchestras – hard work, grubbing about for a living, writing music when he could. By 1939 he had little to show for all that hard work, but a few days after the war actually began, a letter arrived flukily from the enemy country and that started things off. Willi Strecker of Schotts in Mainz wrote to Schotts in London with the decision to take Tippett on and publish his music.

A private recording was made by Phyllis Sellick of Michael's Piano Sonata, called *Fantasy-Sonata* then, plain 'No. 1' now. It was reviewed perceptively and favourably by Edward Sackville-West. I heard it when I was working at E.M.G. and was intrigued by it, but quite frankly the bit I liked best was the series of squishy chords in the last few bars of the finale, put in, Michael told me later, only as a sarcastic back-hander against the Romantics.

My first meeting with Michael was at the Orpheum, Golders Green. Felix Aprahamian had persuaded the LPO to engage Michael and his Morley College Choir to do a Christmas concert there with the orchestra – unaccompanied carols, some Monteverdi, a few things with the orchestra, and the Corelli *Christmas Concerto*. Practically nobody came to the concert and the orchestra mostly did not take to this obviously deeply musical but rather inept conductor who flapped about, joked and shrieked with easy laughter.

It was not that Tippett was not serious or that he was superficial but that he had genuine gaiety in his nature and that his shyness led him to whoop things up. Even now things have not changed all that much. The last time I saw Michael at Covent Garden he took a curtain call after a performance of his fourth opera *The Ice Break*. He came through the curtain very solemnly and cautiously – he cannot see very far – and with the suspicion of a tear rolling down his cheek. The audience suddenly cheered and Michael just as suddenly grinned, made a very camp gesture, wagging his left hand up and down, and departed precipitately.

Backstage at the Christmas concert in 1941 I was fascinated by this bony, handsome creature with lean, mercurial charm and with knowledge and learning worn so lightly. Somehow or other we hit it off and he invited me to go to one of the Morley College 'house' concerts. I joined the choir as a bass, attended rehearsals every week, more often if we had a concert, and I went to the concerts held every three weeks or so.

It was a new world for me, partly because of the musicians I met there and because of the music that I began to soak up. Before Morley, music for me was entirely vertical, in the sense that, although I appreciated melodies, it was harmony, chords, modulations that I enjoyed. Now, singing in a small choir the music of Bach, Purcell, Monteverdi, Gibbons, Byrd, Weelkes and Tallis, I learned to listen more horizontally, to follow lines of counterpoint. I didn't stop entirely loving the more Romantic composers but I increased my range – and eventually understood the irony of those squishy chords at the end of Michael's *Fantasy-Sonata*. Mind you, I still did not understand music that was neither Romantic nor pre-Classical. True appreciation of Mozart and late Beethoven came later.

Choir rehearsals were stimulating. There were about twenty of us, although we were 'stiffened' at some concerts by some cathedral pros among the men. The girls were all potty about Michael, some obsessively so. The best soprano we had was pretty Alison Purves. She eventually married an adorer down the staves called Antony Hopkins, then emerging as a composer. Other composers in the choir at various times were Anthony Milner and Peter Racine Fricker.

The choir pianist was a musician I came to like very much and our friendship continues forty years later. Walter Bergmann had been a lawyer in Halle, was chucked out of Germany for defending Jewish cases, became king of the recorders at Schotts, and co-editor of old music with Tippett. Walter is a good composer and the dedicatee of Tippett's String Quartet No. 2. (I am the dedicatee of Walter's Septet for recorders.)

A whole chapter could be written about Michael's conducting, but certainly it was the spirit rather than the letter that concerned him, and it was the spirit that he was able to convey so penetratingly to us in the choir and the audience. His beat was frequently all over the shop and his ear was less keen than it is now, but if Michael was convinced about the music then so were we.

Sometimes however he would momentarily lose concentration and then dreadful things could happen. At a point where, at the last rehearsal, he had asked for an especially strong entry he would lift his hand decisively but then bring it down as if he had thought better of it, so the entry would come out with all the force of a tired blancmange.

On one occasion HMV engaged the choir to record *Spem in alium*, the motet in forty parts by Thomas Tallis. This meant one singer to a part, eight groups with five singers in each – very difficult to control and impossible to impart much atmosphere to in the dry acoustic of the Abbey Road studio. Tallis intended it for the resonance of a cathedral. Michael conducted us with a wide wavy beat and fragmented blancmange was coming out. In the coffee break we discussed tactics. I counselled a traffic-cop-like four in the bar. After the break he tried it. Suddenly the entries came punctually and clearly. Obviously too clearly for Michael for he soon went back to his wavy beat. He preferred the spirit to the letter – quite rightly so.

Michael is at his best as a conductor when someone else does the early rehearsals, the note bashing, and then he comes in and supplies the top-dressing. The recording of his own *Corelli Fantasia Concertante* string piece was done this way and so was his performance of the Triple Concerto – both miles ahead of any other readings.

During the war Morley College was about the only place where music beyond your hundred best classics could be heard. Only a small part of the college was left unbombed. There was no big hall, only the little Holst Room with Gustav's planets painted on the ceiling, seating for a crowded 150, and a small, raised platform with a tiny but good Steinway in light mahogany.

The atmosphere at the concerts was friendly but highly charged in that hot room. We cursed at the trams – Ah, *trams*! – as they lurched round the corner and blotted out the sound. The people who made up the audience and performers were cosmopolitan, not 'working men' within the meaning of the phrase, and many were professional musicians. Among those who performed at the concerts were many 'Swiss Cottagers' such as Maria Lidka, Walter Goehr and three of the as yet unformed Amadeus Quartet.

Michael Tippett was the nodal point at Morley. He knew all these performers and most of the audience. He had drawn them there because of his passion for old and new music. He would usually introduce the programmes and, in his peripatetic way – with sentences often left unfinished, with one finger poking at eye, ear or nose, never quite looking at the audience – he would somehow, unerringly, put us all in the right frame of mind to grasp what was going to be played. The later Stravinsky was at that time beyond my comprehension yet, after Michael's introduction, I suddenly 'got' it and never looked back. (But I couldn't have told you what he had said, even later that same evening.)

After a few weeks of the choir and a concert or two I was invited to go to Michael's place for the weekend and soon this became part of the pattern of my life. Morley concerts were usually on a

Saturday evening so that after chit-chat in the corridor there would be a rush – Michael liked doing things in a flurry – to a nearby café where we had tea and dreadful Sweeney Toddish pies or, if there was more time and money to spare, we would repair to the Wilton restaurant hard by Victoria Station. Thereafter there would be a scramble on to the platform in time to catch the last train to Hurst Green Halt, not far from Limpsfield, and we would stumble about the fields in the blackout before reaching Michael's cottage, which he always claimed to have designed himself.

Why he was so pleased with the design we none of us could guess, for it was an ordinary and not particularly comfortable little bungalow: kitchen-dining area, two bedrooms and a living room containing armchairs, an animal rug, an early wireless with record player, a black grand piano with just a few remaining ivories (*under which A Child of Our Time had been composed during bombing*) and a work table strewn, like the top of the piano, with correspondence, pamphlets, concert notices, manuscript paper, books and scores, all in great disarray and with a considerable overflow on the floor.

Michael had many friends but sensibly he did not try too strenuously to mix them. Weekends when I was there it was usually the younger set – younger than Michael. Before and after the time I knew Michael best, the friends who shared his double bed had a touch of the delinquent about them, but during my time, from around 1942 to 1946, the only delinquency about the poet Douglas Newton (Den) was that he was, like Michael, a conscientious objector and that the authorities were playing cat and mouse with him.

I slept on a camp bed in the second bedroom, sometimes sharing with a Cambridge friend of Den's, Adrian de Potier, later a film editor but at that time renowned for his expressive eyebrows and his expertise with powdered-egg omelettes. It was not an entirely male establishment – sometimes Tony Hopkins and Alison would come down; sometimes I would take Olive or some other girl.

Sundays would begin with the sound of Michael grinding coffee beans. Meals were protracted at weekends with endless talk, jokes, and plans for concerts, rehearsals and Michael's career. He was also immensely interested in our lives, sympathetic and helpful. He had not so long before tried to analyse himself, during which time he had written down all his dreams. Thereafter most events and fantasies were subjected to Michael's interpretation of Jung so that, for example, if Alison recounted a dream about a swimming pool, it was of prime if semi-serious importance to Michael to know if the pool was round or square. 'Ah, well, poppet, if it was round, then . . . . '

I was sometimes at the cottage alone or during the week – in which case after breakfast Michael would shut himself up in the living room to compose and then a noise would ensue of singing, groaning, shrieking, laughing, a curious declaimed humming and much crashing on the piano, including a hammering *ad nauseam* of certain chords, rapidly spread and repeated as if played on a cimbalom. It was not hard to guess how the piano lost its ivory teeth.

Weekday lunch would be cooked by someone from the farm on whose fringe the cottage stood. Michael had a working arrangement with the farmer and his wife for cleaning, cooking and a supply of dairy and vegetable stuff. After lunch we would take a walk during which wood for the fire was collected and ideas sifted for whatever composition was on the stocks.

Nature has always been a stimulus to him and sometimes I have seen him entranced – in particular one time on the Cornish seashore with the water lapping around his ankles, staring out over the sea and the rocks. He came out of the water and the trance some twenty minutes later, muttering something about quintuple invertible counterpoint. That must have been the genesis of part of the First Symphony.

Home for tea, more work – copying maybe, although mostly he used to compose straight on to full score – then supper, prepared by Michael himself, if possible something 'off the estate', for he has always liked to live off the land. He also lived simply, frugally, nothing fancy or posh, although he likes good things, maybe a glass of wine, never much though. His health was generally good; his constitution sound, wiry; no sign as yet of the later weakness of the eyes. If he was worried, tired, or upset it was his stomach that gave way. (In this respect he was like Britten.)

If Michael is faced with the prospect of something he thinks he cannot do, his body will, almost obligingly, rebel. I have known him to be taken suddenly ill when he has realized that he simply cannot conduct a certain work, either because he hasn't studied the work enough or because the orchestra is not up to it. Once he keeled over actually on the platform when the moment came to give a lecture in a foreign language. He can also collapse after completing a major work.

After supper, more talk, books and bed. But if friends were there – most welcome at weekends, firmly despatched first thing Monday morning, for Michael quickly got fractious if not allowed to work – there might be a record or two; Stravinsky, the Hindemith String Trio, Wanda Landowska playing Scarlatti, the Nadia Boulanger Monteverdi set – but more likely some wild spirituals or Bessie Smith. Last thing at night we might ask Michael what his composition total was that day. The average was about three or four bars. No wonder *The Midsummer Marriage* took so long to write.

Michael was alone in the country for most of the week but he had to travel up to Morley certain days and around those visits to London would be fitted various other business: committees, either to do with musical or pacifist organizations, or visits to his publishers, Schotts, where everything would be gaily disorganized for an hour or so, while he back-chatted outrageously with the two ladies in the showroom or talked more seriously with the bosses or Walter Bergmann.

In 1943 Michael was sent to prison because he disobeyed the conditions of his exemption, as a conscientious objector, from military service. He had been assigned to farm work, notwithstanding Vaughan Williams's big-hearted help. (He did not agree at all with Michael's views but said how important Michael's work was and how important it was that he should be allowed to maintain his objection.) I went twice to visit him, once with Walter Bergmann and Felix Aprahamian, and once with Peter Pears and Benjamin Britten when they gave a concert. (The audience was the quietest I ever came across.)

I got in on the concert day on the grounds that I was to turn pages for Ben. But when we got inside I explained to the chaplain that the turning over was so complicated that we needed an extra person to help, someone who could read music. The chaplain replied he had no one on the staff who could read music. I asked if we could borrow prisoner No. 5832, Tippett, M., who was known to us and could read music. The chaplain said it was against all the rules but he would see what he could do. So Michael came on to the platform with us and we turned alternate pages. It was a very moving occasion. Peter and Ben were also conscientious objectors but had agreed to abide by the conditions – which included giving concerts in prisons – that the Tribunal had placed on them.

If he had pulled strings, it is possible that Michael could have got out of going to gaol but he felt that it would have been letting down the younger objectors he knew through writing regularly in the pacifist *Peace News*. And I know for a fact how much his presence and counsel meant to some of the bewildered and distressed young people in the Scrubs at that time. Incidentally, Michael was tickled pink to take over the prison orchestra from Ivor Novello, who was in for petrol-coupon diddling.

Another incident that Michael recounted was that one day he had managed to wander away from some working party into a room where there was a piano. He was playing away when all of a sudden the Prison Governor came in. Immediately Michael started to strike one note over and over again, inclining his head as though to listen to the tone. Seeing a prisoner at the piano, the Governor asked Michael what he was doing. 'Tuning the piano, sir.' The Governor continued on his way.

Despite his slow progress in composition, Michael is very quick on the uptake. For example, I have never come across a better player of that noisy game demon patience. He keeps up a continual stream of chit-chat as he plays and is constantly asking other players why they don't put this or that card here or there. By the time they have looked to see and found that he is spoofing, Michael has shouted out 'pounce' and won.

Many years after the war Michael's letters from Wormwood Scrubs to Evelyn Maude were published (albeit in photographs of his handwriting) and I was touched to read in one of them: 'I am only really close to you, B.B. [Britten] and John Amis – no one else. And while John is simply a projection of my musical self and therefore often in my mind, Ben is very near just because he is himself. . . . '

On 21 August 1943 Michael came out of jug and had breakfast with Pears and Britten. In the afternoon the ex-prisoner went to the Wigmore Hall where his String Quartet No. 2 was played by the Zorian Quartet. That evening he, Tony Hopkins, Alison Purves and

I took the crowded night train to Cornwall. We got off at St Austell and, by previous arrangement, went to have breakfast with A. L. Rowse. After the excitements of the previous day and a sleepless night we were exhausted, but the sharpness of Rowse's conversation revived us like a cold shower. We then went to Mevagissey where we found a café with rooms, just off the harbour, where we put up. Michael for some reason had neither his ration card nor his identity card returned to him.

A few days later we found ourselves in a secluded bay with the weather suddenly getting warm. There being no one in sight we decided to bathe despite the fact that we hadn't any bathing costumes, although Alison decided to keep her very brief pants on. Imagine our naked amazement when a small rowing boat came round into the bay with a large man in it: a coastguard. He ordered us ashore then went up to Alison, topless still but panted, and solemnly asked her if she had her identity card on her. He then asked us our address in Mevagissey.

That evening we were eating fresh mackerel just out of the sea – is there anything more delicious? – and in comes the local copper, demanding to see our identity cards. OK for three of us but we had visions of Michael being hauled off to gaol again. Whereupon Michael whispered 'Marx Brothers' and we re-enacted a scene from a film in which documents were rapidly handed back and forth, together with a stream of wisecracks and chit-chat. This we did with our three identity cards in the fortunately not very well lit café room, giving a card to the constable and then snatching it away saying, 'Sorry, you've seen that one, try this one' until eventually the copper went away thoroughly confused by the young witty folks into thinking he had seen four cards when he had seen only three.

I spent several holidays with Michael, with our other companions differing somewhat. One of them, in the Scilly Isles, was with Priaulx Rainier, the South African composer. She had a way of making coffee by throwing the ground beans on to hot milk that was delicious but tastes dreadful if I ever try it – but then she is a most accomplished cook. We were amused to find one small vanity in Michael. He thinks his feet are very handsome.

I knew Michael pretty well for about six years, helping him and his career and arranging concerts with him. We started the larger

Morley concerts, away from the college itself, that introduced some of Michael's music, like his Symphony No. 1, and also other composers' music, like Frank Martin's *Le vin herbé*, to London, and presented the first British performance of the Monteverdi Vespers. I was with Michael when he first heard Alfred Deller's counter-tenor voice; I took part in the first performance – in the choir – of *A Child of Our Time*; I played piano-duet illustrations with Arnold van Wyk in Liverpool before the world première of that same Symphony No. 1; I saw the unknown composer gradually become fairly famous, although nothing like as world famous as he is now. His music soon became second nature to me and the best of it moves me as deeply as any music I know.

I don't see very much of him these days, nor have I since the forties, but he always seems the same, quite unaffected by fame. He always had and still has a wonderful way of being at ease with his fellow men and women, friendly with anybody and everybody, never patronizing the humble, never sucking up to important people. At the same time I found then that he knew his worth, knew that his music would eventually win through. That showed incredible confidence. So did his habit of writing on to the full score and publishing his works before the premières. Like all great artists, he had his ruthless side, and that sometimes meant sacrifices for some of us that knew him well, but, since we loved him and his music, we were happy to serve him. After all, *he* has sacrificed everything to his muse. And he is a genius.

Britten and Tippett were very close at times, most after they first got to know each other when Peter Pears had been engaged to sing at Morley. Ben came along too and the two composers clicked.

Michael and Ben shared a love of Purcell, Dowland and all those early composers who gave both their modern counterparts a new vitality based on the old sensibilities and their way of setting the English language. Michael's and Ben's joint festival on the occasion of the 250th anniversary of the birth of Purcell was another landmark. They warmed each other's fiftieth and sixtieth birthdays. Britten dedicated *Curlew River* to Tippett; Tippett dedicated his Concerto for Orchestra to Britten. No comment is recorded from either recipient about the works in question. I should think that by that time they appreciated the actual music as much as Schumann did the Liszt sonata, Liszt the Schumann Fantasia in C.

Britten once said to me that he thought that Tippett could have been just as distinguished if he had gone in for something other than music and that he wondered sometimes why he hadn't. And I know that Tippett did not particularly care for a lot of Britten's later music nor for his choice of subjects.

The names of Britten and Tippett were often coupled in the forties, quite understandably so, for they represented the new order as opposed to Walton, Vaughan Williams, Bliss, Bax and so on. But despite their common interest in Dowland, Purcell *et ceteri* and all they stood for, it is impossible to mistake any Britten for Tippett and vice versa. They are less alike than the music of other composers whose names are often coupled together: Bruckner and Mahler; Mozart and Haydn; Debussy and Ravel.

I count it as the greatest of good fortunes to have been around when these two composers were alive, to have attended so many first and later performances of their works, to have been able to know them, to discuss their works with them, to have attended rehearsals. These things have made my life worthwhile if nothing else. When *Peter Grimes* was first put on in 1945, and *The Midsummer Marriage* in 1955 I went to every performance, to many rehearsals and in between I had the vocal scores and worked at them in something like an ecstasy of discovery and pleasure, savouring this chord, finding relationships, so that eventually I would know the works end to end.

What was so wonderful was that these works, not just these particular operas but so many of their works in other categories, repaid study and repeated performances. So much of other contemporary British music palled with repetition. One saw through it. It wasn't good enough. But work after work of Britten and Tippett was first class – bliss (lower-case b!) was it. . . .

I suppose that one reason why Ben and Michael could get along was because they were so different. In character, *musical* character, I think that Ben corresponded more with Mozart; Michael with Beethoven. Ben worked his compositions in his head; Michael laboriously with piano and paper. Ben always knew where he was going every bar of the piece in advance; Michael had the plan but wrestled with his material and I feel the music dug deeper, aspired higher.

Ben knew when he put a note on paper which finger would play it, on what string or with what technique it would be sounded, where the singer would breathe, how the choir would find the pitch, who would sing the part, whether that person was good at gruppetti or better at single notes, if they had some notes better than others, higher or lower tessiture. Michael has none of this. He asks the virtually impossible from performers, rarely writes for particular performers, lets the artists get on with it, does not even attend rehearsals of premières very often.

Mind you, if artists *do* go to Michael I have known him very perceptive, putting his finger on the spot even with players like the Amadeus. But his tenor parts, for instance, do lie impossibly low – and even Ben, in a letter of birthday friendship, put a PS, 'I wish your piano parts weren't so difficult!'

Ben took everything personally. I think he had one skin less than most people. Maybe because of this he had insight into people's musical capabilities. His writing for individual voices fitted his chosen singers like gloves – so much so that I still hear, for example, in a performance of *The Turn of the Screw*, Jennifer Vyvyan's voice in any Governess, Arda Mandikian's in any Miss Jessel, Joan Cross's in any Mrs Grose, and, of course, Peter Pears in any Quint.

Julian Bream has recounted how, on receiving the guitar part of *Songs from the Chinese* he told Ben that he thought a certain passage would have to be changed. Ben apologized profusely but then asked Julian if he had thought of using such and such a method of playing the offending passage. Julian goes away, tries Ben's suggestion and finds it works.

Osian Ellis similarly rearranged which hand played which notes in a certain passage in the *Suite for Harp* that Ben composed for him. After a performance or two Ben asked him if he would, just for fun, try the original fingering. Osian obliged and had to confess that the composer had been right all along. Typical! Ben hated to be wrong and he almost never was. The exception, the only one I know of, is that he wrote an unplayably low note for the piccolo in 'Billy in the Darbies' in *Billy Budd*. Ben always joked about this mistake – he could afford to!

One result of all these factors is that Britten, tailoring music for particular artists, attending rehearsals, often conducting or playing the piano for performances, had better immediate results than

Michael. Michael in some respects resembles Janáček in his awkwardnesses. In a way Ben conserved, found new ways of using old methods – again, like Mozart. Michael is much more like Beethoven – or Janáček – in striking out.

Even so, it is curious that performances of the works of both Britten and Tippett are both different nowadays from what they were twenty, thirty, forty years ago. Britten was a wonderful conductor of his music and yet recent performances of *The Rape of Lucretia* and *The Screw* by not such good conductors are in some ways better. And when it comes to a really good conductor like Bernard Haitink conducting *A Midsummer Night's Dream* the result is a revelation of new-found beauty. Why? It is difficult to explain. Asked the same question, Michael says (I quote from memory), 'In the old days they played more or less the right notes but it seems that there needs to be time for those notes to settle down.'

Is it that techniques have improved? I think most musicians of any age agree that they have. Tippett's music did have some scrappy performances until Hans Schmidt-Isserstedt came along with the NWDR Orchestra from Hamburg to show us how the pieces should go. But, as I say, Ben was a good conductor: he really rehearsed well and he heard everything.

While Michael was in prison a private recording was made of his Double Concerto for string orchestras. Walter Goehr conducted and Michael asked Ben to go along, there being no producer. The studio at Levy's in Bond Street was an odd shape with most of the players invisible from the control room. There was some detail coming through wrong in the slow movement. Walter asked Ben and me if we could hear what was at fault. Ben went into the studio and asked if any of the violas were doing upbows instead of down. One of them confessed that he was. Ben could actually hear that.

I had seen photographs in the *Radio Times* of the youthful gangling Britten. There was one, often used, of him outside his mill at Snape with attendant bicycle. I remember hearing on the wireless him playing the première of his Piano Concerto at the Proms and also Sophie Wyss singing two or three of the as yet uncompleted *Les Illuminations*. And then I saw him in the flesh at concerts after he and Peter Pears had returned from America.

By now there was a bit more flesh and he gangled less. He was a very attractive figure despite the blobby nose, the somewhat receding chin and the wiry wavy hair. Offstage he always dressed like a young prep schoolmaster, in sports coat and grey bags, and a conventional tie. This is how he looked when I first met him at Morley. We got on, had the odd meal together and I turned pages for him sometimes, both at the Scrubs and the Royal Albert Hall!

I soon learned, however, that with Ben it was not a question of 'love me, love my music' but love every single bit of my music even if I run it down myself. I met him one day in Boosey & Hawkes, just after his Prelude and Fugue for eighteen strings, written especially for a birthday celebration of the Boyd Neel Orchestra, had been performed. Ben made some deprecatory remark about his piece and not only did I agree with him but I went on to ask him why on earth he still needed to accept commissions if he wasn't happy with the result? Wrong. He turned on his heel and did not speak to me again for some time.

I put my foot in it again, in Liverpool, after a performance of *A Child of Our Time*. Singers, composers and friends all had a meal together after the show. In a party mood Joan Cross and Tyrone Guthrie asked me insistently to do my imitation of Peter Pears. At which Peter laughed graciously but Ben looked furious.

Ben simply could not take criticism of any kind nor jokes about any person or composer that he loved. Even a crack about Dowland or Purcell would not be permitted. He would 'loathe' (a favourite word of his) any artist who gave a bad performance. The result was that artists were dropped, cut, snubbed, humiliated on the strength of a bad performance, sometimes because of indiscreet behaviour, jokes, or whatever. After a time newspapers were banned from the house, and most critics were automatically enemies.

Ben used to say scornfully, apropos critics, that sometimes when he was composing he would be completely uninspired and that there would be a place where he felt that he had utterly failed. No critic had ever put his finger on one of these places and so he felt that critics were therefore useless at their craft. I think this was *naïf* of him and shows his lack of confidence in his own craft. Britten was genius enough not to let these places show. He was craftsman enough to paper over the cracks.

Ben worked with the London Symphony as much as with any of the big orchestras. But one time he had a spat with them. One day at rehearsal two double-basses laughed out loud. Ben thought they

were laughing at him or his music and refused to conduct the LSO
for about two years. In fact they were amused at a joke in the
newspaper they were looking at during a 'rest'.

For a time I was still all right because I was married to Olive
Zorian who, with her quartet, gave the first performance of Ben's
String Quartet No. 2 in the afore-mentioned Henry Purcell 250th
anniversary festival. I remember rehearsals of this work at our flat
with Ben present. He was marvellous with the girls, advising,
encouraging, strict but tactful, the model of composer behaviour.

I listened and would occasionally ask about some detail or
comment with delight, 'Oh, I see, this new tune is really the old one
upside down', or something like that, at which Ben would look
hard at his score and say, 'Oh, is it? Fancy that!' Sometimes he
would wink as he said it. At other times it was difficult to know
whether he was fooling or not.

When the time came for the Zorians to record the new quartet
for HMV Ben was persuaded to play, on the flip side of the final 78
rpm record, his viola in Purcell's *Fantasia Upon One Note*. Ben had
only to play this one note which goes on throughout the three and a
half minutes of the piece but he was terribly nervous about it. And
it is very difficult to play one note for that length of time without
getting the 'pearlies'.

Olive led the English Opera Group Orchestra for several years
and she is to be heard on the original recordings, with Ben conducting,
of the *St Nicolas* cantata and *The Turn of the Screw*, given its
première in Venice in September 1954. She and Jennifer and Arda
had stories to tell of the rehearsals for this most perfect of Britten
operas.

For once Britten had composed a work without knowing who
was to sing the crucial parts of the two children, Miles and Flora.
For the boy the future film star David Hemmings was chosen. He
sang well and he acted well – too well sometimes, overdoing the evil
side of Miles so that Jennifer used to get frightened and slap him
down. But he sang accurately and in Ben's eyes he could do no
wrong. The composer seemed besotted with the boy. Cast and
players noticed that Peter and Ben were at odds.

Eventually it was decided by Ben and Peter that poor Olive was
no longer the right player to lead the orchestra, but in typical
Aldeburgh fashion neither Ben nor Peter had the nerve to tell her. A

situation arose when she was the only person in the organization who did not know that she was for the chop. So many artists and people connected with Ben and Peter were dropped. Yet, some years later, when Ben needed Olive for something, he was charming and she went back. I think she was right to do that. Geniuses are exceptional, aren't they? They can break the rules.

It is not generally known but Beth Welford – Ben's sister, the younger one of the two – remembers that when Ben was a few months old, he had a fever so bad that the doctor advised Ben's parents that the child would be an invalid with a bad heart and that if he recovered from the illness had better be coddled ever afterwards. The Brittens decided to ignore the advice, taking the view that Ben should have a normal childhood – no football, perhaps – and take his chance. There was no trouble for another fifty-odd years.

Isn't it curious that the end of Britten's career should have coincided with the legality of homosexuality? Although Ben was prudish and anti-Bohemian, so much of his work seems to be pleading for his homosexuality to be considered normal.

When Bill Servaes was about to take on the job of managing the Aldeburgh Festival he came and asked me if I had any advice, having known Ben, Peter and the set-up for so long. I advised him to enjoy the warmth of Ben's genius but not to get so close to the flame as to get burned. Ben was the best of companions when in a sunny mood. I prefer to think of him in his younger days bowling along in his fast cars, keeping to a hair-raising schedule at Aldeburgh, playing, conducting, producing masterpiece after masterpiece.

His piano playing was incredible, so creative and full of vitality – he made an orchestra out of the piano. His conducting inspired his forces to do more than their best, as I can testify. He came to Dartington in 1959 to conduct *A Boy was Born*, his opus 3, the first of his masterpieces and, incidentally, the first of those 'anthology' vocal works that he excelled in. George Malcolm did the note bashing and Ben came to direct final rehearsals and the performance of the première of the revised version with added organ part in Totnes Parish Church. It was a choice of some two dozen singers picked from the weekly summer school chorus, plus one or two pros and some trebles from George's Westminster Cathedral Choir. Ben was in best form, delighted with the boys, pleased with us. I don't think I have ever felt happier than during that time, even though the responsibility of getting the difficult music right was great. Ecstatic.

I last saw Ben when I went to lunch at the Red House towards the end of his life. It was a comparatively happy time for just that week he had been able to play the piano with both hands, almost the only time since his heart operation that he had been able to do so, and he was delighted. Alas, it was a fleeting moment and soon he stopped playing the piano for good.

I first clapped eyes on – and hands at – Alan Bush at 2.30 pm on Saturday afternoon, 2 November 1940, when he conducted the LPO in a concert of Russian music, including what I think were the first and last performances in London of Myaskovsky's Violin Concerto – quite decent – and Alexander Krein's Symphony No. 1 – absolutely indecent.

I was greatly taken with the leonine, Leninine looks of the bearded conductor, so masculine in appearance and yet with a curious pussy-footing walk. The beard was shorn the next time I saw him for he was then a private in the army. He had come to Morley College either to hear one of his own works performed or one by his friend and non-relation William Busch. I was introduced to both by Michael Tippett.

Michael and Alan had been friends for many years but their paths had diverged when Michael's Communist views turned to Trotsky and later non-politically to Jung, while Alan adhered to Marxism, to which he has stuck through thick, Czechoslovakia, Hungary, Afghanistan, and thin. But as late as 1934 the two had collaborated in the preparation and conducting of the Pageant of Labour, with music by Alan, given in the Crystal Palace, London.

Michael had great admiration for Alan's music, for its strength and its professionalism. He particularly admired *Dialectic* – as does any musician who knows this fifteen-minute masterpiece for string quartet or orchestra. Michael also recalled the wildness of some of Alan's early works, imitating at the top of his voice Geoffrey Dunn's performance of *Songs of the Doomed*, in which he had to shriek the words 'bloody hell' *con tutta forza* on a top A. And when the Zorians were rehearsing Michael's newly completed String Quartet No. 2, there was a place in the finale where viola and cello chase each other in rapid canonic semiquavers and here Michael would turn to me, shouting with laughter, 'I got that from Alan.'

Alan's early music is wilder and sterner than his later music. *Dialectic* can be compared only with Beethoven's *Grosse Fuge* for its intellectual granite strength and its elevated, passionate lyricism. After the 1948 Party Conference Alan dutifully toed the party line and became more national in style – not always successfully. Some of the later works are very good but on the whole I prefer the early granite of the thirties and the gentler lyricism of the pre-Conference forties – in particular the quite haunting loveliness of the Christmas cantata *The Winter Journey* and the love music and minstrel's songs from the first opera *Wat Tyler*. The best of Bush is as good as Britten and Tippett. Bush has been handicapped by his political integrity, the Establishment attitudes he had to contend with as a result, and the unevenness of his output. As a young man Alan began with theosophical studies and I cannot help feeling that if he had gone on with religion instead of turning to Marxism he would have been better known and not so very different in character. I can see him as another Red Dean and indeed his manner is similar to that of many a bishop, and he is as remote from many aspects of life as a bishop, preserving a great and sweet innocence about many things.

His speech is a gravelly mixture of bishop's parlour and Speakers' Corner, including formal rhetoric, and a way of parrying statements not with a negative but . . . after a pause . . . with a positive opposing view. His manner sometimes approaches pomposity and his sentences proceed with many a subordinate clause (he is a master of the parenthesis) and many an interpolated vocative interpolation – my dear friends! – but just when you think that syntax is surely lost he will escape from the apparent grammatical abyss with dexterous and Houdini-like correctitude. (Parse *partout*!)

Alan has been fortunate in two things apart from his great talent. Firstly he was endowed with enough money to be able to pursue his career the way he wanted – and before you curl your lip at the idea of a Party member with a private income, let me say that I understand that Alan has given freely of his money to the Party, just as he has given time and money to friends, students and good causes. The second fortunate thing in his life was that he married Nancy, his adorable and liberal-minded librettist. If his keys vary between a stern E flat minor and gentleness in B or E major,

Nancy's keys contain not more than one flat or sharp and they are none of them in the minor mode.

In 1956 I travelled with Nancy and Ernest Chapman by train to Weimar for the première of Alan's second opera *Men of Blackmoor* (which might be sub-titled 'trouble at t'mill'). It was a rather hairy journey because this was the time of Hungary and there was considerable tension, especially at the border between East and West Germany. However Alan had promised to send us a telegram if he thought that we should not join him at Weimar where he was, of course, present at rehearsals.

This trip behind the Iron Curtain recalled an earlier one, to Czechoslovakia in 1947. At that time I was working as Secretary to the Society for the Promotion of New Music and our office in Shaftesbury Avenue was *vis-à-vis* another where worked a girl called Topsy Levan. Knowing that I knew Alan Bush she bubbled with enthusiasm about a forthcoming trip to Prague to the International Youth Festival with the Workers' Music Association Choir which Alan conducted.

One day Topsy appeared gloomy – might have to cancel the Prague trip, short of tenors. At which point she remembered that I was a tenor of sorts and put her arms round my neck. I will come, won't I? On being reassured that the music to be sung would include some Byrd and Bush, not just a collection of boring workers' songs I went along – after all it did mean a free trip to a country I'd never been to.

The journey was eventful if not idyllic. We were to take a festival train from Paris to Prague but first we went via Folkestone to Paris. At Folkestone M.I.5 pruned the choir of three of its members, all male and fortunately all baritones! (There were only three of us tenors.) We never saw those three again on the trip. At Paris we changed stations. In the spare hour before our special departed I declared my intention of buying some victuals whereupon some of the 'brothers' said huffily that the people's special, they had no doubt, would contain adequate catering.

I'll never forget that train and the journey. There were seats for about 600 people on board but at a conservative – no, that's the wrong word – at a *communist* estimate there must have been more like 1,500 actual travellers. The corridors were impassable because of the bodies and during the nights people were sleeping in the loos and on the luggage racks. I say *nights* because we started late one afternoon and got to Prague nearly forty-eight hours later. Needless to say there was absolutely no food or drink on the train. In 1947 buffets in France were not back to strength; in Germany there were none anyway and Czechoslovakia was a dead loss. It was indeed a people's special.

We English were huddled together and the more militant commies went into committee over every decision. The only trouble was that the other nations behaved like rowdy fascist brutes! If we stopped at a station where there was a water tap we English would form a decent, orderly queue, whereat the more numerous French would just shove us out of the way, jeering. What with all the pushing and shoving very few people got a drink. After a committee meeting it was decided to accept some of Comrade Amis's camembert, pâté, tomatoes, fruit, wine and mineral water.

With such a load on board progress was not quick. In Germany our train stopped frequently. There often seemed to be some kind of *Weinstube* a hundred yards or so away. We would scramble over and in the absence of currency barter cigarettes and so on. After a half-hour or so the train would give three whistles at intervals and it was somehow presumed that if we weren't on board by the third – too bad. We lost a few of our 1,500 that way. It was a wonderful sight to see people chasing after the chugging train waving a *Brötchen* or a beer bottle. Then the inmates took to decorating the loco so that when we finally arrived in Prague you could scarcely see the engine for the trees, leaves, branches and flowers.

We were all completely exhausted and immediately taken to our billet, which was a gymnasium/school where we were each allotted a bed frame plus a palliasse. Washing was in cold water under a crude shower. The brothers went into committee but there was nothing to be done. Alan had gone on ahead by plane and the first thing I did was to borrow enough Czech currency from him to buy myself a ride home on British Airways. Needless to say my stock went down even further with the brothers when they found this out.

Fortunately I discovered that there were two other folks in the choir who were not of the red persuasion so we clung to each other and giggled under the table when the political hoo-ha-ing got too much. This was before the Communists took over, but the festival was totally their show and everywhere we went there were big pictures of Uncle Joe. It was frightening and also embarrassing when Czechs came up to us because we were British, desperately asking us to do what we could when we got home, to tell people what was happening there.

The choir was rushed off its feet, getting up at six, being rather poorly fed and singing three to six times a day at this or that event. The year 1947 was also the time of a heatwave and Prague was one of the warmest places in Europe at the time of our visit. People died in the streets.

The only nice day we had was when the choir was invited out of Prague to a village about forty miles away. We were the guests of the whole village and welcomed by the mayor, his rather sexy plump wife and the town band. We had lunch, sang our Byrd in the local church, gave a concert, were shown the village in great detail and then entertained to a banquet.

We asked them if they would show us some of their local dancing. They obliged but then asked us in turn to show them some of our local dancing. Oh, crikey! We were flummoxed and could respond initially only with the Lambeth Walk. The whole village eventually joined in and that was all right. But they asked for something more like folk dancing. Again, crikey. Then little Aubrey Bowman, the composer, said that he thought he could remember how to do an eightsome reel. Did any of us know it too? No. Well, perhaps if we went outside and practised for a bit he could show us how it went. Mind you, we should have to sing the music at the same time that we were dancing.

Now I am one of the world's least good dancers. Normally I agree with Arnold Bax who said that he thought one should try everything once except incest and folk dancing. However the village had done us proud, honour was at stake and we had the advantage of being half cut by this time. It took us about three-quarters of an hour to sort it all out and then we went inside and did our best or worst. Great success. More slivovitz. Soon I found myself locked in a polka embrace with the plump sexy wife of the mayor.

The climax of the tour was a visit to Lidice. The Germans had taken reprisals for the murder of Heydrich by wiping out the village of Lidice, killing, burning, leaving a totally empty space where it had been. Alan Bush composed an unaccompanied piece, a motet called *Lidice*, a short, concentrated and very touching work, with words by Nancy. One chord tears one's heart out – typical Alan of the forties. Try it for yourself on the piano: prepare a chord of D major with a dominant A as the bass. Let the A subside to G and above it the next E, B flat, F sharp and A and you have 'essence of Bush'.

We sang this motet on the spot where the village had been, with Alan conducting and cine cameras recording it. A fine gesture it was, harrowing and moving. We most of us found that we needed an antidote to that day. I remember getting together with a school-teacher lady and an East End tailor and we conceived the idea of drinking through the list of liqueurs and spirits at the end of the menu. We didn't get very far and we ended up in a tousled tangle on the floor.

Another time I fell off the platform during the middle of a concert. For an encore it had been decided to sing Ben Frankel's arrangement of 'John Brown's body'. This was a piece the choir knew by heart but it was new to me. There were no copies of the music and I couldn't go off as the platform we were performing on was somewhat isolated in the middle of a park. 'You'll pick it up easily enough,' said my tenorial colleagues. All went well until the final refrain when the tenors sang a jazzy descant in triplets that was so unexpected and funny that I suddenly laughed and fell off the edge of the platform. No doubt it looked undignified and, to make matters worse, I picked myself up uninjured and went on laughing uncontrollably. Non-*kulturny*.

I came back from Prague on the plane and sat next to a friendly elderly man with a handsome head. I told him all about our visit and he said he was interested because he was a journalist. It was Kingsley Martin, and he completely mangled what I told him in his next diary piece in the *New Statesman*. Neither I nor the 'brothers' were best pleased.

My friendship with Alan has survived. We never talk politics. We never have. At eighty-three Alan is still reasonably active. He plays the piano most days and not long ago completed a symphony inspired by a recent visit to the Lascaux caves. The piano part represents 'Society' or at any rate 'Man' – otherwise this is a non-political piece. . . .

Twice in my life I have had the devastating experience of the sudden visitation of a disgustingly heavy cold, both times on journeys. One moment perfectly all right; the next violent sneezing and in full flood, just as if some unseen hand has turned on a switch. The first time this happened I was with Olive walking across the causeway to Mont Saint-Michel in Normandy. The second occurred on the boat between Naples and Ischia. I was on the way to stay with William and Susana Walton to discuss a television programme I was making in honour of his seventieth birthday in 1972.

I knew that William had only one lung and therefore had to be extremely careful not to catch colds. How can you satisfactorily explain to your host and hostess, waiting on the quayside, that you weren't such a selfish bastard as to come from England with a cold but that you caught it twenty minutes ago? Graciously they made light of it. 'Just don't kiss William too much,' said Susana.

Who hasn't, after Russell Harty and Tony Palmer have done the walking-through-the-paradise-garden-and-into-the-house-bit with either the Violin or the Cello Concerto as accompaniment, by now seen something of the fabulous setting that *Façade*, *Belshazzar's Feast* and the music for the Olivier Shakespeare films paid for, dreamed up by and worked at by Sue? It is an idyllic and canny use of a hillside in Forio d'Ischia and tucked away on one side are some holiday houses designed and lavishly furnished by Sue which, I hope, bring her in some money now that she lives there all alone after Willie's death shortly after his eightieth birthday. Actually (his favourite word) they were very kind to me and Willie was braveness itself. To wake from a rheumy doze and find the composer of *Portsmouth Point* at the foot of the bed with a steaming cup of char was enough to make one feel quite remarkably chuffed.

Every day William would work morning and afternoon, the piano banging away, sometimes the gramophone too, and a strange noise that might have been Willie vocalizing. I was reminded of Malcolm Arnold's story about the time he stayed with the Waltons. He asked politely what the Master was working on – this was the day Malcolm arrived – and was told that it was some guitar bagatelles for Julian Bream but so far only the first six notes were down on paper. On the day that Malcolm left some weeks later he inquired again, having observed the daily routine and heard the same noises that I had, and William said, 'Well, I'm not doing very well. Still only the first six notes and, as they are the open strings of the guitar, I'm afraid that when Julian plays them the audience will think he is still tuning the bloody thing up.'

Discussing which pieces should be included and talked about in my programme was a bit like treading a minefield because most musicians feel that Walton's pre-war music – *Façade*, the Viola Concerto, Symphony No. 1, *Belshazzar's Feast* – are masterpieces, whereas most of the later music seems like sequels, small fry or even carbon copies of the earlier music. William's hand had lost none of its cunning but the fire had gone out.

Was it respectability that did it, 'the deep, deep peace of the double bed after the hurly-burly of the chaise longue', natural imaginative decline, or cutting off his native roots in order to go and live on Ischia? Probably a mixture of all those but if anybody dared to hint, say, that the Second Symphony was OK but not a patch on the First, they were immediately struck off the dinner list. Susana was particularly hostile to such critics. Loving partners who have no idea of the art of their mates are always difficult to deal with in this respect.

Another interesting feature of Willie's behaviour was his mischievous deviousness, his desire to mislead people, like myself, interested in the background to his life and music. William would either agree with everything you said in a non-committal way or give you various answers at different times to the same question. This was partly due to a bad memory, partly to wanting to cover his tracks because of his various girlfriends in the past and partly because he would often borrow from other composers. At least twice to my knowledge Walton had to pay compensation because of using copyright material, not voluntarily either but after contesting the matter in the courts.

Using the groundplan of other works is quite a common procedure. It is often recommended to students by their composition teachers. Elgar said that it was the most valuable exercise and Ravel openly said that his Piano Concerto in G was thus indebted to Mozart and Saint-Saëns. Poulenc admitted similar borrowings. Walton, however, was cagey about admitting it. Perhaps he thought it rather *infra dig*.

I had cottoned on to the idea that his Viola Concerto was a close relation of Prokofiev's Violin Concerto No. 1 – not only in the basic plans of the various movements but even as to time signatures, the shapes of the tunes, the way things happened. (Look at the way each movement begins.) I asked William about the resemblance three times several years apart. I am (fairly) sure that he didn't remember having been asked before as he gave me different answers. The first time he said no and denied any knowledge of the Prokofiev Concerto. The second time he said yes, very likely as he knew the piece very well. The third time he said no again.

On another occasion both Felix Aprahamian and I, quite independently in print, observed that the shape of the central movement of the then new *Partita* for orchestra by Walton was based on the shape of the saraband of Roussel's *Suite en fa*. Willie again denied knowledge of the piece but I found a score of it at Ischia. (Mind you, I said nowt about it, thinking of the next cup of tea!)

I am sorry that I did not know Walton when he was younger. But he was great fun as an old man, still full of the black sardonic humour that, according to his banker brother Alec, he had possessed even as a boy. In the forties there is no doubt that Willie felt exhausted after his strenuous efforts to keep up with writing music for films during the war and afterwards. This left him with no important works with which to compete with Britten and Tippett, who were then sweeping all before them. Walton was jealous and did all he could to stem the tide against the younger men, homosexuals at that.

Eventually Walton bowed to the inevitable. Britten and Tippett had come to stay in the musical world and in later years he enjoyed their friendship, a somewhat guarded one, with the usual black-humoured quips once he had crossed the lines back to his own camp. Walton enjoyed the hospitality of the festivals at Aldeburgh and Bath while Britten and Tippett were in charge. Willie even wrote an orchestral piece called *Improvisations on an Impromptu of Benjamin Britten*, a good piece, too. And he was genuinely enthusiastic about Michael's opera *The Midsummer Marriage*, although he poked fun at the text. Didn't we all?

Here are two favourite Walton stories. The first he told me himself and the second was recounted to me by Gillian Widdicombe.

At one time William and Susana were invited to stay for the weekend with Bernard Berenson. They were appalled with the general arse-licking atmosphere and the arrogance of Berenson himself, not entering the dining room for Saturday lunch until all the guests were seated and his own dinner-pail ready steaming on the table. After lunch everybody went upstairs for siesta. When they got to their room William said to Sue, 'I don't know about you, but I am going – right now.' And so they packed and sneaked out without a word.

Before the second story you have to know that Willie, having left the UK, was nevertheless rather miffed when Sir Arthur Bliss was made Master of the Queen's Music. Many years later, Gillian recounts, William several times brushed with death and a few weeks before he did actually die, he did stop breathing for a time. Having recovered he was asked by Gillian one day what it was like on the 'other side'. Were they, as often reported, playing late Beethoven? 'No,' said William. 'It was quiet for a bit. Then there was the sound of a fanfare. *Not* one of mine actually. (*Pause*) Bliss, I suppose.'

I first met Malcolm Arnold at one of Felix Aprahamian's 'symposiums'. There was Richard Adeney, the LPO's first flute, and his wife; Michael Dobson, the first oboe, and Malcolm Arnold with his wife, Sheila. Sheila was a young violinist, pretty but a little on the prim side. Malcolm was first trumpet and, like Richard and Michael, very young. They were all only just past their twenty-first birthdays. In fact, Richard and Malcolm lifted the orchestra out of its tiredness and the routine programmes needed during those early war days.

Malcolm's playing was a revelation. His opposite number in the London Symphony Orchestra, George Eskdale, was a fine technician but his tone was like that of a cornet, rather coarse, whereas Malcolm's was the true trumpet sound, shining, glorious. Malcolm was a worthy pupil of the great Ernest Hall, Principal of the BBC Symphony, which was at that time buried in the country.

Malcolm was a slim boyish young man, quite ordinary in looks but with the peculiarity that when he had a solo his face resembled a Disney creature under pressure. It went pink, red, purple and puce, according to the length and strength of the solo. Once having finished, he would lay the instrument on his lap and regard it, at the most with loathing, at the least with icy indifference, as though he bore no responsibility for what it had just sounded.

I shall never forget the way he played the pianissimo muted solo in the slow movement of Shostakovich's First Symphony one afternoon in the Central Hall, Westminster. As I write these words over forty years later my flesh goes goosey and tears come into my eyes as I remember the sound of that quiet trumpet and the gently dissonant harmonies underneath it. It was a performance when the earth stood still, conducted by that remarkable musician Leslie Heward, a performance that still stands in the memory of many musicians – yet a few days later the conductor confessed that he could not recall it at all, because he was half-seas-over at the time.

A few years later, much to our surprise, at one of the orchestral open rehearsals of the Committee for the Promotion of New Music, Malcolm revealed his talent for composition. The first work I remember is *Larch Trees*, then the overture *Beckus the Dandipratt* and Symphony No. 1. It was a new voice speaking music of manic rumbustiousness, nearly pop tunes, cheekiness and a certain curiously urban loneliness, the scores written with great economy and enormous expertise, if with a certain limited emotional scope. The music of Malcolm Arnold has continued like that. Its deceptive artlessness has told against it with the critics. Some of the works are shallow but others stand the test of time.

I used the word 'manic' and I believe that is the condition that has assailed Malcolm for months, sometimes years at a time. He was soon writing movie scores and in the fifties was earning vast sums but living in a way that emphasized his manic-depressive cycles. The producers of films imposed terrible conditions on composers, giving them ten days to write forty or fifty minutes of full orchestral music, take it or leave it.

So Malcolm would write day and night, conduct the result at sessions that needed the ultimate in concentration and then go on the town for a three- or four-day binge. Several years of this took its toll. He grew to twice the size laterally and his appetite for wine and women became gargantuan. His life became a see-saw. It was pathetic to witness and it all but destroyed him.

And yet he has continued to write good music. I believe his Symphony No. 8 to be his masterpiece. I have heard it at least twenty times and it stands the test. But it still has not been played at a professional public concert in London, for the Establishment has written Malcolm off. And his belligerent, irreverent attitude towards the Establishment has done nothing to help matters.

Malcolm's private life has also suffered. There are now two broken marriages, and friends are vulnerable when Malcolm has had a few drinks. Yet there is a lovable, engaging, innocent Malcolm there if one can only locate it. The one person that Malcolm continued to adore was William Walton. He conducted Walton's music whenever he could, and tried to defend him when Walton was humiliated by the producers of the film *The Battle of Britain*, who rejected all but a big aerial dog-fight sequence from his score and got someone else to write new music for the rest of the picture. Arnold's music will come into its own one day. It will be very sad if the composer is not still here to enjoy it.

I first met Bernard Herrmann at a small dinner party at the flat of the composer Richard Arnell. Benny, as I soon learned to call him, was then married to his second wife, an American lady whom he treated with scant respect, in fact he behaved like a male chauvinist pig. He was very Jewish-looking and at first sight slightly repulsive and he was acting in a surly manner as if he resented the presence of two strangers – myself and Olive.

As the evening wore on we talked, he and I, and we found mutual ground. He was pleased to find that I also loved the music of French composers of the Massenet, Chausson, Roussel, Hahn type. I questioned him about American composers that he had known – Ives, Ruggles, Copland, Sessions – and we talked about English composers whose work he had consistently championed and premièred when he was musical director of Columbia Radio in New York.

We talked also about his work with film directors – about Hitchcock for whom he wrote so many scores and, above all, about Orson Welles for whom he wrote the wonderful scores of *Citizen Kane* and *The Magnificent Ambersons*. (I knew not only the music for these last two but a lot of the dialogue.) We got on like a house on fire; and as his shyness wore off – it was that that produced the surliness towards Olive and myself, although not towards his wife (they parted shortly afterwards) – his face changed and I could see that it had at times a strange beauty.

His speaking voice was curious. When angry or contemptuous, he had a low boiling point, and his voice, always in the nose, was harsh and Bronx; when calm and talking of things he loved, literature and music, his delivery became well modulated, pleasing and at least a fourth lower in pitch.

Benny was a curious mix: lovable/irascible, scolding/affectionate, film composer of near genius/concert and opera composer of third-rate quality. Even after all those years of conducting the Columbia house orchestra and the Hollywood picture orchestras he was ill at ease with the London orchestras, whose services he hired for concerts and recordings. These he paid for out of his fat royalties for movie music. It seems that either he or his agent in Tinseltown had been ultra-smart in insisting on a royalty clause for each film. This clause had been pasted into Benny's contracts well before television had become a big thing. Once film rerunning became general on television worldwide Benny became a millionaire.

Benny was like the comedian who wants to play Hamlet but whose talent reaches only as far as the Gravedigger. However, he at least gave the world the chance to decide for itself by ploughing his movie money back into the business, recording his opera *Wuthering Heights*, his cantata *Moby Dick* and other pieces.

I didn't see a lot of Benny in the fifties but we met occasionally and he did some excellent radio interviews with me about Ives, Welles, etc. He was interested in my singing venture (see Chapter 17), scolded me for continuing with my lessons instead of getting out there onstage to sing. 'Why the heck don't you open your mouth in public?'

'Because no one will pay me to sing as yet.'

'Well, I will,' says he.

He was about to record his cantata *Moby Dick* for chorus, orchestra and several soloists. The main part was for a bass-baritone but there were two small tenor parts. I could choose which I liked and I would be engaged. Didn't he want to hear me first – see if I was right? Damn it, no, just say which part you want and you're engaged.

I took a look at the score and decided on Ishmael. Who wouldn't like to deliver some of those lines: 'Call me Ishmael'? Before the recording he did at last hear me. 'Having difficulty with that G sharp, huh? Well, sing any damn note you like, provided it fits the harmony and the declamation.' (Interestingly, almost word for word what Brahms said to the young George Henschel when singing a solo baritone part in one of the Master's choral works.)

Came the recording day, Barking Town Hall, that great recording engineer Bob Auger in charge, Unicorn the label, a small professional male chorus, David Kelly, a helpful old friend, as Ahab. I was considerably beset by nerves as may be imagined but, as usual (I hope) not showing it too much. I sang it reasonably accurately, but on the rare occasions when I listen to it, I can't say I like it. It gets by, it sounds individual, but top notes begin to splay a bit. When the record came out, one or two critics dismissed my singing; one or two said a kind word, like Philip Hope-Wallace who played a bit of me on a *Music Magazine* review, but the BBC has never played the whole cantata nor, I think, any of Benny's 'serious' music. To them he is a non-composer.

Some years later, after I had decided that singing was just not on for me as a career, Benny rang up and said he was making another 'recud', would I sing one of his songs with orchestra on it, and an orchestral song by Delius that had not been previously recorded?

'No,' I said, 'but thank you all the same.'

At which Benny's voice went up in pitch that dangerous fourth and he yelped at me, 'Look I did you a favour way back over *Moby Dick*, di'n' I? Now do me one, cos I want your voice, and nobody else's, singing these two numbers. And the Delius title is kinda suitable. It's called "A Late Lark".'

Irresistible. So I started swotting up my voice.

This time the venue was that church that you can see just beyond the fountains in the Barbican Centre. This time I was less nervous and could observe more – especially how, although the orchestra, the so-called National Philharmonic, a pick-band put together by Sydney Sax, knew that Benny was picking up the tab, it was nevertheless not really on his side. He was fallible. That was the trouble and he knew it. Like Malcolm Sargent, Benny wanted to be loved. But Sargent was better at beating. Benny made a mistake, got cross, tried to put the boys in the wrong. Occasionally he would get a good laugh: 'Horns, why aren't you playing?'

'It's written in pencil.'

'What do you want it written in, *neon*?'

And then when the Delius got beautiful Benny blubbed. Now it's OK to blub when you are listening, but you cannot conduct and blub. Unprofessional.

I quite like myself on the record singing Benny's song 'March'. It's a nice song, too, reminiscent of the sleigh-ride sequence in *Ambersons*. The 'Late Lark' is just a bit too late on my part, veering towards the Peter Sellers record of the old man in the bathroom singing 'You are the promised kiss of springtime'.

I remember a walk one day with some friends, including Benny, in the country. He had brought a bright girl called Norma Shepherd with him, his latest – nice teeth, smashing legs. I had seen them together several times and suggested that he should get married again. 'No, no, never again,' says he.

'Mind if I have a go,' says I?

'You keep your filthy hands off her,' he growls.

And they were soon married right enough. Later we went out sometimes *à trois* and I noticed that he was treating number three in the same rough way that he had treated number two. In restaurants he would stand up and make a scene. Embarrassing. But Norma knew how to handle him, which she did very lovingly. However, when Benny died, his efforts to leave her his money were contested by his earlier family and I believe that poor Norma got very little, if anything, which was very unjust.

Sometimes I have wondered about the fulfilment or happiness or otherwise enjoyed by creative artists, especially these six that I have written about here. Maybe their happiness is immaterial. I think that Benny didn't care much about wealth or domestic happiness. One part of him rejoiced in doing a job well – in the film studios – but I think that he was on the whole unhappy because his serious music was unsuccessful. All these opinions are, of course, merely informed guesses, but I think that applies also to Malcolm Arnold. Like Benny, Malcolm went through three marriages but I think Malcolm's family mental troubles must have dominated his life. Walton's domestic life was happy but he often thought, and said so latterly, that he should have accomplished more. Bush's domestic life has been happy and his philosophy of life will not allow him to admit to being discontented with the number of performances he gets. Britten's domestic life was fairly unruffled and although he said composition got more and more difficult he must have known, despite his melancholic disposition, that he was the tops.

So then what of Tippett? There is no record of domestic bliss. I know now that he enjoys company and has had several lovers of years' standings, but I think that domestically he is the most detached of the six – and the happiest by disposition and nature.

(15)

Quodlibet Amicorum

I thought once of writing some more up-to-date musician's version of John Aubrey's *Brief Lives*. So many musicians of my time have been forgotten or overlooked. Perhaps they were not famous enough to merit a biography but had considerable influence in their day – like Arnold Goldsborough, Thurston Dart, or Walter Goehr. Others may have their entries in the reference books or their biographies potted in publicity handouts, but what were they really like? What did, or do, their contemporaries think about them?

I have made a start towards such a project in this book but it would require research and much more space to do the job properly. So I have done some of it, improperly, in certain chapters in this book. But there are other friends that I want to bring in and that is the reason for this chapter. In the BBC's *Music Magazine* Julian Herbage used to announce that so-and-so would now 'sketch the profile' of X or Y. And that is what I am going to do. The length or detail of the profile has nothing to do with the regard that I hold or held for the person in question. Indeed, there are a number of snap-like visions in my head that seem to want to be put down first.

A shot of bathers floating a few yards out to sea in Anstey's Bay, Torquay. I am in this shot, too, talking to the leader of the Végh String Quartet, Sándor Végh, who is bathing, smoking a cigar and wearing a sun hat all at the same time. I swim a few yards away to talk to the rest of the quartet. This is typical of the quartet. It is always a three-plus-one situation – except when they are actually playing.

Moonlight. I am showing a new visitor to Dartington the gardens. From the bushes I hear the unmistakable giggle of Lionel Tertis, genius of the viola, retired long ago from playing, now in his late seventies. He is a widower but has brought with him this year two ladies, a mother about his own age and her daughter. I cannot tell from the muffled cries in the bushes which of the two he has with him. Time perhaps will tell. (It did shortly after that particular year's summer school. He married the daughter.)

At the bar. I am called away to the telephone whilst talking to Martha, my flavour of the month, so I ask the nearest male to look after her. A mistake. He was Luigi Nono, the composer. He looked after Martha to such a degree that a friendly but distinctly metallic triangle developed of which the apex was a trip in Martha's car to a curious grid of right-angled roads between Ipplepen and Staverton, tiny lanes with hedges twice the height of the car. Gigi (Luigi) asks to drive. Once in control of the wheel he drives at sixty miles an hour down these straight lanes – an Italian version of Russian roulette. He was impatient with the triangle, he said afterwards. (On arriving in Milan some years later I was delighted, nevertheless, to find that one of the streets by the station was Via Luigi Nono, then dampened to discover that it was really named after a French king.) I visited him later in his house. An active communist, he lived in the most conservative city in Italy, Venice, in a house with a tree in the garden. Venice in winter reminded me of the Manchester Ship Canal.

Nono solo was enough of a handful at Dartington. When his pal Bruno Maderna was there with him, the summer school became almost a riotous assembly – hilarious too. Professional amorists, their cockiness led them to make dates for every hour of the day with different girls – but being also busy teachers at the school, they found that they could not keep it up.

Once Britten was there at the same time (1959). Nono made vitriolically scornful remarks in class about Britten and would not even meet him, let alone shake hands. On the other hand, Ben expressed himself happy to meet Gigi, said so several times and couldn't imagine why it did not happen.

Nono refused to speak English in class so a young composer, Peter Maxwell Davies, translated for him. Nono would talk for two, three or four minutes, then wave to Max who would also talk for a similar length of time – in perfect sentences, a great flow of words. When I asked Max afterwards how he could do this so fluently, he answered that he had spent half a year in Italy recently – as if that was sufficient reason! Years later I reminded Max of this feat and he said enigmatically, 'Ah, but I was translating only some of the time!'

Restaurant scene. There are three composers together at the SSoM and I am taking Elisabeth Lutyens, Virgil Thomson and Nicolas Nabokov out to lunch. Apart from having music in common, we are all a bit deaf. Everybody talks rather loudly: Nicolas low and resonant; Virgil high and sharp; Lizzie in between but with a carrying rasp. The restaurant is on the banks of the Dart, one of those half-timbered jobs, inclined to serve dishes like chicken-in-the-basket. Both the younger waiter and the manageress-type waitress are wearing white cotton gloves.

'Makes you think they both suffer from eczema of the hands,' whispers Elisabeth penetratingly. She continues to make adverse comments. The soup has too much pepper; the horse-radish sauce is out of a bottle, and so forth. Nicolas tells scurrilous stories about Igor and Lennie. (Fortunately the apparently mute lunch-munchers around us, so interested in our conversation, do not know who we are talking about.)

Have I been to see *Moses und Aron* at Covent Garden? Virgil asks me. Yes, I have. 'Ah,' says he, 'now in the orgy scene did they have lots of white plastic "come" on the stage?' (This the mutes appear to understand.) And so it continues, myself alternately amused and embarrassed.

While dealing with the bill the manageress advances. 'I couldn't help overhearing part of your conversation,' says she, at which I start cringing. 'And I would just like to say this.The horse-radish was *not* out of a bottle. It was freshly made this morning.' Nevertheless . . . I have not returned to that restaurant since that day.

Artists Room. I am surprised that Charles Ives never reproduced the shindig that a string trio or quartet makes limbering up in the green room before a concert. This particular evening, in 1954, is the first of six concerts at Dartington of the Végh String Quartet. Végh has arrived, looking as usual somewhat like a ghoulash version of Charles Laughton – overweight, little legs. He enchants everybody except the other members of his quartet. Georges Janzer is there, practising different bits of the programme on his viola. Paul Szabó is playing quite different passages from the programme on his cello. They naturally practise in different keys and tempos from each other. The one thing they have in common is that, for this first concert, they are all wearing dark lounge suits.

The door opens and in comes Sándor Zóldy the second violinist – in full evening dress, white tie and tails. Instantly there is pandemonium and instruments are put safely down so as to allow that maximum use of the hands that foreigners seem to find so essential. Strange how foreign languages that one doesn't speak sound so belligerent, never more so than Hungarian on this occasion. I gather that what three of them are saying, give or take a cuss word or two, is, 'We arranged to wear lounge suits on this trip, go away and change'; while the second violinist is saying, 'No, we agreed on tails. And anyway I haven't brought a lounge suit.' So, we had six concerts in which the second violinist was dressed more formally than the others.

Later that evening Sándor Végh and a crowd of staff and visitors were having a nightcap in a ground-floor common room when the sound of jangling bedsprings obtruded from the bedroom above where, we all came to realize, Zóldy and his young wife were housed. There was silence down below as the noise above got louder and louder. Somehow we all turned to look at Sándor who, feeling some comment from him was required, said, 'Very strong player.'

The desire of the various members of the Végh Quartet to get away from each other was so marked that at one time Végh lived in Zurich, the violist and the cellist in Geneva and Basle, while the second violinist was in Paris. This meant that the question, 'Where shall we rehearse? Your place or mine?' was fairly important. I often wondered whether the fact that they did not rehearse much was the cause or effect of their living so far apart. I also remember that once when they were to give a concert in the Royal Albert Hall (chamber music at the Proms, I suppose) they said, 'No, thank you, we won't need to try out the hall because we always play the same anyway. What's the point?'

Concert in a remote country place given by the Martin String Quartet, a member of the audience comes up to Neville Marriner and asks to look at his fiddle. The request granted, the chap looks the instrument all over then hands it back saying, 'Good, I've always wanted to know what a second violin looked like.'

At that time, when I first got to know Neville, he looked like being a second violin for a long time. The son of a Lincoln carpenter, Neville had got himself to the Royal College of Music in London. There he had met a cellist called Diana Carbutt, daughter of a rather up-market stockbroker. When Olive and I got married and settled into a basement flat in Holland Park we saw a lot of the Marriners who lived in Notting Hill Gate.

Next to the old Mercury Theatre there was a cheap but pleasant restaurant where the four of us would have lunch most weekdays. It was a sort of club to which also belonged the New Zealand fiddler Alan Loveday, the Armenian violinist Manoug Parikian, Antony Hopkins and his wife Alison Purves. The Hopkins' soon moved further away but usually there were at least two or three of us.

The latest jokes and gossip of the musical world were sifted over. The badinage was fast and furious, if somewhat on the cruel side because we found it difficult to leave things unsaid. If we thought of something we said it, talking faster, as Irene Worth once explained John Gielgud's brick-dropping, than the brain could censor. A well-known danger sign at these gatherings was Diana's 'contralto voice', which meant that tears were on the way.

More fun was an institution called 'joke-doctors'. If someone told a joke that seemed to have potential laughter in it but had fallen flat, we would analyse it, trying out new approaches, perhaps, or a different wording of the punchline, thus rescuing many a crippled gag. The meetings spread over to some evenings, either at the Marriners' flat, or at ours in Holland Villas Road. In particular, Diana, by now having given up the cello and not going out to work, needed to have company.

After seven years of marriage — three happy ones, the others mixed — it became obvious that I had fallen in love with another girl, so Olive and I split up and the Marriners asked me if I would like to go and live in their new house in Brook Green. I moved in 1955, by which time Neville had packed in the string quartet and was leading the second violins (still playing his *second* violin, naturally!) in the London Symphony Orchestra of which the leader at this time was another old friend from RCM days, Granville Jones.

By this time Neville and Diana had two children, Susie and Andrew. Manoug was now always around the house. One evening Susie was very ill so the four of us were playing Scrabble up in the main bedroom. For once, I was just about to make a very large score, when Diana went to look at Susie. Manoug told her to stop fussing. Diana said something quite rude, at which Manoug got up and prepared to leave. Neville told Diana that she had better go downstairs after him and put things right. Apparently there was an eyeball confrontation and in a flash they realized that they were in love with each other. And I missed my big Scrabble score! Diana got divorced, married Manoug, started another family and became a highly successful antiquarian book dealer.

Back at Brook Green Neville got in a pretty Australian girl called Liz Escott, to look after the house and the children with the help of an Italian girl called Giustina who spoke spaghetti English but cooked us sausages. Her English progressed enough for her to invent the phrase: 'Mr Emmis, you disgustiboy.' Granville Jones moved in and we all had fun, spaghetti and sausages.

The children survived and are now both distinguished in their own fields. Susie and her husband Meirion write books together – including one about the Academy of St Martin-in-the-Fields – and Andrew is one of our best clarinettists. I was able in a small way to help Susie with her first book while Andrew and I collaborated recently in a performance of Walton's *Façade*.

However a big change came into Neville's life as a result of my asking a lovely girl called Mollie Sims to be a trog at the summer school at Dartington. I knew her from the days when she had been Siriol Hugh-Jones's secretary at *Vogue* magazine. Since then Mollie had married and gone to live in Cornwall but was disenchanted and bored. After the summer school I said that if she ever wanted to come up to London for a weekend there was room at Brook Green. And indeed there was, for she and Neville clicked and eventually got married.

The up-market first marriage needed more confidence than the lad from Lincoln could muster, I think. By the time Neville married Mollie he was much more assured. He was quite a scourge to some conductors who wagged the stick in front of his front-of-the-second-fiddles desk in the LSO but he also had the chance of seeing what was good and bad about certain conductors. Nev adored Pierre Monteux – who didn't? – and had the chance to go and study with him in America. This, plus the Academy taking off, has had the effect of mellowing him. He still teases like the devil but there is no malice in it any more. Success has not blunted him. He is still one of the sharpest fellows in the music biz., but he is gentler, kinder and more modest.

He is not the most profound musician in the world and he would be the first to admit it. I used to think he would never make it with works like, for example, the 'Eroica' Symphony, works that need some feeling for tragedy but . . . just listen to that recent record of the 'Eroica' with the Academy! Magnificent, and with depth! Neville has the knack of keeping happy both orchestral musicians and soloists alike. He knows his limitations, he works hard – and he succeeds.

Olive and I used to go to any concert or rehearsal that Georges Enesco directed. In particular we went to the BBC Maida Vale studios when Enesco was to conduct the Boyd Neel Orchestra in Bach's *Brandenburg Concertos* and the Suites. It was there that I first saw a certain musician seated at the harpsichord.

The one thing about Enesco that I thought musically questionable was that he obviously did not like the harpsichord – like most of his generation, including Beecham, who described its sound as 'skeletons copulating on a tin roof' – but suffered it to be there. Perhaps he did not want to deprive a musician of a date. *That* would have been in character. But, whenever he *could* hear the instrument, he shushed the player impatiently as if the harpsichord were some annoying insect.

The person playing the instrument at Maida Vale was somebody new to both of us, which was strange because we knew between us practically any musician in any of the London orchestras, symphony or chamber. This person had the deadest of deadpan expressions, pans just don't come any deader. We inquired his name – George Malcolm. One day I heard George play the solo part in Bach's *Fifth Brandenburg* – wonderful.

In 1952 I got him down to play at the last summer school held at

Bryanston. By this time his pan had suffered a fall from a high window and subsequent facial surgery, so that it looked deader than ever. It was a wonder that it was not a dead deadpan. But George survived. His playing was quite remarkable and gradually I got to know him, which is not an easy thing to do. He is very reserved and reveals himself easily only with children. He was on very good terms with the boys in his own choir at Westminster Cathedral. He kept strict discipline but there was mutual affection.

That fall, however, may have been an indication of some inner desperation. George developed a drinking problem – not helped by his curious taste. (He would drink a glass of cider, followed by wine, then a beer plus a brandy.) And as he got intoxicated easily the result was predictable. One night George entered the bedroom at Dartington where Olive and I were reading just before going to sleep. He went across the room, muttering to himself, opened the wardrobe cupboard and disappeared among the dresses and suits. After a year or two of this George took a grip on himself and went on the wagon – for good. But then one thing George is not short of is grit and determination.

George's mother also had plenty of these sterling qualities and she held on to life. George looked after her like a good son, sharing a house with her until she died, sacrificing . . . well, who knows exactly what? She came at least once to Dartington and was quite fun in her own dour way. I liked her a lot but I could see that there was a slight resemblance to cartoonist Giles's Grandma figure.

There's a story about her that is *molto ben trovato* even if she and George thought it wasn't accurate. When George conducted the weekly summer-school choir he would sometimes revert to the discipline of the choir school which, combined with a headache maybe, accounted for a certain acerbity, particularly towards the altos whose tone was sometimes full of wobble and wrong notes. The story goes that one 'advanced girl' accosted Mrs Malcolm and told her that her son was the rudest man she had ever encountered. Mrs Malcolm was taken aback but, recovering herself, went up to the 'advanced girl', standing by this time in the coffee queue, nudged her with her umbrella and said, 'I'll have you know, my son doesn't suffer fools gladly.'

The last bit is true. George is utterly direct and honest and he cannot dissemble. When I had studied singing for some years, my teachers built me up, but at auditions I was turned down. So I sang to George, knowing I would get a straight and dependable answer. I sang. George said quietly but firmly, 'Well, I'm sorry, John, but it's just not good enough.' I was grateful for that. And I still am.

Britten thought a lot of George, and his feelings were cemented when George did some note bashing for Ben when we did *A Boy was Born*, Britten's earliest masterwork, at Dartington. Ben also adored the boys from Westminster that George had brought to sing the treble parts. I think that it was that, and a performance George did at the Cathedral one Christmas of *A Ceremony of Carols* with Osian Ellis at the harp, that led Ben to say he would one day compose a piece for George and the Choir.

But the piece kept on not coming until there came the time when George resigned from the Cathedral in 1959. He met Ben and told him that he was leaving on such-and-such a date. 'But what about the piece I am writing for you?' said Ben and delivered it within a matter of days. It was the *Missa Brevis in D*.

George kept on coming to the SSoM, finally topping even the Amadeus's score. Some of the best and most fun concerts we had at Dartington were those by George and Julian Bream – Vivaldi on lute and harpsichord was both super music and a super giggle. They were brought together by the man who made both the lute and the harpsichord which the musicians played on – Thomas Goff, an aristocratic figure who turned to high-class carpentry and cabinet-making as a hobby when he was in the Guards, a great friend of the Queen Mother and all that.

He later switched to harpsichords and there were some in the best houses in the West Country. When Tom came to Dartington he would write to all his titled friends in the district and say that he was coming to visit them on the way, a kind of royal progress. They were all so scared of the harsh words he would undoubtedly say about the way that they were keeping his instruments that many of them would shut up their houses and go abroad until September to save themselves the pain of Tom's visits.

I had first met the infant Bream when I had a room in the forties in Belsize Park in the house of singer-guitarist Victoria Kingsley. There were various benevolent people like Victoria who had heard the brilliant prodigy and decided to help him on his way. Some years later he came to Dartington where the situation suited him – a beautiful medieval hall to play in (' 'ere, Johnnie boy, let's have some artistico lighting tonight, shall we? Those big lights are ever so un-lute, don't you think?'), plenty of pretty girls, the company, the chance to play all night if he felt like it, plus the odd packet of Smith's Crisps and the cricket. The trouble was getting him to go. We didn't like to push him out but he did once stay on for a whole week after his last concert.

His masterclasses were instructive and fun. On the first day one year he tried to correct one lad, playing the same passage on his own guitar and saying, 'Go on, more like that. See wot I mean?' At which the lad replied, ' 'S all very well for you. You've got a good box to play on. Mine's a soap box.' Julian conceded he had a point. He hadn't thought of that, so he went round the whole circle of students, playing on every instrument and, incidentally, making almost as lovely a sound on the first lad's box as he had on his own custom-built job.

In cases like Julian's I must confess I wish I could talk to you, reader, instead of writing, because all the stories about Julian are so much better if I could imitate his voice for you. Mind you, Julian talks posher now than what he used to but when he has had a jar or two then he reverts. He turned to a mutual friend on such an occasion saying, 'I don't talk like Johnnie imitates me no more, do I?' Julian comes to life in Tony Palmer's book on him (*Julian Bream: A Life on the Road*) because his speech is reported as it was on a tape recorder.

Some Juliana:

Mutual friend Johnnie Warrack went with Julian to the Royal Academy one year and they went into one room dominated by a large nude. Julian exclaims in loud astonishment, 'Christ, I know 'er!' Silence in that room and the bystanders wait for more. 'What a smashing pair of plonkers!'

Julian once lent his flat to the South American singer Ana Raquel Satre while he was out of the country. She said she found eighteen pairs of evening shoes under the bed, all worn right down at the heels, likewise a cupboard containing forty-seven dirty evening shirts and a whole room full of unopened letters and telegrams.

I was invited once to go down to Julian's Dorset pad to play cricket for his Eleven versus a team of local farmers. It was fairly serious stuff – net practice the night before. Julian has a lovely house with a nice garden and a well-stocked cellar. I asked him to tell me what the opposition team was like. 'Nice fellers but absolute bastards about "walking" when they're given out. They refuse to go and they argue.'

'Well,' I said, 'if they argue it must be important to have a good umpire.'

'As a matter of fact,' says Julian, 'the umpire is the local Jesuit priest.'

We were supposed to start the game at 2.30 but at that time we were mostly still finishing our lunch. 'That's alright, Johnnie boy, all taken care of. I won the toss *in absentia*; we're batting and I sent the opening pair on in advance.'

The first person I see on the field at deep long leg is the composer Harrison Birtwistle. 'Since when were you a farmer?'

I was out third ball. None of us did too well with the bat. Then the farmers batted and eventually in comes Harry Birtwistle. Julian bowls with gardening gloves on so as to keep out of trouble. While he bowls Harry is out of trouble too but then he has to face a fastish bowler. The pitch is none too smooth and soon a ball goes straight and fast to Harry's groin. I am fielding at silly point so I can see Harry's face going into a sort of smiling rictus and he goes down very very slowly on his knees.

'Harry, is it your balls?' I ask him. Julian suggests rubbing them.

'Don't rub 'em,' says Harry, 'count 'em.'

Julian encouraged me to come to the annual English Music Week in the Bavarian Alps at Schloss Elmau. 'Great place, nice people, good tucker and I was knee-deep in girls.' I went the following year: it was, they were, it was and *he* was.

That Tony Palmer book catches the essence of Julian – not only what Julian himself says but also what friends say about him, Peggy Ashcroft especially. Like many other artists, Julian's is a fairly lonely life – all that time on the road, all those special requirements, all that practising. It's no life for having a wife tagging round with you. And yet if the wife stays at home . . . . I fancy that the friends that Julian keeps are the ones that work with him, like Peggy, or like Jimmy Burnett, who records him. Julian certainly has got many things in life sorted out: house, instruments, wine, travel arrangements, tours, arranging his own concerts. And who else has his sort of recording arrangements whereby he records what he wants, when he wants, how he wants? *And* gets paid for it. Good for him. He's worth every penny. He may not play the guitar better than *any* other player but he does communicate better. He plays to and with an audience, and he plays better music than any other guitarist I know.

Even now, nearly thirty years later, on a radiant day or during a good performance of a work that he knew and liked well – during Stravinsky's *The Wedding* the other day at Covent Garden – I remember with affection mixed with anger the pianist Noel Mewton-Wood who took prussic acid.

He came into the Tippett–Morley College circle. I have mentioned the little brown Steinway in the Holst Room. When Noel played Hindemith's *Ludas Tonalis* we used to fear sometimes for its safety. Noel played with a fine technique and quite out of the ordinary sensitivity and musicianship, but now and then the physicality of this young godlike creature would run away with him and he would, as they say, 'go through his tone', i.e., bang.

He was tall and his features were just a shade too coarse to be really handsome. He had a good physique, and tended to hide his shyness by rumbustious behaviour. He was a good craftsman who could make a model theatre, mend his radio, car or piano, breed dogs and compose a string trio. He knew the lives and works of the painters, likewise poets and writers. He knew not just the piano repertoire but all music from Bach onwards. He was a brilliant sight-reader, had most of the piano music of Beethoven, Mozart, Chopin, Debussy and Stravinsky in his head and could play from memory great wodges of *Figaro*, *Götterdämmerung*, *Salome*, *Elektra* and *Pelléas*. He had also made a thorough study of medicine. Noel seemed to love life, gobbled it up. His brain was in perfect order, so was his body. He had a gift for making and keeping many friends. Yet he committed suicide – after more than one attempt.

Since Noel's time I have come to know about the life of Percy Grainger and there are some parallels. Like Percy, Noel was an Australian, born in Melbourne, the only child of a father whose name was scarcely mentioned and a mother of tomboy, dominating character who was determined that her son was to be a god and a musician, determined to control his life, making sure that he did not waste his time with too many friends, women, etc. There the parallels end because Percy continued all his life to idolize his mother and to become a heterosexual – albeit with a sting in the tail!

In later years Noel kept his mother Dulcie at bay although in short doses she was great fun – a craggy witch looking not unlike a Dame Edna grown thinner and older. She was crafty, bossy and had a dangerous habit, if she liked you, of giving you a friendly tap in the balls. She ran a dress shop in London until Noel died, after which she went back to Australia and I never heard another word from her.

Noel began his career in London with the kudos of a Sunday afternoon concerto conducted by Sir Thomas Beecham, and there is a darling picture of the little lad on that occasion. He had a good but not spectacular career. He had his share of Proms, Wigmore Hall recitals, BBC broadcasts, concertos in this country and in South Africa, Australia and New Zealand, but he never quite hit the big time of a Clifford Curzon or a Solomon or a Myra Hess. He had not quite that greatness nor that popular appeal. And he played too much out of the way or modern music. He loved to play Weber, Schubert, Hindemith, Stravinsky, Britten and Tippett – not a passport to popularity in the forties and fifties. You can hear Noel on records: Weber sonatas on Decca 78s; Hindemith on the Concert Hall label, and, as he took over some Peter Pears recitals when Ben was too busy, on Argo, with Peter doing Alan Bush and Tippett.

When I met Noel he was living at Renby Grange with Nancy Eckersley. That is to say, Nancy looked after him, did the cooking, looked after the dogs and provided him with food for thought. It was a large, ramshackle house in extensive, woody, usually muddy grounds. With Noel's help, Nancy bred alsatians. As a guide to the generations the dogs' names went through the alphabet. The dog I remember best was an oldie called Moses, so that's thirteen generations for a start.

Nancy was an ardent Marloweist and quite an intellectual in her upper-middle-class blue-stocking way. She loved Noel more than she did her family, I thought, and certainly more than her husband Roger who sometimes came down for weekends.

Roger had been Controller of BBC Programmes in Reith's day and used to tell me fascinating stories. For instance, when the BBC announced that it was going to form its own dance band, various band leaders took him out to lunch. The interesting thing for Roger was the variations of bribe time. Some fingered their cheque books with the cocktails; others as the various courses came along. He thought one of them was going to miss it altogether but then, as he said goodbye, he slipped a £50 note into Roger's palm.

Nancy was at first almost as intimidating as Noel's mother Dulcie. As I sat down to breakfast she would say menacingly, 'You *don't* want bacon and eggs, do you?' This took me back to school Latin: *num*, expecting the answer 'no'. I complied until I saw that her façade could crumble quite affably. So eventually I would answer something like, 'Oh, *yes*, what a good idea! I see you've both had some, mustn't get left out.'

After breakfast Noel and I would retire to the music room where there were two pianos, one of them a good Steinway Concert Grand. Sometimes I would vocally hack my way through Tippett's *Boyhood's End* and other modern numbers but more often we would play Mozart or Schubert duets at one piano, or Stravinsky and Debussy at two pianos.

I have found that duet partners fall into two categories: those that make me 'all thumbs' and those that can inspire me to play actually better than I am ordinarily able. Noel inspired me – and he needed to, because although I can sight-read fairly well and I have learned the all-important knack of knowing what to leave out, my left hand is even weaker than my right. Thus I am no good at playing 'top' in four hands at one piano because too often the left hand has busy bits, whereas the left hand at the 'bottom' end usually is more stable, providing the harmonic bass.

Playing good arrangements of orchestral works is a wonderful way of getting to know them: our specialities at Renby were Debussy's *Ibéria* and Stravinsky's *Danses Concertantes*, *Dumbarton Oaks* and the Concerto for two pianos. I would also play on a second piano the orchestral part of concertos that Noel was learning. In particular we worked at the Busoni Concerto of which I had a copy. Our sessions were noisy, interrupted by groans and shrieks of laughter. Noel would often shout at me if I foozled a passage or came in late but somehow he never cowed or unnerved me.

Music was punctuated by meals and long walks with the dogs. We discussed music especially but also everything under the sun – except that I never got around to asking Noel if he was queer or not. He appeared to be neutral, just not interested in sex. Nancy was obviously dotty about him but he did not seem to take any notice. I suppose that Michael Tippett must have known that Noel was a homosexual but if he did he never let on.

Then, after some years, our meetings, some of the happiest times in my life, got less. Suddenly, as you might say, *Ecce Homo*, Noel 'came out'. He met Bill Fedricks and set up house with him in Hammersmith Terrace. By now I was married to Olive and after an evening *à quatre* we found that they had reminded us of the story about the soldier, marching along with his squad, whose mother says to her friend, 'Look, that's my boy. He's the only one in step.' We had been made to feel that heterosexuality was abnormal and just a bit dirty.

One evening I went to one of Noel's concerts and told him later that, for the first time in our friendship, he had looked queer as he had minced on to the platform. He thanked me and said, 'God, how awful!' I never saw him mince after that, although he did take to wearing medallions on chains. Bill was good fun in his way but he was very camp and always imagining himself ill. One day he complained of terrible pains in his abdomen. Noel had had enough of Bill's aches and pains and took no notice. Bill died and Noel never forgave himself, almost immediately trying to kill himself with umpteen aspirins. Medical friends had him washed out. A week or so later he rang up in the evening and we talked for over an hour. He thought he was getting over Bill's death. He spoke of the future – he was going to do some concerts with the violinist Max Rostal. I suppose it was his way of saying goodbye because the next day, 5 December 1953, he took prussic acid and died immediately.

He had left a series of notes all over the little house in Notting Hill Gate. In one of them he asked that I should have his Steinway Concert Grand. Dulcie asked me if I would go to the house – this was two or three days later – to help her sort out some of the music. When I got there she remembered she had to go to the bank. Would I mind being alone in the house? I sat sadly in the sitting room dominated by the big piano that he wanted me to have with the smaller grand interlocking it. There on the wall was the remains of the acid he had thrown away. I turned for relief to the piles of music that Dulcie wanted me to sort out. There on the top of one was my own copy of the Busoni Piano Concerto.

That concerto begins with quite a long calm orchestral passage, three or four minutes, before the solo piano comes crashing in. I took the copy to the second piano and began to play the introduction. Gradually I got to the place where the solo begins. As I reached the very bar of the solo entry there was the hell of a noise from the Concert Grand, right on the beat. I leaped up, quite terrified and opened the lid of the Concert Grand to find that a string had broken. It was a C string – and of course the first chord that the soloist plays in the Busoni Concerto is a loud chord of C major. My terror changed to joy so that when Dulcie came back a few minutes later she thought I had become hysterical I was laughing so much.

It was not only for love and remorse that Noel died. He also felt that his career was not advancing. The Royal Festival Hall had been opened some time and whereas his colleagues had played there several times he had only been asked to play there once (by me, for the Apollo Society).

Two years after his death I decided to organize a memorial concert and asked Dennis Brain, Peter Pears, the Zorian String Quartet and Benjamin Britten to take part. I also asked Britten, Alan Bush, Michael Tippett, Arthur Bliss and Cecil Day Lewis to write especially for the occasion. Cecil wrote a poem 'Elegiac Sonnet', for Bliss to set for tenor, piano and string quartet. Alan Bush wrote an elegiac piece for horn and piano which the composer played with Dennis Brain (who died himself two years later in a car accident). I suggested to Ben that he might consider writing a trio and he came up with the wonderful Sitwell setting *Still Falls the Rain*, his third canticle, for tenor, horn and piano. Michael Tippett said, quite rightly, that, without knowing it, he had sometime previously composed the right piece for the occasion. Noel had played it and recorded it with Peter but at this concert Peter sang it with Ben at the piano. It was the last song of the cycle *The Heart's Assurance*, Sidney Keyes's poem 'Remember Your Lovers': 'Young men drunk with death's unquenchable wisdom. . . . '

The Mewton-Wood memorial concert sets me thinking of a happier occasion when I got Noel to play a duet with Eric Harrison, the slow movement of Stravinsky's Concerto for two pianos without orchestra. This was at a party in May 1947 given one month after Olive and I had got married, and it was given us by Gervase's mother Edith de Peyer at her house overlooking Hampstead Heath. The performers were all friends and they included Phyllis Sellick and her husband Cyril Smith, Kathleen Ferrier and Steuart Wilson, who sang a cantata specially composed for the party by Antony Hopkins, who presided at the piano.

The first time I heard Eric Harrison play it cost me sixpence. It was shortly before the war, and it was also the first time that I went to the ballet at Covent Garden. The company was Colonel de Basil's and from that expensive seat in the gods I saw the three enchanting ballerinas, Tamara Toumanova, Tatiana Riabouchinska and Irina Baronova. My chief interest, however, was to see the new ballet *Paganini* based by Fokine on an idea of Rachmaninov, the composer of the music (*Rhapsody on a Theme of Paganini*).

There had been some publicity about the soloist in the papers. Equity refused a labour permit for the German pianist who had previously worked with the company. Cyril Smith was the only famous pianist in this country who knew the piece but he was otherwise engaged and therefore he had suggested a young pupil of his. And it was this young lad who played the solo that afternoon, Eric Harrison. Memory insists that he took a bow wearing a large muffler but I think memory is wrong. Memory must be recalling a picture of Eric in a newspaper. However he did look awfully young and he did wear enormous spectacles.

The war started and by 1943 I was running the London Philharmonic Arts Club. At one of the record evenings I played Rachmaninov's Piano Concerto No. 3 with the composer playing the solo part. For some reason I was in a tiz-woz and it was only towards the end of side 1 that I realized that something was nastily wrong with the sound. Somehow the speed was wrong, so instead of being played at 78 rpm in D minor, it was going faster and higher with old Rachy sounding more like Art Tatum. As I got up to change the record and, I hoped without drawing attention to it, a man got up at the back of the room. He was obviously trying to say something but no words were coming out of his mouth. I put on side 2, now at the right speed and pitch. The chap at the back flashed a lovely smile and sat down. At the end he came up and I met Eric Harrison.

The reason why no words had come out of his mouth was that he had a king-sized stammer. I scarcely recognized him because the spectacles had gone (and the muffler) and also because the photograph and/or the distance at Covent Garden had not revealed that he had the most cockeyed nose I have ever seen. He had been dropped out of his pram and nobody had seen fit to put it right for the poor chap. Eric was Yorkshire and brimming with affection. He was a lovely bloke, incessantly smoking and drinking coffee. His harmonic sense was very strong, which meant that we liked the same kind of music from Tatum to Medtner. We got on like an h. on f. and I was soon visiting him for duets and records. The house I knew best was in Richmond with two pianos in a room leading out to the garden and his serene wife Diana cooking gorgeous meals.

On the right day Eric could play like a dream, especially virtuoso music like Rachmaninov and Medtner. Sometimes he could also bring off Beethoven's later sonatas. It was this very facility that prevented him sometimes from getting deep enough into the music. And he had that incredible talent that I associate usually with organists of making the best of things. Eric's ear was fantastic; his technique was fabulous, as was his sight-reading; and he could get away with practically anything. The result was that he did not work hard enough at knowing his music from the inside.

In the wartime he would perform incredible feats on some of the dodgy pianos. Once the piano keys refused to come up again but he enlisted the help of a singer in the same programme – she had to pull up the notes while he knocked them down the next bar. Another time he was to play Schubert's Piano Trio in B flat, but the piano was a minor third flat, i.e., when he played a chord of B flat what sounded was a chord of G. Anybody else would have cancelled the concert but not Eric. He transposed the whole damn piece! He was also accident prone. A big chance came – to play the *Paganini Rhapsody* at the opening night of the Proms. Eric got a septic finger, the fourth on his right hand. Cancel? Not on your life. He refingered the right-hand part so as not to use that finger at all, first taking off his bandage so as not to worry anybody. And he didn't tell anybody either.

Sometimes this facility led him to brilliant feats of irresponsibility. When he was taking part in a live broadcast, a *Tuesday Serenade*, a mixture of items for soloists and the BBC Theatre Orchestra, the conductor, Stanford Robinson, calculated that the programme needed an extra item. He asked Eric if he knew Prokofiev's *Prelude* (in C minor, I think). Eric said, 'You mean this one?' and played the opening of it. It was the one and Eric played it that night. Seeing him a day or two later I complimented him on what he had played but also commented that in one or two respects what he had played did not correspond with the printed copy. 'Ah,' stammered Eric, 'that's because I've never seen a printed copy. I was b–b–b–busking it.'

This stammer was curious. It always enhanced what he was saying. It improved the joke he was telling, never impeded it. In this respect Eric resembled Patrick Campbell rather than Billy Budd. The curious thing was that Eric, trying desperately to say, for example, 'Johannes Brahms', could say things at top speed in parenthesis. Thus: 'Johannes B–B–B–B– you know the one I mean, that bugger with the beard – B–B–B– you know, four symphonies, violin concerto and two piano concertos – B–B–B– oh, for God's sake – BRAHMS, man.'

Strange to say, two of the musicians whose art and personalities I love best – and I really mean love – will not, I think, be remembered by their gramophone recordings especially. Sándor Végh has made some good records with his quartet (particularly of late Beethoven) but his solo records do not do him justice – any more than do those of Vlado Perlemuter. Possibly by saying this I may have made enemies of these two friends. It is of course a personal opinion but, for me, the magic, the opening of doors, the joy that I have experienced from the playing of this violinist and this pianist is not to be found on their records.

In trying to make programmes to be broadcast about Sándor and Vlado I have been through Sándor's solo Bach sonatas and I have been through Vlado's early Vox records and his newer Nimbus discs. They all sound good from the technical point of view; the notes are all present and correct; the balance is fine. Can it be the effort of putting down, once and for all time, a definitive version for a record that makes these two special artists too careful? Or is it that you need to see them in the flesh? Or is it that their magic simply eludes the microphone?

I have heard musicians say similar things about other artists. I have even heard it said about artists who have made some good records – Toscanini is a case in point. Some of his records are quite staggeringly marvellous. The *Missa Solemnis*, for example, would certainly be one of my desert island discs.

On the other hand, sorry though I am not to have satisfying records of Végh or Perlie, in a way I can take a certain perverse, selfish pleasure in that mine ears have heard the glory, together with lots of other people who have heard these artists at their best in recitals at Dartington. We think so much of records these days that it does give me a certain pleasure to realize that there are some things you cannot capture. But then again there comes that nagging thought that perhaps the magic would be on the records if the artists had produced the magic in the studio. Certainly Vlado does not always produce the magic in concerts. I have heard him not in the best form. The same is true of Sándor, especially if the occasion is a grand one. Both play better away from capital cities. Perhaps that is it. The less crucial the occasion, the better they play.

What makes their playing so magical, then? Well, Sándor's violin playing has authority, profundity and technical ability, of course, but he also has an extra-special feeling for the violin, in particular for fantasy and colour. Too many musicians, I feel, connect music always with the printed page. The greatest performers always give the impression to me that they have also spent long hours improvising so that they develop a sensory relationship with their instruments that they could never get if they only ever played music that has been written down. Végh's feeling for different colours on the violin is what sets him apart. He will change the sound colour not for the sake of changing it but in order to illuminate the music. Another quality he has is that of seeming to add the dimensions of the voice and the dance to the violin.

Vlado has these qualities too. He has left the printed notes behind him a long time ago. The shape and sound of what he plays are conjured out of his brain and his vast experience. And the experience, off the record at any rate, does not dull what he is playing here and now. Vlado can make the fullest forte without sounding too loud. His tenor thumb playing a tune can fill your soul with gladness. Balance between the hands plays an enormous part here, so does the gradation of the various volumes, the relation of *piano* to *forte*. I think that it is no accident that Vlado – as did also Clifford

Curzon – practises from note to note, from chord to chord. I know that nowadays many pianists practise away from the keyboard but there is surely no substitute for the amount of time that must be spent physically with the keyboard in touch with the fingers.

Incidentally, since I have been bracketing their names together, I must mention that, as Sándor and Vlado were at Dartington at the same time one year, I thought it would be great to get them to do a sonata recital together. Surely it would either be the best recital we had ever had at the SSoM – or the worst. In advance I worked on them both and found that they had played together years ago. Maybe . . . perhaps . . . why not? OK . . . green light. They accepted.

It was an awful evening, quite the worst recital. To start with, both were, by this time, a bit deaf. What I had not reckoned for, though, was that both were deaf in the wrong ear for communication on the platform. Vlado is deaf in the right ear; Sándor in the left. Sándor would stand only on Vlado's right. Alice Végh suggested humorously that we should 'change around whole hall including piano'. I have never been so uncomfortable as that night seated on the platform turning the pages for Vlado. There were occasional passages of solo in the César Franck Sonata that were splendid and the sun truly shone, but there were other passages when they were a couple of bars out, both going their own way. In the artists' room each took me aside and complained about the other. Oh dear! Loyalties were racked that evening but I still think it was a risk worth taking. . . .

The numbers DB 5038–9–40–1–2 bring to my mind the sound of Monteverdi in the famous set of HMV 78 rpm records directed from the piano – and why not the piano if played with such style? – by Nadia Boulanger: the plangent dissonances of the 'Lasciatemi morire'; the gentle pounding bass of the 'Lamento' where one waits for natural to turn flat (just as one does in the final round of the chorus in Stravinsky's *Symphony of Psalms*) – the whole world seems to revolve around the difference between two semitones – the sheer joy and pure happiness of the 'Chiome d'oro', the perfection of the chaconne 'Zefiro torna' – and again that feeling of the earth moving when in the middle section G major turns quite simply to E major. Apart from the charm of Princesse de Polignac's incredibly French soprano the pleasure of 'Zefiro' and 'Chiome' derives from the voices of the two tenors Paul Derenne and Hugues Cuénod. There is such a youthful magic about those ever so slightly quivering vibrant young voices that I developed a picture in my mind of their owners: they were quite small in stature and dressed in light, vertically striped blazers with boaters in their hands and bow ties at their throats. If they could dance they would be the young men in the 'Popular Song' of the ballet *Façade*.

One day I saw that a concert to take place in the Victoria and Albert Museum would contains duets sung by Peter Pears and . . . Hugues Cuénod. I sat there waiting for Cuénod to come on to the platform, still expecting somebody small and striped. Wrong. Hugues is tall, slim and *distingué*, with a longish bony face not unlike a younger version of Frank Martin (whom I had met when Morley College had put on the first British performance of *Le vin herbé*). Cuénod was not French but, like Martin, Swiss. But Hugues had a Scottish grandmother and was even, as I saw later at Glyndebourne, entitled to wear tartan, which he did, made into a dinner jacket.

I went round after the V. & A. concert and invited him to come and sing at Dartington, which he did for four years from 1953 to 1956. Hugues is a genuine aristocrat, amusing and amused, laughing with his eyes, and with that upper lip slightly overflowing the lower one. His manners are impeccable. My girlfriend at that time, Angela, used to say that he was the only person who never took advantage of his height and her tininess to look over her shoulder at Glyndebourne to see who else was in the offing.

At Glyndebourne I think his first role was as Sellem the Auctioneer, in which we admired, as with his Don Basilio, how he used to splay his long legs so comically and inimitably. But then one day when I stayed at Merton House, in Ringmer, where so many singers stayed during the summer season, I went into the kitchen where Hugues was boiling eggs for us and at the stove he was using exactly the same comic stance as in the opera. As so often with actors it is the same things they do in private life that they make such effective use of on the stage.

Hugues sang at Dartington in that curious Beethoven cantata *Der glorreiche Augenblick* that Hermann Scherchen 'discovered' and gave several concert outings to. What a strange man Scherchen was! I think he frightened me even more than Beecham did. He was the living personification of the bullying Prussian, tight-lipped, his hair brushed straight back. He came off after the Beethoven performance into the dressing room in a fearful paddy shouting, 'Schweinerei.' And yet I rarely saw him in a temper. It was the potential that I feared – he was like a ticking bomb.

He was a wonderful musician but he nearly always spoiled the performance because he antagonized his forces. He first came to the SSoM to conduct an orchestra made up of ex-members of the National Youth Orchestra. The first concert was one of the best we ever had at Dartington – an orchestration of Bach's *Die Kunst der Fuge*.

By the time of the second concert Scherchen had begun to be disliked and by the third he was hated. And yet he knew his music and he wrote one of the best books ever on conducting. He taught well too. He gave some talks at Dartington, and they were fascinating. He started the first by whistling something and asking the audience what it was. Nobody uttered so he pointed at me directly. Truthfully I said that I thought that he was whistling a scale that included quarter-tones. That unfortunately insulted him because he thought he was in tune. It was the enigmatic scale from one of Verdi's *Pezzi Sacri*.

One day he threatened to cancel the performance. He was staying a few hundred yards away from the main building at Dartington and insisted that Etain Kabraji, the hostess there, find me. I was out for the afternoon, she told him. Find him, he commanded. Was it something she could help with? No, it was something he could not possibly discuss with a woman. When I got back I rushed over to see him, what on earth could be wrong? It turned out that he had bust his braces. I found it curious that Scherchen, who had been married six times to five women (he had a second go at one of them), was too prudish to discuss braces with a girl.

Scherchen, I decided eventually was 90 per cent devil and 10 per cent angel, but the wiring of his make-up had a tendency to fuse. He was better teaching a student or a third-rate orchestra than he was with a really good orchestra – something to do with an inferiority complex, I suppose. (Some of the best Beethoven symphonies I ever heard were conducted by him in Lugano with the Radio-Svizzera Orchestra there – not a world-shaker of a band.)

Years later I went over one afternoon from Cureglia, where I was working, to Scherchen's house and electronic workshop at

Gravesano. One of the things I wanted to see was a room that had been constructed entirely without resonance, a room that was completely 'dead' acoustically. It felt dead physically too – very nasty. This visit was part of an official trip organized by some local Lugano music society. But Scherchen had obviously forgotten all about it. We were kept hanging about in the rain outside for about half an hour while he, we guessed, got out of bed and shaved. I am not sure about the bed part of it but the shaving bit was inescapable because when he emerged, not apologizing because it was a 90 per cent day, he had seven or eight bits of cotton wool dotted about his face from which blood was seeping. Nobody referred to this. He addressed us in macaronic Italian with a frequent use of a word that he imagined was Italian. I still use it myself sometimes: *malheureuseamente*.

Another word he used a lot, as did many Germans in the thirties and forties, was 'quasi', always pronounced 'kvazi'. It quasi gets by in German but it tends to sound silly in English. I went once to Hammersmith Town Hall which the BBC were using for a broadcast by the LSO in which Scherchen was to conduct Symphony No. 6 by the Bavarian composer Karl Amadeus Hartmann. It was a very busy score with lots of percussion, a big orchestra including – if memory serves right – four pianos and triple woodwind, maybe quadruple even. During a break in rehearsal everybody had left the stage except for Scherchen and Steve Trier, who was going over some tricky bass-clarinet passages. The conductor wandered by Steve's desk, listened for a moment or two and then said, 'This piece is quasi very difficult . . . ja, and in some places quasi impossible.'

(16)

Broadcasting Domestically

How to break into broadcasting? I noticed that if there was a new work coming up in a *Wednesday Symphony Concert*, the BBC series of public concerts, there would usually be a talk about the composer or the work in question the preceding Sunday morning on *Music Magazine*. During the 1949–50 season there was to be the first British performance of Stravinsky's ballet *Orpheus*. Nadia Boulanger had taken a small class of us through the newly published score of the work at the summer school at Bryanston. She had played bits of it and I had been fired with enthusiasm.

I had listened most Sunday mornings to *Music Mag* and knew that the programme worked more or less to a formula: three scripted items of approximately a quarter of an hour each. The script was further broken down into units of two or three minutes' talk interspersed with musical illustrations, either recorded or played 'live'. I wrote my script on *Orpheus* and sent it in to the editors, Anna Instone and her husband Julian Herbage.

Anna was head of the gramophone department of the BBC. She was dark-haired and handsome in a heavy Jewish manner. She had a good brain and would have been a good broadcaster if she had not been afflicted with a powerful stammer. She could say 'Julian' quite easily but, for some reason, always addressed him as 'P–p–p –poppet', with the result that the pair of them were always known as the Poppets. Julian had been on the music staff of the Beeb from 1927 to 1944, and was known to the public as a musicologist (in particular for his work on *Messiah* – he made the first modern 'clean' score). His work for the Beeb included planning the Proms as long as Sir Henry Wood was the chief conductor of the series that he had founded. He later became a free-lance but still continued to work on the Proms until William Glock took over the planning, relieving Julian of his job. Even before this it was obvious that the Poppets had no love for William and I had to play down my connections with him.

Julian was fairly nervous and a bit ferrety in behaviour, and had a habit of tugging anxiously at his beard. With rare exceptions he was not a good broadcaster, sounding – it was all 'live' in those times – as if he were going to stumble at any moment. His lack of confidence made most contributors sound better than him but his style was contagious to new broadcasters. However, when my script for *Orpheus* arrived he was only co-editor. Julian didn't take over as linkman until Alec Robertson retired in 1952.

The salutary feature of Alec's broadcasting manner was that he fluffed like anything but with such confidence that his stumbles actually enhanced his work. He was a born communicator despite also a very slightly blurred delivery that made him sound as though he had a plum in his mouth.

Julian and Anna seemed to like my script. I got through it reasonably well but nobody gave me any production. They told me years later that they were slightly frightened by me, although they were both about twice my age and I was an absolute nobody. It was about four years later that Anna did give me some production. Just before the red light came on she flicked down the intercom and said, 'John, dear, s–s–s–s–s–smile.' That was good advice – but it was the only hint she ever gave me. Julian never said anything.

When Julian became the linkman we contributors soon came to notice that anything interesting in our first paragraph Julian would swipe and use himself, which always made our own first words rather feeble, until we learned to write the beginning of a script with Julian's maraudings in mind. His lack of confidence meant that it was a mistake for us to know more than he did. If you wanted another date a certain amount of sucking up to the Poppets was advisable, like slaving across to the canteen to fetch the coffee. (Donald Mitchell once nearly killed himself on the stairs carrying a tray.)

Also it didn't do to fight too hard for some pearl in your script, or some clinching illustration, even when you thought that somebody else's contribution, or Julian's links, would be better meat for the cutting knife. The great thing was to avoid Anna labelling you as 'd–d–difficult'. Too many applications of *that* adjective and you were off the little list. Likewise it was a good thing to hang about after the transmission to go and have a drink with the Poppets.

The drill was that you had to deliver your script by about the beginning of the week but the only person who would look at it was the secretary who would retype it into production formula. When you sent in the script, you would also indicate which records you would be using, having got those out of the gram library and worked on them. On the Saturday morning there would be a rehearsal. First on was the best as otherwise you could hang about for half an hour or more if the previous speaker needed more time to get his or her item rehearsed. It was important – and this was a part I was good at – to time your record illustrations accurately, be prepared for excerpts to be lengthened or, more likely, shortened, and to know the whereabouts of each excerpt on each record.

On Sunday morning there would be a straight run-through, as opposed to the Saturday 'stagger-through'. Contributors would be discouraged from walking into the producer's cubicle but there was a terrible temptation to chatter in the studio. Very often it was a rare chance to talk to colleagues like Martin Cooper (*Telegraph*, in those days), William Mann (*The Times*), John Warrack (also *Telegraph*), Colin Mason (*Guardian*) and many others. Many non-critics took part, too.

In the cubicle would be Anna, with cigarette; Julian or Alec or both; one balancer whose job was to place the mikes and generally act as technical producer, and another operator with the crucial job of putting on the records. If the disc operator was new or too hard-pressed or flustered by Anna, having decided that he or she was being 'd–d–d–difficult', then you could have a right mess on your hands. I was once doing a piece on Alan Rawsthorne's Piano Concerto No. 2 and the girl on grams slipped a disc, so to speak, and there was the danger of a total balls-up, because Julian was at the mike table thinking about his next collection of stumble-fodder, Anna was obliviously lighting a cigarette and the two operators were chatting. Quite fun that was – fairly easily dealt with, but it meant improvising on a live broadcast, which was unusual in those days when everything was scripted.

In fact, everything being scripted was a factor in the programme getting boring from time to time. Julian and Anna seemed, to most of us regulars, to take a fairly easy way out most of the time. The same contributors were used time and again, and when a certain work or composer came up always the most obvious person or expert on that subject was used. Most of the time, yes, but occasionally some big celebrity would be used, like Beecham, and then the Poppets would pull their fingers out and put on a very good show.

In those days the gramophone department of the BBC was responsible for many more presented programmes of serious music than now, particularly on the Home Service and the World Service. Once Anna, the Mother Superior, approved of my work then quite a lot of other dates came my way, so I was often broadcasting two or three times a month. Philip Hope-Wallace, Harold Rosenthal, Scott Goddard, Spike Hughes, David Franklin, Martin Cooper, Sidney Harrison, and then later John Warrack and Andrew Porter would be doing series of half-a-dozen programmes based on some idea like 'Times of Day', 'Ports of Call', or something on those lines, or just some sessions on a certain composer. My familiarity with the recorded repertoire was an advantage and I have always enjoyed planning programmes. Only once was I given the accolade of a Third Programme broadcast and that was for an illustrated talk on Virgil Thomson's opera *Four Saints in Three Acts*.

In those days talks producers took themselves and their jobs very seriously. They would bone up on the subject the speaker was talking about until it often seemed as if they should be giving the talk. The script was weighed very carefully in advance: 'i's were dotted and 't's crossed; every comma was important – for all the world as though it were being printed and not spoken.

Walter Todds was at that time on the way to becoming a friend but he was also very Eng. Litt. – good fun off duty, a bon viveur, but inclined to be pedantic on the job. We had a two and a half hour rehearsal with a half-hour break before live transmission. Walter really put me through the mangle at rehearsal, so much so that we encroached well into the half-hour break. I kept on saying to him, 'Walter, don't forget, I simply must go to the loo before transmission.'

'So you shall, dear boy, but we must first do something about that floating participle on page twelve and while we're about it just look at page fourteen. . . .'

And so it went on until finally, at three minutes to the hour, I had to run for the loo. I came back into the studio with my trousers still round my knees just as the red light started to flash. After it was all over, 'Well, jolly good, Johnnie, but you sounded curiously breathless on page one. . . .'

My first television was a film made in 1961 about Paul Tortelier for *Monitor*. Humphrey Burton was the director and the plan was to go to Paris with a crew to interview the cellist, to see him in his flat among his family and also to shoot him conducting an orchestra of twenty-four cellists, led by Maude (Mrs T.) playing an instrumental version of his *Hymn for the United Nations*.

I was the new boy but Humphrey, the old boy in telly, did not come up with any scheme and allowed me to suggest one and also the musical illustrations. We chewed the plan around and it worked. The new medium was fascinating although the long periods of waiting for the technical boys to work out the lighting were tedious. Tortelier proved himself an actor, able to repeat his answers to my questions again and again with the same amount of sincerity and spontaneity. The children were delightful. I adored Maude, whom I always referred to as 'la petite ange', mistakenly convinced that so feminine a being as an angel had to be of the female gender in French. Tortelier is a *naïf* when it comes to politics and humanism. His hymn sounded succulently sonorous on all those cellos even though its style is more akin to that of Donald Swann than to similar appeals for brotherhood by Beethoven.

My next TV foray was disastrous, an interview with the great violinist, Nathan Milstein. The thing about interviews is that they must appear to be spontaneous. The trouble with some TV producers is that they always want everything rehearsed.

'Couldn't I ask other questions in the rehearsal?'

'No, dear, only the ones you are going to ask in the transmission because we want to know the length roughly and get the right angles.'

Milstein was talkative at rehearsal but when it came to the show he cut all his answers down to half a sentence because he was bored and he had already said it all before to me. I wasn't helped either by being out of shot and, even worse, with no eyeline to him as two close cameras were in the way. It was my last TV for a long time, until . . . .

Until I happened to write to John Culshaw, then boss of BBC Television music. BBC2 had a magazine programme called *Music Now* which they were committed to for at least another season; but it had been going wrong. William Fitzwater had been the editor. He was a brilliant, imaginative, forward-looking director, but he had taken the selfless course of not directing any of the items, excepting some of the studio bits, instead sticking to producing – in the sense of commissioning and doing editorial work. Which he was not the right man for. Bill was an original. I came in on the last programme of his series, summed up the situation and asked Bill if he would stay on and let me be the editor while he directed some items.

We had struck up enough rapport for him to agree and for the first of the new series, transmitted on 27 September 1970, which I introduced as well as fronted, Bill produced a superb 35-minute film of the Academy of St Martin-in-the-Fields with Neville Marriner. The orchestra was performing at Bruges in the Flanders Festival. Bill went over to recce and found out that there was a medieval carnival taking place at the same time as the Academy was in Bruges. Bingo! He intercut the two and I interviewed Neville on a barge on the canals. Game, set and match. It was a wonderful start and we got rave reviews. The all-important viewing figures started to snake up.

Bill made some more interesting films and we varied the rest of the programme with more conventional items: interviews, Janet Baker singing, Walter Legge talking about Dinu Lipatti, Michael Tippett talking about his music at Avebury – that sort of thing. It worked quite well despite those who sneered that it was just radio with pictures.

Our title got confused with the generic title *Music on 2* however and John Culshaw suggested that we should change our name after one year. So we called it *Counterpoint* for the second season and the figures immediately went down to a few measly hundreds of thousands. Then someone had the idea of incorporating *Counterpoint* into a new arts programme for the following year, so my baby went down the plughole and I found myself a kind of music correspondent in this new *Full House*.

I stuck *Full House* for a year then quit. It was soul-destroying. It wasn't so bad for me being free lance, but worse for the regular BBC types because they could not quit. Quite a good team had been assembled but the programmes suffered from the story-board committee process, the endless meetings of the twenty or more various art-form representatives, who were mostly trendy blown-by-the-wind long hairs, all smoking madly and contradicting each other interminably. Those miserable meetings were redeemed by the presence of one or two kindred spirits, chief among them the young, ebullient, corn-haired, chubby and very bright director Vernon Lawrence. We found we had both been at Dulwich College – in different centuries as he was always pointing out – and struck up a friendship.

In spite of my asking for discretion, it wasn't young Vern's fault that, immediately after Yvonne Loriod and Olivier Messiaen had played on two pianos one of his *Visions de l'Amen*, a hat-check girl wearing next to nothing came on to make an announcement while applause for the music was still dying down. The two page-turners and I tried to make a body shield so that Messiaen should not see this insulting juxtaposition but, to our surprise and Yvonne's amusement, the rather small Messiaen jumped up and down repeatedly in order to try and see the girl over our shoulders. Oh, *garçon*!

Having a wider audience noticing what I was doing was pleasant, of course, but after radio there were so many strands of television that either were uncontrollable or, at any rate I was told, were uncontrollable. In the magazine, for example, my personal assistants spent most of their time telling me that such-and-such a thing could not be done. 'You're not in radio now,' they would say, witheringly. Half the time they were right. Certain things were, for instance, against the union rules, but a lot of things could be done, simply by reversing some recent tradition. And that is one of the troubles with working in television. So many habits are quickly formed and in no time become Holy Writ in the White City. Everybody there speaks a special language, mostly consisting of initials and acronyms, and anything that happens outside the television screens and studios is beyond their ken or their wish to ken.

The Music Department at BBC Television was a rum outfit. 'Department for televising programmes connected with music' would be a more accurate designation. The brilliant Decca music man John Culshaw lost his shine at the BBC. His chief interest seemed to be in getting back to the recording industry and producing his own not very good TV programmes. It was a joke at the weekly meetings that he seemed to see only about one programme in six that the department put out. He was always out that night or his set was on the blink.

Some very good directors were let go from the Beeb – like Bill Fitzwater who returned home to Australia – while some others were allowed to produce only one show a year. Those who produced most shows seemed to me to be unmusical. They spent all their time organizing or keeping up with the hardware, i.e., the new technical developments. Their shows proclaimed their lack of musicality in the way that shots were always chosen for visual effect, never to enhance the musical effect. I never saw any of them at a concert or an opera.

The most impressive feature of working in television was the number of young committed technicians with real talent, and standards that transcended union or other restrictions. These were the designers, video and film editors and some of the lighting and sound people. The gulf between the good film/video editors and the bad ones was unbelievable, as were the improvements that the good ones could make to the final result. As an example of perseverance beyond the call of duty, I remember one night when Bill Fitzwater was video-editing and he had said that it might take until midnight. I was then editor (in the sense of being responsible for the series) and working on another project in the early evening but I resolved to go along later in case they needed cheering up.

In fact we were there right up to nine the next morning with another shift about to come in. Bill was working with his assistant and the BBC video editor was Peter Francis, one of these technicians I am talking about. By 5 a.m. we were all pie-eyed with fatigue and even Bill was saying, 'OK, sport, I think that one will do.' Whereat Peter would say, 'It's not 100 per cent, Bill. I think you might regret that in the morning. Mind if I have one more crack at it?' And the next time it was perfect. These are the local heroes, the ones that make television, once in a while, a joy to behold.

After my year with *Full House* I made a few 60-minute documentaries: one on the Amadeus Quartet; one on Holst, with his daughter Imogen; a celebrity birthday portrait on Walton (in which I persuaded Hans Werner Henze to write a *pièce d'occasion*, in fact one of his most pleasant works, a 2-minute *Stückchen* for a few instruments including, I recall, an ocarina part played by the lovely Judith Pearce) and, best of all I thought, one on Poulenc, for the tenth anniversary of his death in 1963. My director on this last was Denis Moriarty, with whom I had worked very happily on *Music Now*. We went to Paris, filmed Georges Auric and Jacques Février playing a duet at one piano and I did an interview with Darius Milhaud.

I had done a chat for radio once with Milhaud and he had been very snappy and slappy. Perhaps he had been feeling ill. I had to ask him about some late works he was performing/conducting with orchestra at Maida Vale for Radio 3. His answers were one sentence long, so, running out of steam a bit, I asked him whether the longer movements were based on sonata form. 'There is no such thing as sonata form, so that is a very silly question.' Ouch! Anyway, in Paris Milhaud was quite different, friendly and touching on the television film about his old friend Poulenc. 'You know that Francis was a compulsive telephonist. And now when I am in Paris and I hear the telephone ring, I always think that it will be Francis. But it never is and that makes me always very sad. I loved him like a brother.'

By now Milhaud himself had not long to live. He had been so nice at the interview that I asked him if I could get him anything from England. He said that he was fascinated by the Thomas Tallis Motet in Forty Parts and would like to have a score of it. I sent it to him and received a postcard of thanks from him just a few weeks before he died in 1974.

From Paris Denis and our film crew went to Rocamadour to film the church of the Black Madonna where Poulenc was inspired to write his first religious work, after the death of a great friend beheaded in a motor accident. We also filmed in the grounds and house that Poulenc had owned near Vouvray, on the banks of the Loire.

We took with us Pierre Bernac who had a wonderful partnership with Poulenc for many years – Bernac a high baritone, Poulenc at the piano. For their concerts Poulenc wrote scores of songs and, since Poulenc was queer, most people have assumed that theirs was a relationship akin to that of Pears and Britten. Wrong. But before I had got around to observing that in Poulenc's voluminous correspondence Bernac was always addressed in the second person plural – unlike most of his correspondents – I naturally wanted Bernac to talk about their relationship. The camera rolled, we talked, I probed gently, Bernac parried. Eventually while the film magazine was being reloaded, Bernac looked round furtively and then said in his well-produced voice, 'I cannot discuss this matter too frankly for your programme. You see, Poulenc was a *homosexual.*'

It was Denis's charming conceit to get Georgina Parkinson from the Royal Ballet out for a day with us, to dress her up as the pageboy in blue velvet jacket and to get her to dance the *Adagietto* from *Les Biches* actually in the hall of Poulenc's own house while in the next room his old friend Jacques Février played the music in the famous piano arrangement. Georgina was superb and it was touching to see how the old pianist fell in love with the young ballerina.

It was my conceit to contrast the little formal garden of Poulenc's house with the grand formal garden and the château of nearby Chenonçeaux, using music of the *Concert champêtre* for harpsichord to accompany the former, and the Organ Concerto for the latter.

Television at least has the resources to enable one to do something worthwhile and stimulating like this Poulenc programme. It got good notices and drew an enthusiastic letter from Humphrey Burton who was at that time working with commercial television. Shortly after this Culshaw resigned from the Beeb and Humphrey came to the Corporation, much to my joy, because Humphrey was so appreciative about my TV work that I thought he would give me plenty of jobs. It turned out to be quite the reverse. For some reason I didn't get any more dates at all from the Music Department, and I subsequently heard from one former colleague in the department that my name was put on the Index at a weekly meeting. Ah well, back to the old radio drawing board!

Like the Lord, the BBC giveth and the BBC taketh away, as I have found many times. And if there is a barney, then the Corporation closes ranks. And if an individual questions authority, Auntie becomes severe. The BBC has been both generous and harsh with me. The harshness occurred when, after I had been running *The Week Ahead*, later rejigged as *Music Now* on Radio 3 for seven years as a successful magazine programme, my producers took advantage of the appointment of a new Controller, Ian MacIntyre, to minimize the extent of my involvement in the programme. I was given the push and various new presenters were put in. I organized some protests, supported by rave reviews in *The Times*, but such protests are useless and I have not been forgiven in those quarters. (And *Music Now* soon died.)

However, I am still grateful to the BBC for what it does by and large, and for what it has done for me. I might be selling matches otherwise. Meanwhile *My Music* continues on television and radio (touch wood!) and the BBC External Services give me work continually. Recently the BBC Transcription Service gave me lunch to celebrate the 300th edition of the quasi-monthly programme I do for them under the title *Talking About Music*, rather a confusing title in Britain since Antony Hopkins has been using it longer than Transcription. However the choice of title was Malcolm Frost's, not mine – apologies nevertheless to Tony!

I am very happy with my Transcription producer Betty Jowitt. We recently went on a promotion tour together in North America and are still good friends! For some years now I have done a weekly magazine programme for BBC World Service called *Music Now* (titles get somewhat inbred in the BBC), first under the benign hand of Julian Budden, that supreme Verdi scholar, and latterly with Piers Burton-Page who is so talented that I am sure he will go on to tasks (even) greater than being Music Director of BBC World Service. But for more about the External Services see a later chapter.

(17)

Singing

The singing began in 1959 at the summer school. Professor Frederick Husler came to Dartington to give a class and lectures, and he brought with him his assistant, the Hon. Yvonne Rodd-Marling. Husler had trained for opera but gave up being a singer when still a young man because he developed a gift for teaching and a distaste for public performing. He spoke little English and Yvonne did the preliminary liaison work. I don't think that William Glock had previously met either of them. The recommendation came from Priaulx Rainier, an old friend of Yvonne's.

From the start Yvonne managed to invest Husler with an aura of fame and an almost magical key to the mystery of singing. Yvonne made more preliminary fuss about Husler than any agent, accompanist or relative had ever made before about a teacher or artist at the summer school. The rooms must be this and that and, above all, must have connecting doors. It all caused a mental raising of eyebrows with myself and Bee Musson.

It was arranged that Husler should bring with him a quartet of singers trained by him who would demonstrate not only in his classes but also, in a more general sense, in the end-of-week choral concert when they would sing the solos in a Mozart or Haydn Mass. They were an international bunch: Marilyn Tyler, the soprano, was Rumanian–Jewish = American, attractive, something of a prima donna, a good raconteuse and witty; Pamela Bowden, English, for many years the organizer for the Incorporated Society of Musicians after a good career as a mezzo-soprano; Naan Pöld, a Finnish light tenor; and Robert Titze, a German baritone with a smallish voice but great intelligence and skill, and his own way of speaking English – he didn't clean his teeth, he 'washed his bitings'.

Classes began but all the students attending were girls. Were there no men, asked the Prof? In Germany, Husler is known, Yvonne put in quickly, as the tenor maker. I said I would try and find some male students but there were none to be found. The Prof expressed disappointment. This was my big chance and I asked if I could have a lesson. Was I trained, he asked. No. Why?

I explained that in the old Morley College days I had got interested in singing, sang in the choir, imitated Peter Pears and Alfred Deller and even, one time, sang some eight bars of a counter-tenor duet in a Purcell verse anthem, in a broadcast conducted by Michael Tippett. I had started off as a bass in the choir but latterly had discovered that I could manage tenor parts more easily. During my many weekend visits to the pianist Noel Mewton-Wood we had often bashed through works like Tippett's *Boyhood's End* and one or two of Britten's song-cycles. At one time I had thought of having lessons but when I asked singers like Peter Pears or Alfred Deller or Joan Cross they gave names of teachers that, on cross-checking, the others considered voice-killers. So I dropped the idea.

I had my session with Husler and he got quite excited, called Yvonne in, and she got excited too. 'You could be heldentenor,' he pronounced, but with the proviso, 'You would have to come to work with me in Germany for a trial period to make sure.' So then *I* got quite excited too. Yvonne eagerly told William Glock. 'He'll never be any good,' he said, brutally if prophetically – but then William tended to think that anything that tampered with the future of the summer school was treachery and should therefore be discouraged. Perhaps that is why he said it.

After that year's Dartington was over I went back to London and thought about it all, delighted at the prospect of going to the other side of the footlights and having a shot. Knowing so many artists I wanted to be one of them, and if my voice did miraculously change from a fifteenth carbon copy of Peter Pears to heldentenor that would be terrific – and quids-in too. The world was always short of this species of robust tenor. But was I too old, at thirty-seven, to start a full-time singing career? There *had* been cases in the past of singers starting that late – though never of course of instrument-alists, especially string or keyboard players, where the fingers have to begin to develop the necessary technical flexibility in single-figure age, at the latest in early teens. On the other hand, how strong was my determination? Obviously not really strong enough, otherwise I would have found a teacher before now.

Sometimes people come to me for advice. Should they take up music? Should they give up their jobs and become craftsmen? Should they get married? My advice has always been that if *not* doing whatever it is, is really going to make their lives miserable, then do it. Otherwise, don't touch it. In my own case I didn't ask myself the question. As with marriage, alas, I went ahead on the same basis. Give it a whirl and if it doesn't work, then back to the old drawing board. I could always go back to another job on the safer side of the footlights.

I went over for three weeks to Husler in Germany for a voice trial and he gave me the green light. Therefore I went to discuss matters with Malcolm Frost, Head of BBC Transcription Service, with whom I then had a two-days-a-week job as his own personal consultant on music matters – since he did not trust his own music man, the composer Ivor Walsworth.

Malcolm generously allowed me to do my two days in week A on Monday and Tuesday, then I took the night ferry to the Hook of Holland, went to Husler in Germany, spent Wednesday to Wednesday having lessons every day except Sunday, and then came back home to do Thursday and Friday at the Beeb in week B. I came quite to like that journey. The Harwich–Hook night boat was full up only the very first time I went, so full in fact that on that occasion I shared a cabin with three Indians some of whose feet produced an amazingly nasty pong. At six in the morning one staggered on to the station platform at the Hook to find two trains at the ready: the posh, elegantly blue, *Rheingold* and the more common dull grey-green one that took me through the Nethers into Germany as far as Wunsdorf where Yvonne, by now a firm friend, was waiting to collect me in her old green Ford.

At first I wondered why so fastidious a person as Yvonne had such a filthy mud-bespattered car. When we got to Steinhude, three-quarters of an hour later, I realized why. The last mile of the journey off the main road from the dreary village down to the lakeside where the Huslers lived took us along unmade roads and I never saw these tracks, even in summer, without deep puddles in the midst of the nastiest mud in Europe.

The Husler residence was a wooden summer house, ferociously cold in winter, without central heating. In each room there were stoves which the elderly Frau Professor (yes, we went in for those cumbersome un-Salic methods of address that the Germans cultivate) laboriously tended, but it was rare for more than one room in the house to be warm. You could bet your bottom Mark that the warmest place in the house would be occupied by Farida, the apple of the Frau Professor's eye, a large Hungarian shepherd dog, quite white and quite stupid.

If the Professor was such a famous teacher, what was he doing in this neck of the muddy woods? Well, it seemed that during his heyday between the two wars as a fashionable teacher in Berlin — pupils came in one door and departed through another so that the celebrated singers should not meet each other or give away that they were having lessons — Husler had decided that he must have a summer house away from the madding crowd (he had a Garbo complex) and he found this house hundreds of miles away from Berlin in the heart of Westphalia, where the pigs look like the people and vice versa.

Steinhude-Meer was a local beauty spot, famous for the eels that were abundant — live in the lake and dead in the shops. In the middle of the water was an island where there had once been a famous chocolate factory. Steinhude was obviously a cooler spot than Berlin in a war and Husler had stayed here unmolested — he had been born in America of Swiss parents and had fortunately retained his Swiss passport — and after World War II he had become professor of singing at Detmold Academy not too far away, spending every third week during termtimes there, but coming back afterwards to Steinhude.

On our side of the lake the rushes grew high with channels between. In a rowing boat you could imagine yourself in some jungle swamp. In colder weather the lake froze over which made for good sport but it never froze solid, so the eels flourished below, emerging in the thaws. Alas, we students ate them rarely because we were poor.

Most of the students lived up on the made-up road near the village in a guest house but Yvonne had arranged for me to stay at another, much smaller establishment, where I was the only guest during the winter months, run by a middle-aged couple with an enormous floppy male puppy, a Tibetan wolfhound I think, which was already twice the size of Farida – and she was as large as any normal large dog. My room had a balcony overlooking the rushes and the lake beyond, so I spent many happy breakfasts reading and watching the water birds, enjoying the quietness and solitude. The event of the week was my bath. I discovered that in this part of Germany it would be considered unreasonable in a guest house to bath more frequently; and indeed preparations for the event took several hours.

Intention of bathing had to be stated the night before and throughout the day itself confirmation was sought: 'Heute abend, ja?' In my room itself there was only a basin without hot water (in a very up-to-date West German house in the late fifties!) so goodness knows how the water for the bath was prepared! The scheduled hour for the big dip was nine o'clock in the evening but it was never ready until at least an hour later. And what was in the bath, when all was said and done and prepared, was some four inches of what looked like brown Windsor soup frothing with Badedas foam. The event was still topical the following day: 'War schön, nicht's wahr?'

Two or three times per week I would eat with the Huslers – Frederick and Marion were their names – and Yvonne. Otherwise I took my lunches and high teas up at the student guest house. Some of the students fed themselves in their rooms but there were usually anything from two to six of us at table. It was friendly and there were often invitations to a drink afterwards in the evenings but, apart from a special friendship with Joy Mammen, the Australian soprano, and Pieter van der Stolk, the Dutch baritone, who later married each other, I found that the conversations tended to get too local tittle-tattley or fixed on the state and health of their throats with all that entailed, or about how much anything and everything cost. This pricing was an especial obsession of the Germans. Since most of us had never tasted success this was understandable, but it was boring. Half of them were down-to-earth, the other half lived in a fantasy world.

A lot of the time, too, was spent in the Professor's waiting room. Crazily, there was no timetable. Everybody waited and when one lesson finished the Professor would come in and call out a name. Sometimes we would have a singabout up at the guest house but down at the Prof's there was no music-making, no weekly house concert. In fact we were discouraged from singing on our own in case we ruined the effects of our lessons. These lessons were strenuous. For ten or fifteen minutes at the most we arpeggioed or scaled up and down, attacking variously certain notes. Once a week perhaps he would ask me to sing something, an *aria antica* usually or a Mozart concert aria.

Husler had his own views on training voices, a method I suppose it would be called, and he wrote a hefty book on the subject. Maybe it is the reason why I never made it as a singer, but I never saw that his method differed all that much from other teachers whose lessons I have occasionally attended. Husler had studied the physiological aspects of the voice, however, and his teaching was sensible and without gimmickry, though I could never see how a quarter of an hour a day for three, four or five years was going to build anyone's voice. Imagine, say, training a horn player that way. So, why did I continue to study with Husler for over four years? Partly because he was a man with charisma and partly because he was the only man who ever said I could be a heldentenor. And partly, perhaps, because within me there was a reluctance to being taught except when I found a real teacher like Husler – like my French master at prep school, like my Latin master at Dulwich – who had tremendous authority and was something of a father figure.

The lessons at Steinhude took place in a studio, a shack apart from the house. The heating was never quite adequate but there was a small grand piano and, since neither the Professor nor Yvonne could play as an accompanist, I played on the few occasions when one was needed – perhaps when an ex-pupil or non-student would come for a refresher lesson and then return to his or her opera house in Germany. Sometimes a singer would come from further afield, like Heather Harper, Marilyn Tyler, or David Kelly.

The star ex-pupil, however, held up to us as the supreme exponent of the Husler teaching, was Sándor Konya, a Hungarian tenor who appeared a few times at most of the great opera houses of the world, including the New York Metropolitan and Covent Garden, where I remember him singing the part of Calaf in *Turandot*. In fact he was on the edge of the Big Time, not quite good enough or astute enough to be taken up by the recording companies, for example. Konya was not a particularly good actor or musician and his voice, though beautifully produced, did not have sufficient guts or personality to warrant his large fee in the world market for very long.

In Germany Yvonne was not Husler's co-teacher. She taught only at the weekends, perhaps one of us regulars, maybe someone from outside the student circus. She lived most of the time that I went to Steinhude in a rather small hut in the garden with minimal heating and comfort. Her special task was translating Husler's magnum opus from German into English. Her fidelity to the original was such that she had made a completely unreadable translation. For several months I went over the translation with her and we argued about every word, plus all the punctuation: me trying desperately to produce something that would not be laughed out of countenance because of its grotesque Teutonic clumsiness; Yvonne trying to produce the feeling of the original text because it was like Holy Writ to her, the sense of which she knew a hundred times more about than I did.

Yvonne's devotion to Husler was 100 per cent. She had met him in Berlin in the thirties and presumably fallen in love with him. Yvonne had been an actress and somehow illness had shattered her voice. Having discovered the Prof she had gone to Berlin to live, giving up, so we understood, her husband and two sons to do so. After the Second World War she had gone out to Germany to try to find Husler again and, having found him, stayed. It seemed as if, to Husler and Marion, Yvonne was the girl who came for the weekend and remained forever.

Had the love of the English girl been returned, recognized even, let alone consummated? Who could tell? We students, friends and even relatives could not. All we could do was to piece together, as best we could, an enigmatic relationship. Yvonne lived in a way that was romantic, heroic even, but vague. She abased herself like a saint. As thin as a rake and often not well, she lived in conditions that would have killed a person without her faith and determination and – love for Husler.

Yvonne had a truly noble side to her. She would do anything for a friend. I am convinced that if I had rung her up and asked her to rescue me from prison, say, she would have done it, or really risked a lot to try to do so, without questioning whether or not I deserved my fate. And of how many of one's friends could one say that? But, on the other hand, it was awfully difficult to get a straight answer from Yvonne about most everyday questions. She lived for Husler and for her friends, and rather in the past.

According to Yvonne, her friends and relatives were the best in the field. She built them up into gods and paragons, just as she built up the voices and reputations of Husler's pupils. Questions such as, if so-and-so was so perfect why hadn't he or she made the grade, were swept aside with the implication that even to ask was disloyal, unworthy or uncomprehending. Her father had been an ambassador and while Yvonne pooh-poohed the idea of grandeur and snobbery, she clearly revelled in it all.

Husler was a well-built man, with a reputation as a mountaineer and a botanist. He knew a great deal about all sorts of scientific matters and animals but, I thought, rather little about music and musicians, although he had an incredible feeling for style. His ear was fantastic when it came to voices. His face was handsome, and he had white hair, a heavy face, with the nose too large for beauty perhaps, gold in his teeth and a generous laugh. Sometimes he was a little short of breath. He reminded me somewhat of the Great Man, the principal character in the libretto by W. H. Auden and Chester Kallman for Henze's opera *Elegy for Young Lovers* – a great man but with feet of clay.

'Feet of clay' would be going too far where Husler is concerned but he was rather the great German Professor. He didn't want to be bothered with awkward questions. He liked to sweep such things under the carpet or refer them to Yvonne. He was shy and embarrassed about money, personal relationships and many other subjects. But he had an aura of greatness, he was big, kind and, as I said before, charismatic.

I continued going to Germany for nearly two years, usually staying at Steinhude and occasionally at Detmold, where my stay was made bewildering and enchanting by the presence of Marilyn Tyler. But when Husler reached the age of seventy he retired from the Academy in the little town where the young Brahms had once lived. He thought it was time to leave the cold lakeside house and move back to the land of his fathers. Yvonne drove him around Switzerland. They found the French section too clinically clean. It would be like living in an operating theatre. The German section was too provincial with its baby-talk dialect and an atmosphere that provoked the thought that, if the Swiss had created their own mountains, they would have been much flatter. Finally they looked at the Italian-speaking Ticino, across the Alps and facing south, with a bit of Latin dirt in the mixture.

They found a house in a little village called Cureglia, about five miles to the north of Lugano. It was a fairly big house with wistaria growing round the front door and a moderate-sized garden with a few fruit trees and vines; unlike the Steinhude house this one had central heating and it had a courtyard at the side where student quarters could be and were eventually provided. The view was either down the valley towards Lugano, into the Benedictine establishment over the road or across a valley towards higher hills of two or three thousand feet. Idyllic. The village had a church, a post office, one or two dim pubs, a shop or two, including a *latteria* where we bought not only milk but groceries.

It was there that I first saw that primitive superstition was not dead in this peasant-like population, only a few miles from a big little town like Lugano. A certain old lady was obviously not liked, and coming into the *latteria* one day I noticed that most of the village shoppers awaiting their turn had the two middle fingers of their right hands bunched up so that the first and fourth fingers made the sign to ward off the 'evil eye' accredited to this old lady.

The standard of physiognomy was noticeably low. The men were slightly less ugly than the women. Even in Lugano where we went at least once a week to visit the supermarket the standard of beauty was no higher. If you saw a pretty girl you soon knew that she was a foreigner, either a tourist or one of the many who had come to live in that part of the Ticino. There were so many Germans settled there that eventually a law was passed prohibiting any more land buying by foreigners.

At first we students had to live out in the village in digs until the *casetta* in the courtyard had been done up. There was eventually room for six or eight people with a communal kitchen and a sitting room. The village digs were much more primitive than they would have been in the other parts of Switzerland. I stayed in several, including one that had an outside lavatory built on a balcony on the second floor with crude ill-fitting slats so that it was like giving a public performance – even less fun when the weather was cold. At one time I shared meals with an intelligent Dutch girl because her digs had some elementary cooking facilities.

After some months the summer and her mother arrived, and a strange coincidence came about. Annajet, the Dutch girl, had said, 'Now, please help me to be nice to my poor old mother. She's not pretty and she's not happy.' I did my best for the two weeks of the visit. Mother was certainly hideous, not particularly agreeable, and absolutely square in shape. Two weeks came to an end but Mother said that although her hotel could keep her no longer she wanted to stay a few days longer. I thought nothing of it, even when I found she had taken a room in the same building that I was living in at the time (the one with the public inconvenience).

One night as I lay reading in bed the door opened and in came the Dutch mother in a shiny nightdress. She bore down on me like a battleship about to crash into a tug but instead of crashing she took my head in her hands, kissed me, and told me that she was in love with me. It was too much of a shock for me to hide my horror. In the words of a well-known song, 'she sighed, she cried, she damn near died', but I could not 'haul her into bed just to keep her from the foggy, foggy dew' and excused myself as gently as possible.

She went next day back to Holland and her daughter explained to me that the reason why Mother had taken such a shine to me was because I reminded her of their doctor in Amsterdam, a young man who apparently looked very like me. She even mentioned his name and with surprise I found it was the same Dutch doctor that Olive had fallen in love with after she and I became 'ex'. One day at the Edinburgh Festival I had unexpectedly seen Olive walking down the street accompanied by a man that I immediately recognized as not only having the same build as myself but who even resembled me facially.

When the *casetta* was ready I moved in and found that the only other occupants so far were two young German students, Billy and Klaus. Soon others joined us. There was an English girl as fat as Billy was thin. She soon had a romance going with one of the local bus drivers. We seemed to go in for stout parties – heaven knows I was one of them – for soon a curious middle-American girl came. She set the cat among the pigeons by falling in love with Yvonne. Then there was a rather handsome German baritone who fell in love with *everyone*. Down the road there were two German baritone students who made their tuition money by being bakers. For birthdays they made the most marvellous confections.

The lessons continued and I persuaded Yvonne and the Professor to keep to a timetable so that we didn't have to hang about as we had in Germany. I also persuaded them to have a weekly house concert where most of us sang. I did most of the piano playing and spent much time practising and acting as *répétiteur* with the singers.

I found one curious thing: that the Germans 'owned' their German composers so much that they were not prepared to be at all flexible about their interpretations. One of them would start off a Schubert song or a Mozart aria and I might suggest a certain modification of tempo. 'No, it goes faster, John.'

'But have you considered the sense of the words, or that bar where there are so many little notes to get in, that surely determines the musical flow and tempo?'

'In Germany we make it so.' End of discussion.

Most of the German students had poor voices and musicianship. Sometimes they could scarcely 'read' music. They mostly ended up singing small parts or in choruses in German opera houses. It is difficult in England to understand that most towns of any size or standing in Germany have opera houses and that the members of orchestra, chorus, stage and administrative staff are all, technically, civil servants. If Devon, for example, were in Germany there would certainly be opera houses in Exeter, Plymouth and Torquay, and there would probably be theatres in Paignton, Ilfracombe and Barnstaple which the other companies in the bigger towns would visit regularly.

Some of my fellow students did better than chorus line. Gerd Feldhof for example is a regular Herald and similar parts in good houses, such as the Bayreuth Festival. Occasionally a singer would come from England for a period. Such a one was Annon-Lee Silver, a soprano originally from Nova Scotia.

I had met her first when she came as a student to the summer school at Dartington. She was blonde, very pretty, naïve, yet in some senses knowing. She sang like a bird – as freely as a bird, that is, and with a voice that, like a bird's, had a thread of hard material in the middle. In Devon at our weekly student concerts she sang and won everybody's hearts with one of the *Bachianas Brasileiras* by Villa-Lobos. Fortunately we had a cello class that week so I was able to collect eight cellos together and direct the performance. It so happened that we were short of really good sopranos in the choir that week for the Bruckner Mass in E minor which Reggie Goodall was directing so I asked Annon-Lee if she would join in, adding, 'I'm sure that if you do the conductor will fall on your neck.'

'I've had enough of that already this week, thanks,' said she in her unusual speaking voice, entirely in the throat, with no chest resonance. Indeed, in her white court shoes and with that high voice, it was no wonder I used to call her Minnie Mouse. She had heard so much about Husler from me and others that she decided to come out to Cureglia for a year.

Annon-Lee and I spent many happy hours together, working at her repertoire with myself at the piano, although we would sometimes swap roles and she would play Fauré songs for me. Working with her, especially at Schubert and Wolf, was a heightened experience, giving me not just happy hours but supreme pleasure, such as I have also experienced making music with William Glock, Noel Mewton-Wood, Eric Harrison, and Donald Swann. Those were regular duet partners at one time or other, all pianists.

Other great moments have been when I have played chamber music, the Haydn piano trios, the Mozart piano quartets and the Shostakovich Quintet. Of course I can't play all these pieces well – the finales of the quartets and the scherzo of the Quintet are devils – but I can keep up most of the time. One of the secrets of amateur music-making is knowing what to leave out! One other great experience was playing through Bloch's wildly orgasmic Hebrew Rhapsody *Shelomo* at midnight with the young Jackie du Pré.

But all that is really in parenthesis. The great joy of that kind of music-making is that you are both, or all, concentrating so hard, and you know the other person's musical personality and playing so well, that you anticipate and coalesce without having to talk or gesture. You become the music, as Eliot wrote.

There was little of this joy with most of the other students at Cureglia but it was sometimes fun. Sometimes I felt that I had been able to help or open doors. At other times it was a thankless plod and at moments I wanted to bang their silly heads because they were behaving like singers without having the saving grace of a good voice or musicianship. I don't know why Husler and Yvonne didn't chuck some of the duds out. Was it the money or did they see some potential that was never realized?

I sometimes felt that the lessons were too similar for everybody, that these technical exercises were like some endless belt, and not really geared to the very different needs of each individual singer. I wish they had told me that I obviously was not going to be the, or even a, heldentenor. But then singing, like most skills, is largely a matter of confidence. Part of training a skier, runner, singer, whatever it may be, is to build up confidence. The strange thing was that all those lessons that I had, good things in themselves no doubt, were less productive of steps forward than talks I had with Joy Mammen, Pieter van der Stolk and Annon-Lee Silver.

Poor Annon-Lee. Poor us. Just when her career was beginning to take wing – small parts at Glyndebourne, recordings coming up and so forth – cancer gripped her and destroyed her in her early thirties. Not so long before she died she took part in one of my television programmes, still looking beautiful and singing exquisitely. She sang with the Amadeus Quartet one of Mozart's most marvellous tunes, the aria 'Ruhe sanft' from the unfinished opera *Zaide* –the one that Beecham had growled at me.

I enjoyed my time in Cureglia. My visits there were longer than the ones to Germany. I no longer worked for the BBC Transcription Service but was free-lancing and this meant that I could come to Ticino for the whole of the three terms. After earning some money in London I would go out to be a student for two months at a time. At the late age of thirty-seven it was as if I was going to a University – of a kind. It was the first time in my life that I lived out of London, and the first time for many years that I was free of the telephone and the distractions of musical events in London and a large round of friends.

Having changed my room from one facing into the courtyard of the *casetta*, I was further away from the road, overlooking land that ran on a gentle slope for a few hundred yards and then dipped out of sight into a valley running parallel with the horizon and then up into wooded high hills or young mountains. There was a tiny village and church opposite at Arosio. It was a wonderful view. There were no aeroplanes in this part of the world but there were sometimes large birds, in particular an eagle that the Prof recognized as a 'Mailand' – a fair enough name when further down the valley after forty or fifty miles you would come to the town the Germans call Mailand (Milan).

One night after we had done a show for the village of Cureglia in the courtyard of our *casetta*, we went to dinner across the lake at Campione, an Italian enclave in Switzerland where gambling goes on and the restaurants stay open late as a result. After that, feeling tipsy and in no need of sleep, we walked up one of the little mountains by Lugano and laughed so much that we literally rolled down again. On returning to my room at dawn with the birds making a noise that was quite deafening I saw on my wall a butterfly so brightly coloured and so massive (about seven inches in wingspan) that I thought, in my light-headed state still, that one of the students had painted it there. I went to touch it and found that the glorious object moved. A bit later, the early-rising Prof came to have a look at it, gave it a name of course, and prescribed honey in a saucer, and mulberry leaves from the garden. I kept it a few hours for the sheer joy of looking at it, then let it go.

This village show that I mentioned became an annual summer show. I think it helped public relations. In particular the children loved it. Everybody heard the curious noises that came out of the big *casa* and the *casetta*; they saw us all wandering about the tiny village of Cureglia, two or three hundred people I would guess, and they saw us in the two pubs, in the two or three shops, waiting for the bus, or in the post office. So it was a good idea that they should connect up the voices and the people, see us singing and acting little pieces in their entirety, some in chorus, some solos, some concerted items – all popular stuff. It was all done on the cheap. We dressed up a bit and draped the open-air stage with fishing nets and so on.

One rehearsal showed Yvonne's indecisiveness at its quirkiest. A Danish tenor, nicknamed by me 'Danske' (from *Billy Budd*), his head completely shaved *à la* Yul Brynner, totally queer, great fun, moody, who walked by himself most of the time but could be excellent company, and who when he wasn't at Cureglia earned money as a taxi driver in Copenhagen, was in a duet with me. At one point he had to go offstage, so he asked Yvonne, our producer, which way he should go off.

Yvonne mumbled.

'Sorry, Mrs Rodd, didn't catch it.'

Mumble.

'Left or right, Mrs Rodd?'

'I should have thought it was obvious,' Yvonne managed to get out.

'Well, it isn't. Which way?'

'Really, Danske. . . . '

'Mrs Rodd, you are the producer. Just tell me, do I go out to the left or the right?'

And so it went on for a bewildering two or three minutes. Yvonne couldn't or wouldn't commit herself. Danske was determined to have an answer. It was typical of them both.

The only similarity between Yvonne and Auntie in *Peter Grimes* is that Yvonne had two nieces. I fell in love with Miranda who was an actress. She was blonde, very pretty and frightfully upper middle class, talking about 'scoff' instead of grub, and asking 'What's the form?' and things like that. Miranda arrived broken in health and spirit after a bad car crash in Africa in which she had lost her memory, including any recollection of the man she was engaged to marry. With loving care she was fairly soon restored to health. Her sister Harriet was pleasantly nutty, very bright and greedier (even) than I am. We all got on well, thanks partly to Yvonne's generosity in taking us about – she was the only one with a car.

Dagmar was a young German girl with a truly lovely mezzo-soprano voice and a natural musicality. When she arrived she was very gauche and coltish. She took a fancy to me and with a quite unconscious animal sense of aggression ousted Miranda. Having been taken possession of by Dagmar she and I remained lovers for many years, in spite of the difference in age and the frequent separations we suffered because she came from near Düsseldorf.

One of the good things about Cureglia was that it encouraged and stimulated letter-writing. I still have several hundred letters from Dagmar and she has a similar number from me. Her singing career suffers because she has no sense of ambition. She came once however to Dartington and sang, with great success, the *Four Poems of Saint Teresa of Avila* by Lennox Berkeley with Neville Marriner and the Academy of St Martin-in-the-Fields.

Another great friend of Cureglia days was called Kurzbein (Shortleg) – a mongrel of intelligence, fidelity and affection that I found wandering about the village one day, took for a walk and kept as a companion as long as I remained in Ticino. Cureglia was in open country and there were countless small and larger walks.

One minute and the village had gone. There were woods, hills, mountains, a few small lakes and of course the big lake at Lugano.

One place I particularly liked was a valley leading out of Locarno called Verzasca. What was unusual for Switzerland was the wildness, the unkemptness of this valley, which, added to its grandeur, made it very rare. Half-way along the part of it that had a made-up road one came to a really lovely hump-backed bridge, said to be of Roman origin. On hot summer days there was good sculptural bathing to be had on both sides of the bridge. Up river a hundred yards or so the river bank was all stone: there were large lumps of stone in the river, all rounded but with small lumps on top of what looked like torsos – the whole effect was as if Henry Moore had combined with nature. But if you went back to the bridge and a hundred yards further down, the whole scene switched to Giacometti: here the stone was all narrow and elongated. Rushing water abounded, clear as crystal.

Incidentally at Locarno the water was sometimes less than crystal. Several times I leaned over the lake edge looking down into the water and saw hundreds of turds. It was sometimes the same in the lake at Lugano. Annon-Lee refused to believe it, saying the Swiss would never allow anything like that, but one day a little later on she did admit that when bathing she had been surrounded by curious-looking sausages. Which reminds me of a train I took once from Locarno to Domodossola. I nearly missed it because it didn't go from the train station but outside in the street. This train behaved just like a tram until it got way outside the town, then it changed its character and the track became enclosed.

The ticket collector wanted to see what I had to show him but what he had to show me was irresistibly risible to an English-speaking person. His cap was new and it had printed in large gold letters the initials, without full-stops, of the company that he worked for: Ferrovia Autolinea Regionale Ticinese. Had the company been going long, I asked, commenting on the newness of his hat. No, he said proudly, the Autolinea part had just been added, hence the new lettering. I was tempted to pinch it to bring it back to England but he was so proud of it that I couldn't take it, even when he left it unattended on a seat for several minutes.

I must admit that up to this period I had a rather typical (at that time) antipathy to America and Americans. I hadn't been there and the sort of Americans that I had seen as tourists and the sort that had been in the UK during the war did nothing to make one like them, despite one or two really nice musicians I had met, especially those at Salzburg in 1947 at the school organized by Princeton that Donald Swann and I went to for the month of May.

For that reason I avoided visiting the American School just down the road from our singing outfit. I also disliked the Welsh student who suggested I go there. He went there, he told me, because they gave him free meals. But one day one of our Australian students at Cureglia, Janne, introduced me, in a café in Lugano, to two architects working for TASIS (The American School in Switzerland). One was a funny little bald-headed guy from Texas called Sam, the other was Jerry Wells, and there was also Adèle, his girlfriend, later wife, later split up. It really took me some time to get used to their lingo — I'm not kidding, it did — but then they introduced me to Dave Mellon, the headmaster of the Postgraduate school in part of Lugano called Loreto.

TASIS was started in a small way by Mary Christ Fleming at Locarno — in a house coincidentally occupied later by the English composer Benjamin Frankel whom I knew and visited there — but she had seen it grow, damn it, she *made* it grow — she's a ball of fire, an educational tycoon and an entrepreneuse with a drive like a bulldozer only nicer — into a junior and senior school for children of American parents living in Europe. Then she had the idea of a postgraduate course for American children to bridge the gap between leaving school and going to college, a one-year programme instructing them in French, German, and Italian, plus the arts, taking them on extensive tours of the surrounding countries, and including the spring term (it changed somewhat later) up at Andermatt where they could all learn to ski. Later Chris expanded her activities to include a school at Uzès near Avignon, one in Florence, one in Athens and one at Thorpe near Windsor.

Dave Mellon asked me if I would like to give some talks on music to the students. Why not? I started by talking to the entire school, about sixty of them, I think, plus staff and wives, in the salon at Loreto. Not knowing how much, if anything, they knew, I began with Benjamin Britten's *Young Person's Guide to the Orchestra*. That seemed to hit the spot and a very pleasant liaison with the school began and prospered until I left Cureglia four years later, by which time I liked Americans, and had made many friends among staff and students.

The postgraduates were average age eighteen and rarely musical, but most of them were really nice, socially rather more adult than Brits of that age, but less well educated. A number of them spelled clarinet with a k! They were very naïve and could easily get hysterical. On the night of Kennedy's assassination some of them were near to suicide. They were all of them north North Americans – except one year there was a mighty pretty gal from Down South and they were horrible to her. I thought she was cute, although I must admit that the first time she spoke to me I answered first in French, then German, then Italian before I realized what language she spoke. Eventually I used to tease them about their little American foibles and they teased me too about my frightfully British ones. Sometimes it was more real than teasing.

There was a party just before 'Commencement' and the speaker (Admissions Officer at Harvard) for this culminating ceremony came round to talk to everybody. When my turn came round he looked up at me and said, for all the world like an irascible Charles Coburn, 'You're kinda British, aren't you?' Of course I was and I often put it on for effect, pretending not to know, for example, when talking about Prokofiev's ballet *Cinderella*, that *Fairy* Prince meant something quite different to them.

Sometimes I went up to Andermatt for the weekend, doing a lecture or two, and then taking a skiing lesson. I never stayed long enough to ski properly but on the one occasion when I managed some 300 yards *before* inevitably I fell face first into the white stuff, I thought it was a magical experience.

The formidable Mrs Fleming soon became a good friend. So did her daughters and her son Tom. Lyn used to come sometimes to La Scala with me to the opera and her driving of her sports car got us back home in double but scary quick time. Her older sister, Gai, I co-opted into helping me several years at the summer school where she became my right hand and other things.

All in all my time abroad, learning how to sing or how not to be a singer, was just the change that my life needed. I think most people could do with a 'change of life' in their late thirties. Most by then are committed to families or jobs in such a way that they cannot change, but there I was – I had 'had marriage' as Madame Binnie put it that day on Brighton Pier; I was not at all rich but financially independent; Cureglia was the university I never had. I read extensively, walked, played the piano a lot, learned about singers, conducted choirs at Cureglia and with the American School, sang in public, lectured, taught in class, had time to think. I gave up criticism at this time but kept the summer school going by correspondence and maintained a certain contact with the BBC.

I brooded about the singing – I guess I knew that I had started too late, and I also knew that I had stayed too long with Yvonne and Husler. I did some auditions. I even did one in Graz at the opera house, travelling a thousand miles to do so. I sang for less than three minutes. The Intendant said, 'Do I understand that you have done music criticism? Ja? Then why don't you stick to it? Goodbye.' It was a thousand miles back too.

Back in England I did some auditions – about a dozen of them. They included two at the Royal Opera House, Covent Garden, including one on the stage, singing Mark's aria from Tippett's *The Midsummer Marriage*. They didn't even bother to let me know the result. I sang for the BBC but my voice 'was not suitable for broadcasting'.

Singing was up and down. One day I thought my voice wasn't bad. The next day I knew it *was*. Of course, your true singer would have gone on plugging away. A dozen auditions is nothing. I should have been prepared to do fifty or more. My teachers had given me the impression that I was quite a way up the ladder – all part of the confidence building process. But I realized I was down at the bottom – where even was that first bloody rung? Was I prepared to do school concerts? Take the night train from Crewe?

One more go. I sang to Peter Pears, daring to do the Prologue from Britten's *The Rape of Lucretia*. Viola Tunnard, that great and wonderful person and musician, played for me and afterwards she said kindly that I had not done myself justice. Peter rubbed his chin for a bit and then said rather tentatively, 'Well, my dear, it's a *useful* voice . . . . ' Oh boy!

Could I abandon it just like that? Pride came into it somewhat – when does it not? – because a lot of people in the music profession in England knew what I was trying to achieve. I went to see Lucie Manén, an old friend, a singer, a teacher and an amazing researcher into what the voice really is. She suggested that I go to her for six weeks at Igls, near Innsbruck.

Cureglia had been such a large part of my life that it was sad, although not difficult, to say goodbye. I am very rarely tearful on such occasions. My tears are shed (reserved?) for music, plays, cinema and for pity. I may suffer from self-pity, but I don't cry about it. When I was married I discovered that I could cry to order but I only once managed to use it to good effect – on all the other occasions just when I have achieved my aim and dispatched two tears, one each side, on their journey down my cheeks, I start to laugh at my success. Cut!

Igls was just outside Innsbruck, a skiing village in winter. One winter it was the scene of the Olympics and an enormous jump was constructed. I often ate with Lucie and her husband, Dr Otto John. We have remained firm friends, whereas, alas, when I met Yvonne Rodd subsequently we seemed to have nothing to say to each other.

Lucie gave me long lessons, explained everything about how the voice works – too much, I think. She did this I am sure because at the back of her mind there was the idea that I might take over the Gospel of Singing according to St Lucie. Her lessons, unlike the Rodd–Husler ones, were geared to me and my personal failings and strengths, if any. But although I loved this time with her, I had the feeling finally that it was all too late – at forty I could not make this jump.

To sing well is like standing naked on the stage. I could not give my all, only part of me. Maybe it is the story of my life. Where I can give my all is in radio and television, in giving talks, in organizing concerts I believe in, in the summer school – and in friendship. Friendship – maybe not love. Making love maybe; just loving . . . How did I get on to this? (You see? I'm trying to grab my hat and change the subject.)

Most of the time at Igls I stayed in a flat above the Johns. It had belonged to a lady with a taste for flounces, ostrich feathers, pink carpets, soft white rugs. Dagmar came and we had a pink and white honeymoon. This girl, who occupied my life for seven years, was tall and boyish looking, very downright and German in many ways, and yet with a strange sense of fantasy and fun. I don't think we ever quarrelled for more than thirty seconds at a time. It is disgusting how fond of food she is but she never gets fat. We could never pass a restaurant without her wanting to look at the 'card'.

'Card' was typical for there are one or two tiny gaps in her otherwise excellent English where she will translate literally from the German: 'card' (*Karte*) = menu; 'When will you get your hairs cut?'; 'Let's have spaghetti – how would you like *them* cooked?' And, best of all, 'Enough of your backside driving!' Our friendship continues, despite the distance between us. Our love dwindled, mainly because she came round to my way of thinking, i.e., preferring girls to men – and you can't both think that and continue.

At Igls I continued to walk, this time in wonderful forests instead of the Ticinese woods. I brooded more on the singing, and while I brooded I saw cruel things; crows hunting squirrels up and down trees; crows attacking a new-born deer and pecking its eyes out before I could stop them. Otto would go into the house to get a rifle because he hated crows as much as I did. But the crows seemed to know why he had gone into the house. For the rest of the day there would not be a crow in sight.

Otto had seen much in his day but he never gave up his wish to be vindicated in the eyes of his German fellow countrymen. For this was the famous Otto John, one of the chiefs of the post-war German Secret Service, who had been drugged in West Berlin, taken across to the East and kept a prisoner there for two years. He had managed to escape back to the West and reported for duty again with pride at having outwitted the Communists. He was gaoled for several years by the Adenauer government and, contrary to the Geneva Convention, put in solitary confinement for eighteen months. It is a wonder that the man wasn't a mental wreck. Sometimes his obsessional desire to have the case retried drove him to despair but Lucie managed to keep him sane. We had some wonderful times together, including one evening when Dr Kurt Schuschnigg came to dinner.

The crows and, in some curious way, Otto's case helped me to decide to give up singing. . . . But when I got back to London I went to dinner one evening with the American composer Bernard Herrmann and he persuaded me, as I recounted in chapter 14, to record for him his cantata *Moby Dick* and then, some years later, his song 'March' and the Delius 'A Late Lark'. And that really was the end of my singing – except for a few concerts with Donald Swann and the little party pieces that I sing on the radio/television show *My Music*. But more of that later.

(18)

Externally Yours

On the first day of 1957 Benjamin Britten's only full-length ballet, *The Prince of the Pagodas*, was given its première at Covent Garden. I went and was enchanted by the music which had many features that were intriguing as well as beautiful. The pagoda music reproduced in an extraordinarily successful way the sounds of Balinese music – which I experienced later on the spot – and at other points it was clear that Ben had sensibly and sensitively been looking at other scores by composing masters of the ballet – a glance or two at the Stravinsky of *Apollo Musagetes*, but more at Tchaikovsky and Prokofiev. Another feature was that in the second act Ben had composed the only convincing male and female love duet music he ever wrote, though admittedly without words.

I had been to some of the orchestral rehearsals and had run into Ivor Walsworth. Ivor asked me if I would be interested, since I obviously liked the music and knew it as well as anybody at that stage, in doing some commentary on the ballet for a recording about to be made for BBC Transcription Service.

Now the world in general, or at least the English-speaking part of it, became aware of BBC Transcription Service as such only in 1981 when the British government put this part of the BBC on the chopping block and announced its intention of applying the axe. Even then few seemed to grasp what it was and how it was different from the BBC World Service. Both the World Service and Transcription are part of the BBC External Services. Broadly speaking, the World Service broadcasts directly live whereas Transcription, as its name implies, transcribes, parcels and packages material, mostly from the domestic services in Britain, and sends it out to its subscribers abroad for transmission in the various places and countries on their own domestic services in their own time.

Certain countries, Australia, New Zealand and, for many years, Canada, take everything Transcription offers – maybe Hong Kong does too. Other places, South Africa, for instance, take certain programmes, and so do many of the radio stations in the USA, both university ones and the bigger cultural stations like WFMT in Chicago. I was out in New Zealand in 1981 and the dismay there was widespread and rather touching. They do feel isolated out there and the large number of BBC programmes in the domestic output kept them in touch. Australia is more independent; Canada broke away in the eighties; South Africa is limited because of the attitude of Equity and the Musicians' Union in London; but drama, stories, music, features, talks and comedy programmes all figure to a greater or lesser extent in all English-speaking places and countries in the world.

The *Goon Shows* are even more popular in other countries than they are in the United Kingdom and, as *The Times* stated in 1981, *My Music* and *My Word* are the two most popular currently running radio shows that the BBC puts out – in the Transcription Service. In New Zealand, Hong Kong, Australia, Canada and South Africa any of the *My Music* team are rapturously received, as I know from personal experience. People come up to me all the time: 'Don't let it stop'; 'Tell your mates we love the programme'; 'We never go out on Monday evening' – or whenever the regular transmission day is. In fact I think we are more famous *there* than at home.

Ivor Walsworth (1909–78) – you won't find him in *New Grove* – was a composer. Quite a lot of his music is published; some was played by his pianist wife, Joan Davies, and there is a good Cello Concerto but otherwise not much of great interest. In 1957 he became musical boss of Transcription, and it seems that asking me to do the *Pagoda* job was about the first thing he did. It was curious, considering that he had no great love for me – nor I for him.

He was a spacious man, quite handsome with a lot of white hair. He was attractive to look at but few liked him. He was generally lazy. At Maida Vale he usually had two lunch hours, one in each of the canteens, and was most often to be seen in his office, with his feet on the desk, snoozing. But he could work very hard, long hours and he was absolutely brilliant as a balancer and microphone placer.

Typical was one day when Ivor was about an hour late for a session in which we were to record Barry Guy, the virtuoso double-bass player. The engineer just could not get it to sound right. Eventually Ivor walks into the studio, his overcoat on, the inevitable cheroot hanging from his lips, takes in the whole situation at a glance and says to the engineer in his annoying drawl, 'Try turning the mike round the wrong way.' It worked, dammit!

I tried to dislike Ivor and I certainly did not trust him, although I was in his company at Transcription a lot and found him entertaining. He had been vile to Olive and, indeed, to any artist who was nervous and vulnerable. Ivor was at his most deadly in the days of live broadcasting. Just as the red light was flickering he would saunter from the mike to the control room and drop one well-chosen acid remark or question: 'E string playing you up, eh?' or 'Watch that cadenza' or 'Pity the octaves are flat.'

The overall boss of Transcription was a rather eccentric, seeming bumbler called Malcolm Frost. He had been in M.I.5 and was straight out of John Le Carré. Apparently Frost had the idea of a transcription service in the thirties, failed to sell the idea to the BBC, started one on his own, was quickly bought out by the Beeb and kept in charge. He tended to cut through red tape, to go his own sweet way and thoroughly annoyed the top brass who grudgingly conceded that he was brilliant at his job.

Malcolm excelled in public relations all over the world and he had the true impresario's flair for waving his finger about in a dither and then landing it squarely in the right place at the right time. Whereas the high-ups thought that he should provide a service that would fly the flag at all times, Malcolm provided one that comprised the best that the domestics served up, although including a good percentage of flag-flying material. For example, if the Edinburgh Festival had Boult and the BBC Orchestra doing British music and the Leningrad Philharmonic under Evgeny Mravinsky, Malcolm would not just take the British programme but also the Russian one, something that neither the Beeb brass hats nor the Russians would have done.

Frost also 'initiated' programmes which included taping concerts that the domestics did not, or, if he felt there was a gap, he would plug it by recording material he chose. He recorded many programmes annually at the Aldeburgh Festival years before BBC Music Department did so on the domestic services. In this he rendered incalculable benefit to Britten. Only once did I find, in music, that he misjudged something and that was when Swann and Flanders were just beginning. I told him that they were playing at Notting Hill Gate, that they had made such a success that they were coming into town – and what about it? Get in before they recorded commercially? 'No,' said Malcolm, 'I've seen the show. It'll never sell abroad. It's pure Streatham.'

In 1957 I was broadcasting quite a lot – music talks, high-class disc-jockey programmes; fun to do but with nobody taking much notice. Then I did this little job for Ivor. The thing was that for packaging the Britten *Pagodas* it was necessary to 'place' Britten for abroad; to 'place' Covent Garden and the première; to skate round John Cranko's not wildly good choreography; to tell the story and to highlight some of the musical features so as to fill out the time. (Most radio stations prefer programmes in slots of quarter-hour, half-hour, hour, hour-and-a-half and so on. It was no good sending out something that lasted 55 minutes, or 64. Therefore the presenter – Transcription preferred a presenter to an announcer – sometimes had too little time, sometimes too much, or very occasionally just enough.)

I had just the right amount of time; Ivor did a great job recording the music in an empty Covent Garden (before they ruined the acoustic a year or two later, raking the stalls and adding extra seats, which has rendered the sound almost as dead as at Glyndebourne).* I was impressed that, unlike *Music Magazine* or any of the Broadcasting House lot of producers, Ivor really took the trouble to 'produce' me. He let me listen back to my speech, suggested different inflections and so on. It was an eye-opener, or, rather, an ear-opener. Of course the essential difference was that here I was working on tape instead of live.

A few weeks later I got a call. The boss of Transcription wanted

---

*Transcription took Busoni's opera *Arlecchino* from Glyndebourne, and played the packaged disc to John Christie and his music staff, who congratulated Ivor on his success in handling the dry acoustic. Ivor never let on that what he had done was to play the tape through in the large empty Maida Vale studio and re-record it. Clever.

me to have lunch with him. The Head of a Service! Malcolm took me to lunch in Abbey Road and amazed me by saying, 'I like very much what you did. We need musical presenters, we can give you lots of work.' No doubt the shock make me preen and look pleased. Upon which he said, 'The thing is that most of your music critic colleagues are unsuitable. They are either too la-di-da, or have heavy accents or they are so queer that we have to add balls to their voices by adding bass resonance. Whereas your voice is nothing – just normal, unregional, slightly cockney if anything. Don't get big ideas.' That took the smile off my face. Then he said, 'If you have any ideas for programmes, let me know.'

I came up with the idea of a music magazine. It was not very original but, as I explained to Malcolm, whereas Anna Instone and Julian Herbage in their *Music Magazine* on the domestic radio scarcely ever used interviews but nearly always had a scripted talk, I wanted to have nearly all interviews. If Britten had a new work, get him to talk about it, and don't have a scripted talk by him or a talk about him by someone else. By 1970 the interview or the talk by the artist himself had become the norm but in 1960 it was new. Malcolm said yes and I was given as producer a bright lad from New Zealand called Laurie Constable. He was a good producer, painstaking and, as he knew little about music, he was a filter that rejected anything that the man in the street would not understand.

The first programme had Britten in it, talking about his new realization of *Dido and Aeneas*; Winton Dean and Arthur Jacobs arguing about putting Handel's oratorios on the stage, and some material nicked from a domestic feature about Glyndebourne with John Christie being the English eccentric and Carl Ebert doing a virtuoso act, rehearsing simultaneously in German, French, Italian and English.

The eye-opening factor of Transcription to me was the immense trouble that everyone took. When five o'clock loomed at Broadcasting House engineers would, if the show was not complete, stay on perhaps for a few minutes but they wouldn't stay for the retakes that would give the programme a touch of class. At Transcription nothing was too much trouble. These programmes were in competition with the best in the world and were commercial at that. We would spend a lot of time to get it right. Even when Laurie and I were satisfied, one of the engineers – there was one in particular called Dick Goff, with a lovely West Country burr, near retiring age, tactless but sharp – would say, ignoring the producer, 'Now, John, that wasn't quite right and you know it' or 'That may be all right for you two, but the sound was wrong. Please let's try it once more.'

These early shows were very satisfying although I was only then learning how to interview. I also began to learn about editing with tape and scissors. Sometimes we got in a mess. Laurie decided to transpose some things that Britten had said, but we were stuck at one point for a 'reaction' from Ben so we searched all the way through forty-five minutes of tape for him either grunting or whatever as long as it sounded like an affirmative. Eventually we found him saying 'Yes' in a very desultory fashion. Dick and Laurie fiddled with it until it sounded all right when you listened to the whole interview. But we fell over backwards every time we heard it. Now this may sound like making a fuss or nit-picking but that is what editors and engineers have to do all day, every day. We never falsified anything but you could easily do so if you were unscrupulous or unguarded.

For instance, one day Laurie was busy and asked me if I would start editing an interview with Neville Cardus. I knew that I had to hack about twenty minutes out of the talk so I stopped at the point when Neville was saying, 'Beecham was, of course, the greatest conductor in the world of tenth-rate music.' And I cut seven minutes out and let him continue with, 'Take Delius, for example.' You see the dangers?

Interviewing meant a new evaluation of many of the people in the musical broadcasting world. There were many people who were first class at script writing and reading but not at all good at being interviewed.* And vice versa. It was a joy (programme two) to work with H. C. Robbins Landon, the Haydn expert. You asked him a question and out would come five or ten minutes of wonderful quick talk about going round the monasteries of Austria and

---

*Of course, one could go too far with rejecting personalities for broadcasting. Scene: Vienna, 1807.
PRODUCER: So, who do we interview about that new opera, *Fidelio*?
LINKMAN: Why not Beethoven himself?
PRODUCER: Jeez, no. He's hopeless at the mike. North German accent you can cut with a knife, coughs and splutters, and he can never hear the questions anyway.

Czechoslovakia looking for Haydn manuscripts, secondary sources and so on. Then there was Ralph Kirkpatrick, the great harpsichordist, describing how he had come across a descendant of Domenico Scarlatti one day by idly glancing through the Madrid telephone directory.

In programme three I interviewed Percy Grainger (not long before he died). I adored his music and even used the opening bars of his *A Lincolnshire Posy* as the signature tune for my magazine programme *Talking About Music* and that pleased him because he thought that no one knew any of his music except *Country Gardens* (which was more or less true at that time). We got on famously. He told me how he collected folk songs in Lincolnshire with a phonograph. 'Ah, 'ee's learned it quicker nor I,' said one of his singers as he played back a cylinder one day.

And he told me the story behind the very tune that I was using as sig. tune. He started to collect a song called 'Lisbon' from a Mr Dean in the workhouse – this was in 1905 – and as he sang it he began to cry. The matron said, 'He hasn't sung these songs for years and it makes him think of his youth and it upsets him and it might kill him.'

'There was nothing to be said to that,' said Grainger, 'so I left it uncollected – or, rather, badly collected. I came back the next year and went to Mr Dean in the workhouse and he said, "Oh, I can't sing for you jung man, mah head's too bad." I said, "You don't need to sing for me, Mr Dean, but I'd just like you to listen to some of the others who have sung for me."' (A cunning ploy.) 'So he listened for about a verse and a half and then he said, "I'll sing for you, jung man."'

J.A.: And *did* it kill him?

P.G.: No. Anyway I thought it was better to kill him and get the song than let him live and not get the song. What use was that?

J.A.: You're a *real* collector.

(UP GRAMS.)

People sometimes ask me about interviewing. It depends a bit, of course, whether you are doing it 'live' or whether you can edit afterwards. Mostly the ones I do are the latter sort in which case it is simple: know your subject, look the interviewee in the eye and listen. This rarely fails. Musicians, like most people, like to talk, especially (a) if it's good publicity and (b) if the interviewer listens, does not interrupt and can easily lead on to the next point. However, you will happen occasionally on musicians who cannot start or finish a sentence, hesitate, 'ur' all the time, try to remember dates (which are unimportant in interviews usually), are over-coy. Another point is to observe courtesy: don't be aggressive, play second fiddle; don't swank or try to obtrude your own personality.

I can recall only two musicians who wouldn't look me in the eye: one, not surprisingly, was Sir Malcolm Sargent – nice enough until the mike was on and then totally self-absorbed; the other, curiously enough, was Sir Adrian Boult, but for totally opposite reasons, i.e., not self-absorbed enough and shy. Virgil Thomson, a superb broadcaster nevertheless, had the awful habit of 'ur-ing' louder than the rest of his phonation. It was a chore for the engineers to remove each sforzando, even though we reminded them that to err was human. Virgil was one of those interviewees who made lively material by slapping down the interviewer.

I find that too many of my colleagues don't listen. They are too worried about the next question on their lists – even Bernard Levin suffers from this. Beware of jumping in too soon, lads, you may miss the pearl. Mind you, it is often difficult to decide whether to follow your quarry down a side street or to try to get him back on the straight, but I have frequently found that the side alley may be more interesting than the main street. It depends whether you want a neat package or a slack parcel that may or may not contain wonders but that will certainly need tidying up.

Another problem is whether or not to help interviewees over a stumble or a word that eludes them. I was given a lesson on this early on by Joseph Szigeti whose vocabulary was wide and his English idiomatic but halting. We had got on to the subject of record reviewers. He talked of those who compare performances and was saying, 'They approach their task with. . . . ' There was a long pause which I punctuated with some cliché like 'careless abandon'. 'No,' said Szigeti. 'They approach it with . . . *blithe nonchalance.*' Wow! In future, I waited.

Collective interviewing is tricky. I would sooner talk to one member of a string quartet than all four together. If you talk to the four of them together, they interrupt each other as they never do when making music, or they are silent and self-conscious in each other's company, realize that their colleagues have heard the same comment or wisecrack before, and so forth. Likewise in discussions I find that three is the maximum for good results. How many television discussions are ruined by having five, six or more experts, so that *none* of them gets a good whack at the subject?

Awfully boring is the subject who agrees with whatever you say. William Walton was like that. The nearest semblance to a good interview with him – and it needed hours of editing – was after Gillian Widdicombe had broken the ground previously by endless questioning for her biography (which has been 'forthcoming' for at least ten years at the time of writing these lines).

I dislike and try to avoid the sort of question that doesn't really ask but tells: 'Now in 1929 you went as chief conductor in Birmingham, doing forty symphony concerts a year and sharing the choral ones, after which you went to Cape Town to do seasons as well as teaching at the University. How did that come about?' Crude. Sometimes interrupting is necessary but not often. For me Bernard Levin often ruins the flow by doing this – this week his interview with Ralph Richardson was rerun.

It is difficult but one should try to avoid clichés and the repetition of certain words. At the moment I have the interviewer's habit of beginning too many questions with a peremptory 'now'. Sometimes, in order to get a certain answer, the interviewer has to play the charlie and lay his head on the block but with some quick thinking it should usually be possible to avoid appearing too stupid – 'Exactly how many piano sonatas did Beethoven write, Mr Brendel?' – or too clever – 'Of course we all know that Beethoven wrote thirty-two piano sonatas.' That's too *de haut en bas* – the kind of 'we' that implies a barrier between the intelligent interviewer and the crud of a listener.

One of my worst moments was when I allowed myself to be persuaded by a producer into asking Dame Ninette de Valois a question about a ballet subject that I knew nothing about. She mauled me, quite rightly. Another floater was many years ago when I asked Janet Baker if it wasn't a sacrifice for her never to have married. Clang – she had been married for x years. (I hadn't met her husband at that time.)

I have been pleasurably slapped down not only by Imogen Holst,

Nadia Boulanger and Madame Prokofieva, but also by that great actress Katrina Paxinou: 'You think Enesco was the greatest all-round musician you ever met? Have you ever *heard* any of his compositions? You have? Then you talk like a fool!' Why did I interview Paxinou? Because when she was a young girl she was a singer, made a stunning success in Athens singing Saint-Saëns's Dalila with the equally young Dimitri Mitropoulos conducting. She told me also that at one time she had a flat in Berlin adjoining Busoni's. Late at night she had free concerts through thin walls.

Sometimes an interview can become almost a flirtation. It did with Irmgard Seefried – so much so that after we had finished one of the engineers asked if she was a girlfriend, past or present. I told him I had met the lady five minutes before the interview started for the first time. With some artists one question is enough. One time Isaac Stern answered and went on from there for twenty-five minutes without stopping for breath. At other times important things get said while I or the engineers are changing tape reels. And at others the interviewee will say, 'Turn that damned machine off and I'll tell you what really happened.'

Stalk an interviewee? Yes, occasionally. Ivor Newton was an outstanding raconteur, with an ear for telling detail and an engaging way of chuckling a few seconds before the punchline. But he had never broadcast and was very nervous of doing so. Couldn't we talk it through in the studio before recording so as to get the feel of the studio, etc.? I knew that his idea would kill the freshness of his story (about playing for Fyodor Chaliapin and the scenes after he died) so I arranged with the producer and engineer that we should set up the mikes, get a rough balance in advance and leave the tape running, but if Ivor were to look through the glass panel they were to duck down and keep out of sight. Ivor saw no one, thought he was just talking to me and delivered his goods perfectly. Then he found I had fooled him, listened to the tape and was never nervous at the microphone again.

He did perfect interviews about Conchita Supervia, Oda Slobodskaya, and with Gracie Fields, with whom he had toured factories and aircraft hangars during the war – new venues and a new repertoire for him, although never rehearsing with her alarmed him at first. He had a touching story about one time they had played at a factory and were just going through the exit gates when a tramp came up to the window of their car and said, 'They wouldn't let me in, Gracie, said I was muck.' Gracie said to him, 'No man's muck that can do a day's work', tore her bouquet of flowers apart and gave the tramp half of it.

What I have enjoyed and learned from so much with interviews is how spoken comments enabled me, and my listeners, to read between the lines of written biographies – often small things but, as the song says 'Auch kleine Dinge'. Alfred Swan – Donald Swann's uncle (yes, one 'n' for Alfred) – knew Medtner and Rachmaninov and used to stay with the longer-named at his summer house near Lucerne.

Teasing, said Swan, was a great part of Rachmaninov's life in company – teasing the guests who stayed with them and teasing Medtner in particular. Medtner always complained that Rachmaninov was his oldest friend and yet he could never manage to have a conversation with him about music. Instead Rachmaninov always teased him. They would be having a serious talk about something chez Rachmaninov and one of Rachmaninov's daughters would tie yellow ribbons round Medtner's legs while he wasn't looking and when the time came to get up from table and go into the sitting room Medtner was the butt of everybody's laughter. But Rachmaninov's laughter was entirely silent. All the muscles of his laughter-saturated face would be quivering, yet there was never a sound.

The house, said Swan, was all gaiety – quite a different picture from the usual impression of Rachmaninov as 'six and a half feet of Russian misery', as Stravinsky put it. Another revealing touch is that Swan said that Rachmaninov's favourite author was not Dostoevsky or Tolstoy but Chekhov. He read his letters incessantly. Swan also let out that the disastrous première of Rachmaninov's First Symphony was partly due to the fact that the conductor, Glazunov, was drunk – according to Mrs R. who was present. Rachmaninov was so tense that he left the hall. There were some faint calls for the composer at the end but he was not there. He was still riding back and forth on the local tramway.

Later Artur Rubinstein told me of a historic dinner party in Hollywood during the forties. Stravinsky and Rachmaninov lived near each other but did not meet – understandably, in view of their music. However the wives met a few times at the local supermarket and thought that their husbands should get together, so a dinner party was arranged: the two couples and Rubinstein as buffer. The Stravs arrived chez Rachmaninov.

Drinks. Desultory conversation between the composers. More drinks. Stravinsky strolls to the bookshelves, looks at two or three before Rachmaninov tells him that the books are not his, that they have rented a furnished house. Silence. More drinks. At dinner Stravinsky says what a pity that Rachmaninov sold for a few roubles the copyright of his famous C sharp minor Prelude. Silence. Rachmaninov comments how unfortunate that, as Russia had not signed the Berne Copyright Convention, Stravinsky received no performing rights on his three famous ballets. Silence. Stravinsky begins to speculate on how much money he *would* have received if Russia had. . . . Rachmaninov begins to speculate how much money *he* would have received if he had not sold the copyright on the Prelude. They get pencil and paper and begin to calculate the respective amounts. Thaw. And general relief from the other guests.

I shall always regret not having had the chance to interview Stravinsky while he was at Dartington during the summer school. I had thought of asking him but decided to see how Colin Mason got on with his intended interview for the *Guardian*. Stravinsky asked to see the questions in advance. Colin submitted about thirty. Stravinsky said that thirty answers amounted not to an article but to a small book. His charge for a book would be minimum 10,000 dollars. Colin went away without his interview. So I did not even ask.

Some interviews have gone out more or less as made; others need hours of work. Nicolas Nabokov, Roberto Gerhard, John Cage, Karlheinz Stockhausen, André Previn, Gillian Weir, Leopold Stokowski, Aaron Copland: no 'ums', no stumbles, straightforward, thinking on their feet. Michael Tippett, Pierre Boulez, Madame Prokofieva, William Walton, Elisabeth Lutyens, Nicholas Maw, Priaulx Rainier, Zubin Mehta, Yehudi Menuhin, Eartha Kitt: hours of editing involved. This is not to say, I quickly add, that one category is better than another. Incidentally, Lina Prokofieva was delightful, so pretty in her eighties, volatile; slapping me down when I asked her if her husband was boorish, yet condemning him in the next sentence for not suffering fools gladly, for being rude to people right, left and centre, and writing offensive letters; not blaming him for the break-up of their marriage, or for not attempting to help her when she was arrested and sent to the detention camp at Vorkuta (where the extreme difference between winter and summer temperatures could be 108°F).

Boulez shows similar extremes: from the music, so meticulous, to his speech, so messy. Deciphering his speech is hard – meaningless turns of speech translated from French or German like 'on the contrary' instead of 'furthermore' or 'however', and always with each interview the addition of some new incomprehensible word or expression which he used to excess and which could not be entirely eliminated. One time the word 'fuckus' (he was mispronouncing 'focus') was used nine times. On the other hand what a delightful, thoughtful, helpful, unselfish person Pierre is.

The two last adjectives could not be applied to Stockhausen. He arrived over an hour late; he was unapologetic, and impolite to the technicians, but once the interview started he exuded what I can only call 'charisma'. He won me over in two minutes flat. If he'd asked me to kiss his feet I would have done so. He made me think that Wagner must have had that same kind of magnetic personality.

Bad temper? I can only remember Sir Arthur Bliss when, one minute after we had started recording, the producer came in – startling Arthur, I admit, while he was talking – to say that inexplicably the sound had stopped coming through. The Master of the Queen's Musick went berserk. That's the only expression I can use, because not only did he trumpet abuse, but his eyes went red, as an elephant's are said to do when enraged.

Me bad tempered? It showed only once that I recall, in a talk with Willy Boskovsky. He kept on floundering, interrupting himself, making noises, tapping the table, asking if he could say something again, flying off at a tangent. It was unforgivable of me but I did sound quite short with the poor old waltzer.

What I found interesting was that, though very occasionally I would behave in a manner of speaking quite opposed to that of my interviewee, most of the time I fit in with him or her so chameleonly that, if the person I'm talking to stumbles, or has an accent or whatever, then so do I. There's a priceless interview with Jon Vickers in which I sound more Canadian than he does! And, of course, it was quite unconscious on my part, just playing along like a competent second fiddle, trying to match my tones to his.

(19)

My Music

I used to listen as often as I could in the old days to the radio programme *My Music*, and among my many delights in being in the programme nowadays is that now I *never* miss it.

When David Franklin was a member of the panel I went to a couple of recordings at the old Playhouse Theatre in London as his guest. I had got to know David when he was a bass in the Covent Garden company at the Royal Opera House. His was not the most beautiful of voices but he was a first-rate actor with a fine sense of character and comedy. His Baron Ochs (in English) in Strauss's *Der Rosenkavalier* was extremely stylish, not least in that David never became too coarse. He never forgot that he was supposed to be playing a seedy aristocrat, not a jumped-up plebian like his potential father-in-law Faninal.

He was at least six foot five which means that he was two inches taller even than Denis Norden or Frank Muir who are, in turn, an inch or so taller than I am. David had a very slow speaking voice, deliberate, excellent in solo turns. I happen to talk much quicker than David, so the show speeded up a fraction when I joined the team.

One of the nights I went to the Playhouse was an occasion when David recounted how he had once been a member of the Cambridge University Madrigal Society, always, he said, known as CUMS. He had then joined the Birmingham University Madrigal Society, always known as (*pause*) the Birmingham University Madrigal Society. David embarrassed the hell out of me on one of those occasions when he could not identify a piece of Elgar, by flinging the question at me in the audience. But as I was sitting very near the back I was desperately 'off-mike' and the producer probably cussed like anything.

My chief joy in the show then as now is the wit of Denis Norden. The lovely Frank Muir is often witty but on the whole is more of a comic than a wit *in person* – he writes very wittily. Trying once in Australia to compare the two, I used a cricketing analogy. Frank hits in front of the wicket: square cuts, hooks and on-drives; whereas Denis's shots are all behind the wicket: fine glances to leg or late cuts.

David had a stroke, became incapacitated, and later died. He left *My Music* at the end of a series, so the organizers of the show had several months in which to find a replacement. *My Music* is recorded usually during the first quarter of the year. Until quite recently the senior parent of the show-organizing body was the Transcription Service; Ernest Stancliffe was one of the Transcription men concerned with the programme and, after the others had failed to come up with anybody, Stan (as he was known) suggested me.

Having worked with the Transcription Service a long time Stan had experienced my stories, imitations and bursts of song at the lunch table in the canteen because he was one of a group that ate together on the days when I worked there. Eventually Stan managed to persuade our dear producer at that time (1973), Tony Shryane, that I should be tried out – just two or three shows to see how it went. I was on nodding terms with Steve Race; Frank and Denis were quite unknown to me personally, while Ian Wallace I knew quite well because we were mutual friends of Siriol Hugh-Jones, a close friend of mine who was at one time features editor of *Vogue* magazine, and of Michael Flanders and Donald Swann.

The big night came and I was naturally nervous. It was rather like deputizing for a member of the Amadeus String Quartet, with the added disadvantage that there was no music to play from. Steve Race was a great help and nursed me as much as he could. He and I had a preliminary meeting or two, because the feature of *My Music* is that most of the questions are tailored for each of the four of us. The questions are in the areas of music that we *should* individually know something about or could improvise an answer to – or, if Steve occasionally feels that we have had it too easy, something that is right *not* up our street. Thus he will fling a Gilbert and

Sullivan at me, knowing that I hate the stuff, and knowing that Ian will know the answer for sure, in order to stimulate me to invent something. On the whole, however, I don't get what I call the Johnny Mercer questions, while Frank and Denis do not get the Shostakovich ones.

Even so, sometimes they can none of them believe that I am not being toffee-nosed when I say I don't know, for example, a song called 'Doggie in the Window'. How can I have lived through the era when that song was so popular (whenever that was) and not know it? I suppose the answer is different listening and viewing habits. I listen almost exclusively to Radio 3 between eight and nine in the morning, maybe to *This Week's Composer* and occasionally to other radio programmes. I don't watch the sort of television programmes in which such songs would be played. I mean 'Doggie' wouldn't get played in *The Kenny Everett Show, Soap, Dallas, Laugh-in* or even *The Benny Hill Show*, to name but five programmes I have watched fairly regularly over the years – and even then I might use the musical numbers for having a pee or a cup of tea.

That first night the thing I remember most is Denis being asked during the warm-up for his definition of a haggis, to which he replied, 'It's a sort of mousaka of Glencoe.' Wow! I can remember being scared but none of my answers or what I sang. I do know that in the early days, because of nerves, I used a lot of funny voices, German and Italian accents, and a John McCormack singing voice.

Ian was as helpful as he could be. He is a super bloke, as kind and generous a colleague as anybody could wish for, never nasty about anybody. Frank and Denis know each other so well after working together so long that a raised eyebrow or a nod across the stage enables the one to know what the other is thinking. They tend to keep themselves somewhat to themselves. They are both tall and slim, and both shy by nature, so they can sometimes appear stand-offish, but if you are prepared to go up to them and nudge your way in, they will respond. They say of themselves that they know they lack small talk but are too old now to acquire any. On the whole they don't like jokes and they don't suffer fools gladly. Ian's and my paths cross sometimes, because we have musical friends in common but I don't ever meet the others socially. In a way that is a good

thing, because when we meet professionally there is a more stimulating impact.

I think the show works because we are all so different. Steve puts
the right questions most of the time – and so we all knock sparks
off each other. *My Music* is not, I think, cosy in the manner that
Face the Music sometimes is/was – showbiz people being coy about
music. Tell a silly joke in *My Music*, or get sentimental, and you get
a verbal lash from Denis; or Frank will shout 'Resign, resign!' I like
it that way.

After two or three shows I asked Frank for 'notes', advice, hints.
'Well,' he said, 'fwankly you're not very good at the wepartee, but
that's all wight, lad. Stick with your anecdotes.' So I have.

The drill is as follows. About August, Steve will badger me for
my list of songs or tunes that I would like to sing or whistle.
Occasionally he will suggest a few that he or listeners have asked
for, or perhaps one that will fit into a scheme that he wishes to
follow – all about flowers or whatever. We all choose our own
songs, I believe. I don't know for sure – we just don't inquire about
such things. Then we sort out the dates a bit. Lately we have taken
to doing two special Christmas shows: one for radio, one for telly.

We start recording the series in the New Year: thirteen evenings
we meet at around seven, wherever it is, the Westminster Theatre or
some other venue, and have a drink. Steve will maybe ask me to
hum a tempo for a song but we do not rehearse anything, nor do we
know questions in advance, except on (I speak for myself) the
rarest occasion – like what I call genre questions, such as 'Supposing you wake up in hospital, what music would you least like to
hear?' Never on identification of tunes, factual questions and so on.

Steve goes on stage to do the warm-up and we follow after ten
minutes or so. Our scorer goes on first. The rest of us follow one by
one. We test out the mikes by a little bit of chat, usually saying what
we have been up to since we last met. We record the first programme, and then the second, meanwhile checking with the producer to make sure nothing has gone astray. Sometimes a tiny bit
has to be done again for some technical reason. Very occasionally
one of us will want to do our song again, although since neither
Frank, Denis nor myself are professional singers we don't mind too
much if something goes agley – it adds to the fun. Ian, being a 'pro'
naturally repeats his if he and Steve have come unstuck, or if he has

a frog in his throat or something. The first quarter of the year is the worst time of year for colds and things like that, and it is not easy to sing after gabbing for half an hour or a whole hour.

We all tend to groan when the piano medley comes up but it is because those tunes whirling past quickly are difficult to spot. Classical tunes are made more tricky for me because the piano is rarely the original medium for the ones Steve chooses, nor does he play them in the original keys, both of which factors tend to faze me. I must say Steve does these medleys very artfully – and while I'm on the subject, his playing for the accompaniments of golden oldies and ballads is very well done, with interesting, intriguing harmonies.

The reason why the chemistry in *My Music* works is not only the interplay of the four quizees and the skill of the quizmaster, but also the fact that our lives are not closely entwined. We meet regularly but briefly in the first quarter of the year only and are stimulated by the encounter. If we went on tours, spent hours in trains or dressing rooms together, we should know each other better but I doubt very much if it would improve the show. In fact, I am sure it would detract from it.

The only time that we have ever been together for any length of time was when we went to Hong Kong to appear at the festival there in February 1983. Even then there was only one occasion that we met face to face for a whole day and that was when we were taken for a boatride and picnic by our hostesses from the festival committee. Great fun. The rest of the time we were mostly separated. We all did one-man shows or speeches. We didn't avoid each other, but we didn't all stay at the same hotel. Steve Race brought his wife Lonnie and Ian Wallace's daughter Rosie was there part of the time. I saw more of Ian because we at least did both stay at the wonderfully picturesque Garden Hotel.

We recorded the usual brace of shows in Hong Kong and they were especially good ones. We had brought our producer, Pete Atkin; Leonie Lawson, our adorable scorer, and Pete Freshney, our chief engineering expert. Local lads from Radio Hong Kong worked all day in preparation for the show in the evening. Everything eventually got sorted out and Pete said to them, 'OK, chaps, see you for the show' but they then let him know that in Hong

Kong they work shifts. So a new lot of engineers turned up and there were some hitches. But these hitches were turned to advantage because instead of doing the usual ten-minute warm-up we fooled around for nearly fifty minutes, thus giving the receptive audience a longer show. Incidentally, I saw only one Chinese person in our full house. It was essentially a 'blighty' audience – ex-pats having a night out. Our show was the first of all the festival events to sell out.

My Music is the only radio show to be shown on television. What happens is that Douglas Hespe and his crew bring their cameras to seven of the thirteen evenings and video us. Sometimes there is an extra round with some added visual interest, photographs and the like, otherwise it is the same show. The TV version, apart from Eire, is not shown abroad. The viewing figures, when I last heard them, were often near the 3 million mark, which is a lot for BBC2. And, as I write, BBC1 is putting on the old shows at nine o'clock in the morning and the figures are creeping up.

This sort of coverage has quite an effect on life. People come towards me as if they know me and then do a double-take. Some grin when they see me; some openly laugh; some just look puzzled. I find this rather delightful. Folks come up in theatre lobbies or country lanes. The only time that I get embarrassed about being asked for an autograph is if I happen to be with a musician friend whose work is, unlike mine, really distinguished. Then I feel that it should not be me signing the autograph but my companion.

Occasionally Steve Race will mention songs that listeners have requested and if they are very popular ones that I do not like, or think that Ian or Frank would sing much better than I would, I try and get out of them. Sometimes Steve will say, 'but surely you want to give the public what it wants?' and I say, 'not particularly.' By which I don't mean I want to give the public what it does *not* want, but I really enjoy giving the public what it might like if it heard it. After all this is a large and captive audience. That is why I like to find interesting and beautiful folksongs or unknown little bits of arias or songs – it's the mini-musico-evangelical in me again; like Glock : 'I try to give the public what it will want to hear *next* year' – by gad, sir, Reith was right!

In 1983 I got the Australian pianist and composer Penelope Thwaites to make a setting of a poem by Phyllis McGinley called

'All the days of Christmas' which I found in John Julius Norwich's enchanting commonplace book *Christmas Crackers*; in 1984 Donald Swann found in his desk a Christmas jingle by Michael Flanders and set it for me to sing and whistle; the same year Steve Race's muse nudged him to set for me Hilaire Belloc's poem 'On a Sleeping Friend'; and even as I write Malcolm Arnold has come up with a little morceau for siffleur et piano which he has called 'Thème pour mon Ami(s)'. All these oeuvrettes are fine examples of their composers' craftsmanship, especially in writing something that can capture an audience in no more than seventy-five seconds (pity that Anton von Webern isn't still around!)

P.S. Just back from Cornwall where I was introduced to a Countess. 'Oh, you're in *My Music*. I love it, *do* tell me about the fat one.' Rather nastily, and hopefully, I asked her if she meant Ian Wallace. 'No, not him, nor those two frightfully witty ones, nor the question-master; no, the fat one, tell me about him.' Oh dear! but at least she was interested, wasn't she? I wonder what she wanted to know? Perhaps I had better send her a copy of this book when it is finished.

Which it is.

Index

Figures in italic refer to plate numbers